Copyright 1994

by

Faye C. Brydels

Donna B. Jenkins

All rights reserved — no part of this book may be reproduced in any form without permission in writing from the authors, except by a reviewer who wishes to quote brief passages in connection with a review written for inclusion in a magazine or newspaper.

ISBN 0-935545-19-0

1st Edition	December,	1994
2nd Edition	October,	1995
3rd Edition	September,	1996
4th Edition	December,	1997

Printed by
Land and Land, Publishing Division
196 S. 14th Street
Baton Rouge, Louisiana 70802

INTRODUCTION

This collection of recipes had its beginning many years ago in the Home Economics Department at Woodlawn High School where we taught together from 1974 to 1983. We often talked of writing a cookbook yet until recently our lives were too full to begin.

Louisiana offers the world a unique cuisine due to its diverse cultures. We grew up in north Louisiana, yet spent our adult lives in south Louisiana. Since Louisiana above and below Bunkie are quite different worlds, we are a blend of both. We tend to take the basic ingredients of one area and flavor it with the spices of the other.

Froggy Bottom is an area in a small town in north Louisiana. It also reminds us of the night sounds of a south Louisiana swamp. We thought this name was fitting and proper for our diverse collection of recipes.

We would like to thank our many friends, neighbors, and students who have shared their treasured recipes with us over the years.

To our wonderful families, we say thank you for your patience, encouragement, and endless taste testing of recipes. Without you, our book would not have been possible.

Please visit our Internet homepage:
www.froggybottomcookbook.com

TABLE OF CONTENTS

Party Menus iv
Appetizers and Beverages 1
Soups and Gumbos 27
Salads 37
Breads 49
Eggs, Cheese, Pasta 69
Meats 77
    Beef 78
    Pork 97
    Poultry 102
    Game 116
    Seafood 119
Vegetables 139
Sweets 157
    Cakes 158
    Desserts 179
    Pies 187
    Candy 195
    Cookies 206
Preserves, Relishes 217
Children's Corner 223
Party Ideas 231
Table Settings 241
Facts from the Chef 247
Index 259

Party Menus

Cajun Delight - It's Crawfish Season

Lake Charles Dip
Assorted Crudites

Boiled Crawfish
with
Corn   Potatoes
Artichokes   Mushrooms
Green Beans
Dipping Sauce
Saltine Crackers

Keg of Beer

Freezer of Ice Cream

Louisianians are crazy about crawfish and they frequently hold "crawfish boils". These get-togethers are casual dining at its best; guests pick the crawfish apart with their fingers and suck the meat from the head, claws, and body. Served piping hot, piled high on newspaper-covered tables, crawfish are a true delicacy.

A Summer Evening Repast

Artichoke Dip
Assorted Crackers
Wine Punch

Texas Barbecued Pork Chops
Marinated Vegetable Kabobs
Cold Pasta   Pesto Sauce
Sliced Homegrown Tomatoes
Italian Dressing
Joe Kelly Bread

Iced Tea   Imported Beer

Bits and Berries

A summer evening on the patio with good friends and delicious food is a Southerner's idea of heaven. Succulent pork on the barbecue pit and garden fresh vegetables are the basis of an easy to prepare meal. Casual dining, balmy weather, and lush southern patios go hand in hand.

Tailgating Under The Oaks

**Football Party Dip   Mountain Caviar
Assorted Crackers
Rolled Tortillas   Picante Sauce**

**Kozan's Ham and Cheese Rolls
Natchitoches Meat Pies
Shrimp and Pork Eggrolls
Italian Marinated Vegetables**

Kathy's Fantastic Brownies

Tailgating under the beautiful oak trees on the LSU campus before a Saturday night Tiger football game is a tradition in Baton Rouge. The campus is alive with fans moving from the tailgate of one vehicle to the next sharing food and friendship. Saturday night, tailgating, and "Death Valley" — there's nothing like it!

Candlelight and Elegance

Artichoke Soup
Crackers
White Wine
Marinated Eye of the Round
Ratatouille Nicoise
Potatoes Stuffed with Crabmeat
California Spinach Salad
Sour Cream Dinner Rolls
Red Wine
Grasshopper Pie
Demitasse

Relaxed elegance is the keynote of southern sophistication. The evening hours offer the chance to enjoy the subtle aspects of southern ambience. Plentiful and delicious food, cherished friends, and china sparkling under candlelight create a simple graciousness. From the cotton fields of the north to the sugar cane fields of the south, Louisianians always offer guests a warm and genuine welcome.

Mardi Gras Magic
— Breakfast after the Ball —

Champagne
Orange Juice
Brunch Casserole
Delicate Grits
Marinated Fruit
Angel Biscuits
Peach Jam
King's Cake
Coffee

Mardi Gras or "Fat Tuesday" is celebrated with exciting parades and elaborate balls in many southern cities as a last fling before the Holy Season of Lent. After the ball family and friends gather to culminate the festivities with a leisurely, late breakfast. Toasting with champagne and cutting the King's Cake typifies the classic southern hospitality of the Mardi Gras.

Let's Celebrate!
— Child's Birthday Party —

Cheese Straws
Sausage Pizza Rounds

Watermelon Whale
filled with fresh fruit
Fruit Yogurt Dip

Old Fashioned Ice Cream

Hershey's Prize Chocolate Cake

Party Punch

— Party Favor: Small plastic bag filled with Nutty Putty and tied with brightly colored ribbons.

When birthday time approaches, girls and boys almost explode with excitement. They anxiously await "their" party complete with refreshments and a rousing version of "Happy Birthday"! When the games are over and the presents opened, they crowd around a festive table to consume mountains of lucious cake and creamy, homemade ice cream washed down with generous servings of cold fruit punch.

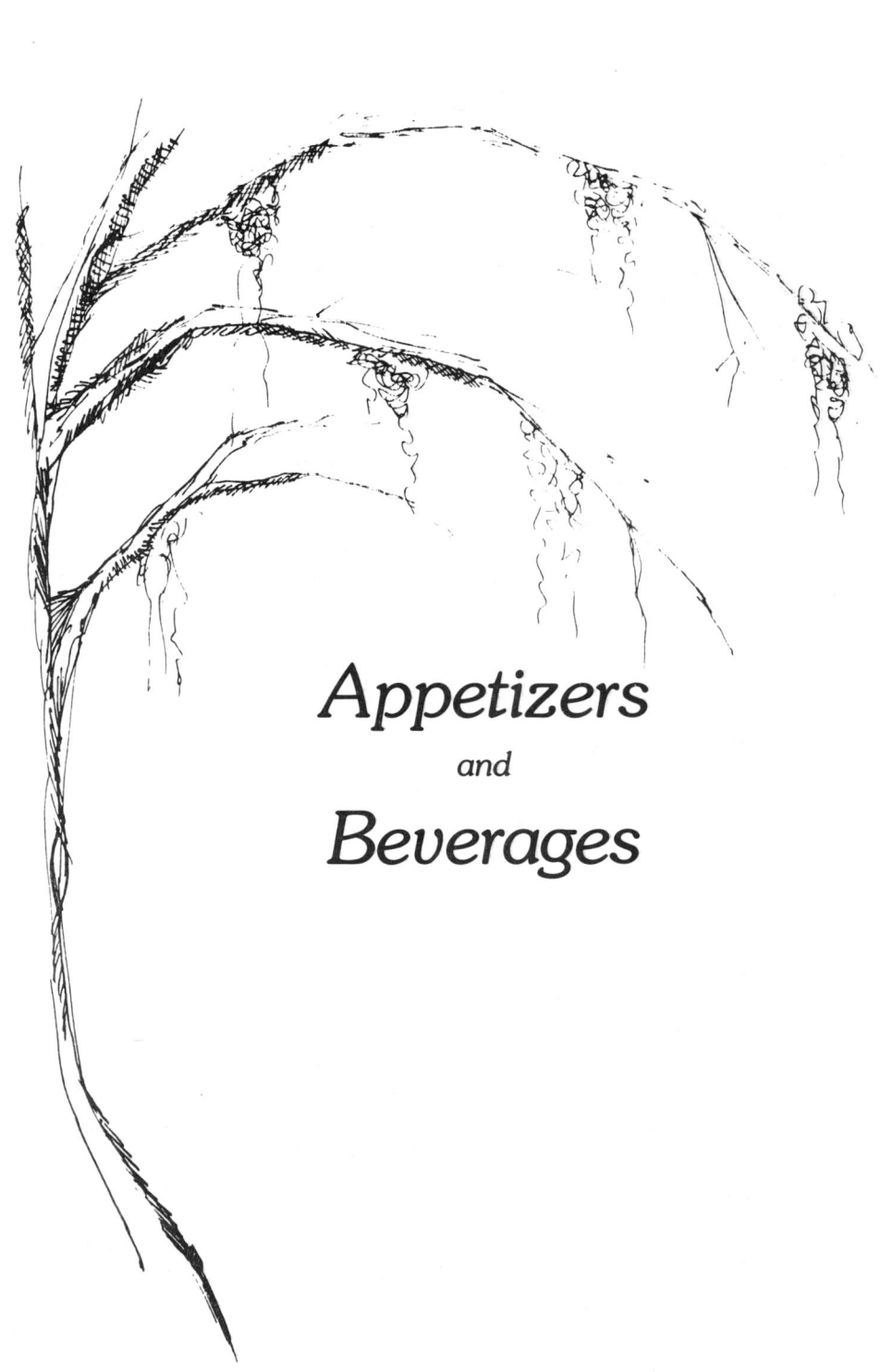

Appetizers
and
Beverages

ZINGY STRAWBERRY BRIE

1 cup strawberry preserves
1 tablespoon horseradish (or more to taste)
8 ounces cream cheese
Crackers

1. Mix strawberry preserves and horseradish together.
2. Pour over block of cream cheese.
3. Serve on crackers.

   Delicious with any jelly or jam.

HAWAIIAN BRIE

1 (approx. 1-pound) baby Brie wheel
1 (8-ounce) can crush pineapple in syrup, drained
3 tablespoons honey roasted peanuts
2 tablespoons firmly packed light brown sugar
2 tablespoons flaked coconut, French bread or crackers (optional)
Fresh fruit (optional)
Gingersnaps (optional)

1. Remove rind from the top of the Brie round; place on an ovenproof serving platter and set aside.
2. Combine pineapple, peanuts, and sugar in small saucepan. Cook until thoroughly heated.
3. Spoon mixture over cheese, bake at 400 degrees for 8 to 10 minutes or until cheese is softened.
4. Sprinkle coconut over pineapple topping and continue to bake just until coconut is lightly toasted.
5. Serve with fresh fruit or gingersnaps as a dessert or with bread or crackers as an appetizer, if desired.

   Yield: 6 dessert or appetizer servings.

CHEDDAR CHEESE BALL

5 ounces sharp Cheddar cheese
13 ounces Colby cheese
2 tablespoons mayonnaise
Juice of 3 cloves garlic
Tabasco 2-3 drops
½ cup chopped pecans

1. In food processor combine cheeses, add mayonnaise, garlic juice and Tabasco. Stir in pecans. Divide in half, shape each into apple. Roll in paprika. Add toothpick stem and mint leaves.

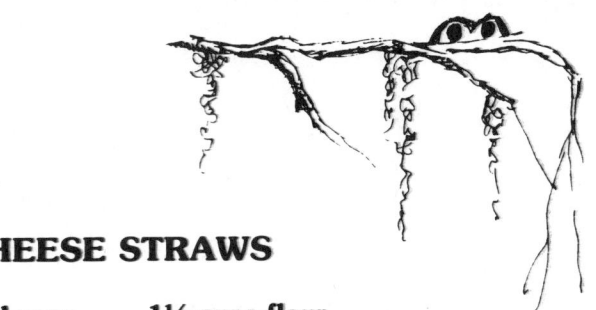

CHEESE STRAWS

1½ cups grated Cheddar cheese
1 stick or (¼-pound) butter
2 tablespoons ice water

1½ cups flour
¼ teaspoon salt
¼ teaspoon red pepper

PREHEAT OVEN TO 350 DEGREES

1. Cream cheese and butter with blender.
2. Add ice water. Add flour and seasonings and chill.
3. Roll out of pastry tube or on slightly floured board ⅛-inch thick. Cut strips ½-inch wide, 4 to 5 inches long. Place on ungreased cookie sheet. Bake at 350 degrees for 15 to 20 minutes.

   Makes 40.

HERB-CHEESE SPREAD

1 teaspoon Dijon mustard
1 (12-ounce) package Havarti
   cheese
1 teaspoon dried parsley flakes
½ teaspoon freeze-dried chives
¼ teaspoon dried whole dillweed

¼ teaspoon dried whole basil
¼ teaspoon fennel seeds
½ (17 ¼-ounce) package frozen
   puff pastry, thawed
1 egg beaten

PREHEAT OVEN TO 375 DEGREES

1. Spread mustard over top of cheese; sprinkle with parsley flakes and next 4 ingredients.
2. Place cheese, mustard side down in center of pastry. Wrap package style, trimming excess pastry. Seal seams.
3. Place seam side down on a lightly greased baking sheet.
4. Brush with egg; chill 30 minutes.
5. Bake at 375 degrees for 20 minutes; brush with egg, and bake an additional 10 minutes or until golden brown. Serve warm with assorted crackers or sliced apples or pears.

   Yield: 8 to 10 appetizer servings.

CHEESE CRISPIES

2 sticks margarine at room temp.
8 ounces Cheddar cheese (grated)
2 cups flour
2 cups Rice Crispies

Pinch salt
½ tablespoon red pepper
1 teaspoon of water (or a little more)

PREHEAT OVEN TO 325 DEGREES

1. Using an electric mixer, mix grated cheese and margarine.
2. Slowly add flour.
3. Using a fork add Rice Crispies, seasoning and water.
4. Make into small balls and place on greased cookie sheet; press with a fork. Bake at 325 degrees for 15 minutes.
    Makes 75.

"PHILLY" CHEESE BELL

1 (8-ounce) package Cracker Barrel Cheddar cold pack cheese food
1 (8-ounce) package Philadelphia cream cheese
Margarine

2 teaspoons chopped pimento
2 teaspoons chopped green pepper
2 teaspoons chopped onion
1 teaspoon Worcestershire sauce
½ teaspoon lemon juice

1. Combine cheese food, softened cream cheese and 2 tablespoons margarine; mix until well blended.
2. Add remaining ingredients; mix well. Mold into bell shapes, using the Cracker Barrel container coated with margarine.
3. Chill until firm. Remove.
    Yield: 2 bells.

GARLIC CHEESE ROLLS

½ pound sliced pimento cheese, grated or ½ pound processed cheese and 2 pimentos, chopped and drained
1 pound grated American cheese
8 ounces soft cream cheese

½ pound blue cheese
3 cloves of garlic, grated
2 medium onions, grated
Red pepper to taste
1 teaspoon salt
½ cup Parmesan cheese

1. Mix ingredients well.
2. Shape into 4 rolls about diameter of cracker.
3. Roll in paprika and parsley; wrap in waxed paper. Chill for a day.
4. Slice thin and use on toast rounds or crackers.

HOT CRAB/CRAWFISH ARTICHOKE DIP WITH PITA TRIANGLES

1 large bell pepper, finely chopped
1 tablespoon cooking oil
2 (14-ounce) cans artichoke hearts, drained and chopped
2 cups mayonnaise
1 cup finely chopped green onions
1 cup fresh Italian Romano cheese
2 tablespoons lemon juice, freshly squeezed
½ cup pimento, diced
1 tablespoon Worcestershire sauce
3 fresh jalapeño peppers, seeded and minced
1 teaspoon salt
1 pound lump crabmeat (1 pound crawfish tails may be substituted)
½ cup blanched almonds or roasted pecans, sliced

1. In a small heavy skillet, sauté the bell peppers in oil until softened. Set aside to cool.
2. In a large bowl, combine the rest of the ingredients except the almonds or pecans. Check for seasoning adjustments you may want to make.
3. Transfer the mixture to an oven-proof chafing dish or baking dish and sprinkle the almonds or pecans on top. (This dip may be prepared up to this point one day in advance, kept covered and chilled.)
4. Bake the dip in a preheated 375 degree oven for 25 to 30 minutes or until golden and bubbly. Serve with pita triangles.

Serves 10 to 12.

PITA TRIANGLES

8 large pita bread loaves
1 stick (½-cup) melted butter

Salt and pepper

1. Cut each pita loaf into 8 wedges and separate each wedge into 2 triangles. Arrange the triangles rough side up in one tight layer in a jelly roll pan. Brush lightly with melted butter; season with salt and pepper to taste.
2. Bake the triangles in the upper third of the oven for 10 to 12 minutes, or until crisp. Let them cool in the pan. The triangles may be made one day in advance and kept covered in an airtight container at room temperature.

Makes 128 triangles.

STUFFED MUSHROOMS WITH CRABMEAT

12-18 large fresh mushrooms
2 tablespoons butter
2 tablespoons minced garlic
2 tablespoons parsley, chopped fine
2 tablespoons finely chopped green onions
3 tablespoons chopped mushroom stems
1 full cup crabmeat
¼ cup unseasoned breadcrumbs
3 ounce Chablis wine

1. Remove stems from mushrooms and save for filling. Sauté mushroom caps in 1 tablespoon butter until tender. Do not overcook. Set aside and save butter stock.
2. In another pan, use the remaining tablespoon of butter and sauté mushroom bits with minced garlic, parsley, and green onions. Stir constantly and cook over low fire for about five minutes.
3. Add crabmeat and stir mixture constantly. Sprinkle in plain bread crumbs to make filling more solid. Add Chablis wine for flavor and liquid. Also add butter in which mushroom caps were cooked.
4. Remove pan from burner and carefully stuff mushroom caps with mixture, placing them on broiler tin that has been covered with aluminum foil. Garnish with thin strips of Danish Havarti cheese or substitute with a similar cheese. Place in broiler and thoroughly heat. Remove when cheese strips show signs of melting. Serve at once.

PARTY PIZZAS

1 cup mayonnaise
1 cup chopped black olives
1 cup Cheddar cheese, grated
1 cup chopped dried beef in jar

1. Mix together and spread on party rye bread.
2. Broil about 4 minutes, 4 inches from broiler top.

NOTE: I add chopped green peppers and onions sometimes.

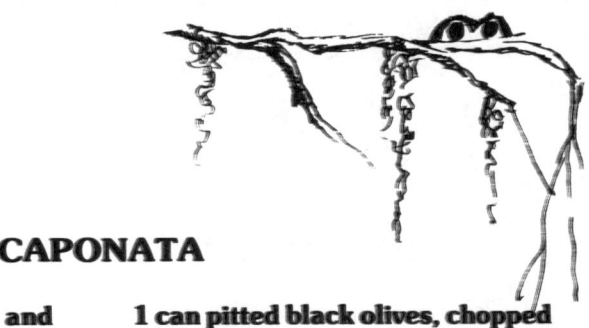

CAPONATA

- 2 medium eggplants, cubed and not peeled
- ½ cup good olive oil
- 2 medium onions, chopped
- 1½ cups sliced celery
- 2 medium bell peppers, chopped
- 2 garlic cloves, chopped
- 1 jar Italian olive salad
- 1 jar stuffed green olives, chopped
- 1 can pitted black olives, chopped
- 1 jar capers
- 2 cans Rotel tomatoes, chopped
- ⅓ cup red wine vinegar
- 2 tablespoons *each* salt, sugar, dried basil, tomato paste
- ½ cup chopped parsley
- 1 teaspoon black pepper

1. Heat olive oil in a 5 to 6 quart pot; add eggplant and onions. Sauté until light brown.
2. Add rest of ingredients. Simmer covered approximately one hour, stirring occasionally.
3. Remove lid and simmer until thick. (Note: Cook until most of the liquid has been cooked down.)
4. Serve at room temperature.

   Yield: 3 quarts.

NOTE: Excellent served with home-made pita crisps. Freezes well in plastic bags. Serve in hollowed-out eggplant surrounded by mounds of pita crisps. Pita crisps may be stored in freezer indefinitely, packaged in plastic bags. Bring to room temperature to serve.

Pita Crisps

- Pita or pocket bread, cut into 8 wedges like a pie and separated
- Butter, melted
- Salt, black pepper, garlic powder
- Tabasco to taste
- Tarragon, thyme, marjoram, freshly grated nutmeg to taste

1. Place pita wedges, bottom-side down, on baking pans.
2. Mix seasonings into melted butter.
3. Brush butter mixture generously on each wedge and bake in a 200-250 degree oven until golden brown, approximately 1½ to 2 hours.

KOZAN'S HAM AND CHEESE ROLLS

1 box Pillsbury hot roll mix
½ pound sliced turkey, julienne
  (cut in long thin strips)
½ pound sliced ham, julienne
½ pound sliced roast beef, julienne
½ pound grated Cheddar cheese
½ pound grated mozzarella cheese
Italian dressing

PREHEAT OVEN TO 350 DEGREES

1. Mix hot roll mix according to directions. Knead dough and let rise for 5 minutes. (Turn bowl over dough.)
2. Divide dough in half.
3. Divide ham, turkey, roast beef and cheeses in half.
4. Roll out dough 10 x 14 x ¼-inch. Brush top of dough with Italian dressing.
5. Place a layer of ham, roast beef, turkey, Cheddar and mozzarella cheese on dough. (Use half of ingredients in each roll.)
6. Roll (like a jelly roll), place diagonal on large cookie sheet. Seal edges.
7. Brush with a mixture of ¼ cup milk and 1 egg yolk.
8. Bake at 350 degrees for 25-30 minutes.

Serve with Dijon Mustard or Beer 'N Brat Mustard. Delicious for a tail gate party.

ROLLED TORTILLAS

1 can refried El Paso beans
1 package large flour tortillas
  (8-10)
1 (8-ounce) carton sour cream
1 (8-ounce) package cream cheese
1 (4-ounce) can chili peppers,
  chopped, drained
3 green onions, chopped
1 (4-ounce) can chopped black
  olives, drained
1 tablespoon picanté sauce
Salt, pepper to taste

1. Place refried beans in food processor and blend.
2. Cream cream cheese with electric mixer. Add sour cream and mix well.
3. Mix all ingredients except tortillas and refried beans.
4. Spread refried beans on tortillas.
5. Spread the sour cream mixture thinly on top of refried beans.
6. Roll, wrap in waxed paper, and refrigerate until ready for use.
7. Slice to desired thickness and serve with picanté sauce. These will keep for at least a week in the refrigerator.

BARBECUE SAUCE FOR LIL' SMOKIES

½ cup finely chopped onion
3 tablespoons vinegar
2 tablespoons brown sugar
1 cup catsup
3 tablespoons Worcestershire sauce
1 teaspoon celery seed
1 tablespoon prepared mustard
1 cup water
Dash hot sauce, if desired

1. Combine ingredients in saucepan; bring to a boil.
2. Pour over Smokies in baking pan. Place in slow oven (300 degrees) for 1½ to 2 hours. Serve in chafing dish. You can make the sauce ahead of time and heat with the Smokies in a slow cooker.

STUFFED EGGS

6 eggs
⅓ teaspoon salt
2 tablespoons mayonnaise
1 teaspoon mustard
2 tablespoons finely chopped sweet pickles
2 tablespoons chopped fine onion
1 tablespoon pickle juice
Black pepper, red pepper to taste
Paprika

1. Place eggs in saucepan of cold water. Bring to hard boil, and reduce heat slightly. Let boil slowly 15 minutes. Peel under cold running water.
2. Cut eggs lengthwise and remove yolks into bowl. Mash thoroughly with fork.
3. Add mayonnaise and all other ingredients. Fill the whites with mixture. Sprinkle lightly with paprika and garnish with parsley. If mixture is too dry, add a little more mayonnaise.

Serves 6.

NOTE: If you like a sour taste use lemon juice instead of pickle juice.

BACON-WRAPPED CRACKERS

Waverly wafers   Thin sliced bacon

1. Wrap a Waverly cracker with a thin slice of bacon. Sprinkle with thyme, oregano, red pepper and garlic powder. Bake in a 250 degree oven for 50 minutes.
2. Serve immediately or store in an airtight tin.

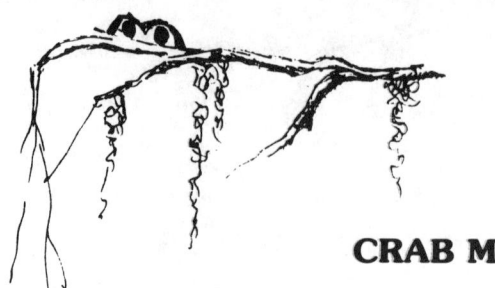

CRAB MUFFINS

1 (5-ounce) can crab meat, drained
1 stick margarine or butter, softened
2 teaspoons mayonnaise
⅛ teaspoon salt
1 package (6) English muffins
5 ounce jar Kraft Old English sharp Cheddar

1. Mix butter, cheese, mayonnaise and salt.
2. Add crabmeat.
3. Top each muffin with mixture (12 halves). Cut each half into fourths.
4. Freeze for at least 30 minutes (can be kept in freezer for weeks.)
5. When ready pop under broiler unit until brown and bubbly. Serve hot. Makes 48.

NOTE: To remove fishy taste, rinse crabmeat in cold water.

SAUSAGE PIZZA ROUNDS

½ pound sausage
½ pound ground beef
½ pound grated Cheddar cheese
½ teaspoon basil
½ teaspoon oregano
⅛ teaspoon garlic powder
1 tablespoon parsley flakes
1 loaf small party rye bread

1. Brown meats lightly in skillet, drain. Add cheese and spices.
2. Stir until melted and blended.
3. Spread on rye bread slices.
4. Freeze on cookie sheet. Put in plastic bags. Store in freezer.
5. To serve — thaw, then broil about 5 minutes or until bubbly.

Optional: Spread a little pizza sauce on top of each.
Yields: About 36.

CHEX PARTY MIX

6 tablespoons butter
4 teaspoons seasoned salt
4 teaspoons Worcestershire sauce
2 cups Rice Chex
2 cups Corn Chex
2 cups Wheat Chex
1 cup peanuts

1. Melt butter and then add the rest of the ingredients.
2. Cook 45 minutes at 250 degrees, stirring every 15 minutes.

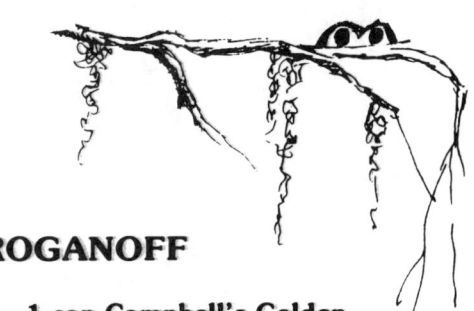

PARTY STROGANOFF

1 pound round steak, cut into thin strips
½ cup sliced onion
2 tablespoons butter or margarine
1 can Campbell's Golden Mushroom Soup
¼ cup white wine (Sauterne)
⅓ cup water
½ cup sour cream

1. In skillet, brown meat and onion in butter until tender.
2. Stir in soup, wine and water. Cover and simmer 45 minutes or until tender, stirring occasionally.
3. Mix in sour cream only until well blended. Serve over noodles.

   Serves 4.

OYSTER WRAPPED IN BACON

3 jars oysters, drain only 2 jars
2 cups seasoned bread crumbs
1 pound bacon
Red pepper to taste

1. Combine bread crumbs, 3 jars of oysters, *drained* two jars, and add juice from one jar in food processor using the chopping blade. Mix.
2. Give the bread crumbs a few seconds to absorb juice. Shape in a roll about the size of your thumb. Wrap ½ slice bacon around it. Secure with tooth pick. Place on broiler pan.
3. Broil until bacon is brown (turning).

   Makes about 60. Delicious!

MINI-MUFFALETTA

2 packages Pepperidge Farm Party Rolls (20 count)
½ pound sliced ham
⅓ pound sliced salami
⅓ pound sliced provolone cheese
⅓ pound sliced mozzarella cheese
1 jar Zatarain's Italian olive salad mix

1. Slice pan of rolls in half horizontally. Layer ham, provolone, mozzarella and salami on bottom half of bread.
2. Drain olive mix and chop fine. Spread on top of meat and cheese. Replace top half of rolls.
3. Wrap in foil and bake at 425 degrees for 20 minutes.

SPINACH, FETA AND PHYLLO PURSES

1½ cups finely chopped onion
½ cup olive oil
2 (10-ounce) packages frozen spinach, cooked, drained, squeezed dry by handfuls, and chopped

2 cups grated Feta (about ½-pound)
2 teaspoons dried dill
4 (16 x 12-inch) sheets of phyllo, stacked between 2 sheets of wax paper and covered with a dampened kitchen towel

PREHEAT OVEN TO 375 DEGREES

1. In a heavy skillet cook the onion in ¼ cup of the oil over moderately low heat, stirring occasionally, until it is golden, add the spinach, and cook the mixture, stirring, until it is combined well.
2. Remove the skillet from the heat, stir in the Feta and the dill, and let the filling cool.
3. Lay 1 sheet of the phyllo with a long side facing you on a work surface and brush it lightly with some of the remaining ¼ cup oil.
4. Lay another sheet of phyllo over the first sheet and brush it lightly with some of the remaining oil.
5. With a sharp knife cut the sheet lengthwise into thirds and cut each length crosswise into fifths, making 15 sections, each approximately 4 by 3½-inches.
6. Put a level teaspoon of the filling in the center of each phyllo section.
7. Working with 1 section at a time gather the corners of the phyllo over the filling and twist the phyllo closed gently.
8. Transfer the pastries to an oiled jelly-roll pan and make pastries with the remaining phyllo, oil, and filling in the same manner.
9. Bake the pastries in the lower third of a preheated 375 degree oven for 25 minutes, or until they are golden. (The pastries may be baked 1 day in advance and kept covered with plastic wrap and chilled. Reheat the pastries in a 375 degree oven for 10 minutes, or until they are heated through.)

Makes 30 hor d'oeuvres.

TIP: Make garnishes a couple of days before party. Seal in plastic bag. Mark on outside of bag which dish it is for.

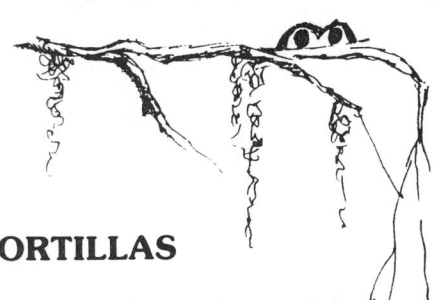

TOUCHDOWN TORTILLAS

8 ounces lite cream cheese
8 flour tortillas (7-inches in diameter)
8 slices Muenster cheese
½ cup yellow mustard
1 medium red onion, thinly sliced
4 ounces chopped green chilies
24 spinach leaves (approximately 3 leaves per rollwich)
16 ounces prosciutto, ham or turkey, thinly sliced

1. In a small bowl, combine the cream cheese and chilies. Mix well.
2. Spread a thin layer of the cream cheese mixture on each tortilla.
3. Layer each tortilla with spinach leaves, 1 slice of cheese, 2 slices of meat, 1 tablespoon of mustard and a thin layer of onions. Tightly roll up jelly-roll style.
4. Using plastic wrap, cover tightly and refrigerate until ready to serve.
5. Serve tortilla whole ("burrito-style"), or cut into 1-inch rounds and serve as bite-size snacks.

Makes 8 servings.

COCONUT BANANAS

Beautiful on any fruit platter.

4 bananas, peeled
4 tablespoons lemon juice
1 pint sour cream
1½ cups shredded coconut

1. Cut bananas into 1-inch pieces. Place lemon juice, sour cream and coconut in separate bowls. Dip banana pieces in lemon juice.
2. Roll in sour cream and then in coconut, making sure all sides are coated. Cover with plastic wrap and refrigerate several hours or overnight.

Makes about 24 pieces.

SPICED PINEAPPLE PICKUPS

1 can (29-ounce) pineapple chunks, undrained
1¼ cups sugar
¾ cup vinegar
8 whole cloves
1 small cinnamon stick
Dash salt

COOK DAY OR TWO BEFORE SERVING

1. Into medium saucepan, drain syrup from 1 can pineapple chunks.
2. Add sugar, vinegar, cloves, cinnamon stick and dash salt.
3. Cook over medium heat 10 minutes. Add pineapple chunks and heat to boiling.
4. Refrigerate. To serve, drain pineapple chunks and serve with cocktail picks.

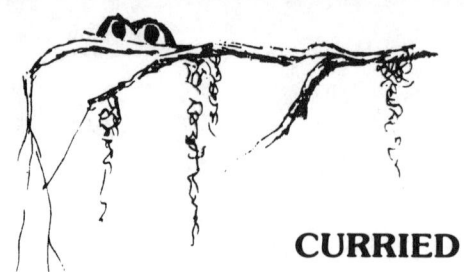

CURRIED SNACK MIX

4 cups bite-size squares bran cereal
1½ cups bite-size twist pretzels
½ cup unsalted dry roasted peanuts
¼ cup cooking oil
1 teaspoon curry powder
⅛ teaspoon ground red pepper
1 cup snipped dried apple
½ cup raisins

1. In a 13 x 9 x 2-inch baking pan combine cereal, pretzels, and peanuts.
2. Stir together oil, curry powder, red pepper, and ¼ teaspoon salt. Drizzle half of the oil mixture over cereal mixture. Toss. Repeat with remaining oil mixture.
3. Bake mix in a 300 degree oven for 30 minutes, stirring after 15 minutes. Stir in the apple and the raisins.
4. Spread mixture on foil to cool. Store in an airtight container for up to 2 weeks. Makes 8 cups snack mix.

TIROPETES

1 (8-ounce) package cream cheese
3 ounces Gruyere shredded or aged Swiss cheese
8 sheets filo dough
⅓ pound feta cheese
1 egg
2 tablespoons chopped parsley
½ cup melted butter

PREHEAT OVEN TO 375 DEGREES

1. Cream the cream cheese and feta. Mix in Gruyere.
2. Add egg and beat until well blended, add parsley.
3. Lay out filo and brush lightly with melted butter. Cut strips 3 x 14-inches.
4. Put 1 teaspoon mixture into one corner of dough and flag fold.
5. Place on ungreaed (lined with foil) baking sheet.
6. Bake 10 minutes - puffed and golden brown. Cool and freeze.
7. Reheat from frozen state in 375 degree oven for 10 minutes. Serve hot.

VEGETABLE DIP

1 cup mayonnaise (not Miracle Whip)
1½ cups sour cream
1 package Knorr's Vegetable soup mix
3 chopped green onions
1 can chopped water chestnuts
1 package frozen chopped spinach

1. After defrosting spinach, squeeze liquid out. You may use paper towel so that dip will not be runny.
2. Mix all above ingredients.
3. Serve with French bread morsels. Cut middle out of round loaf and fill with dip (use middle pieces to dip).

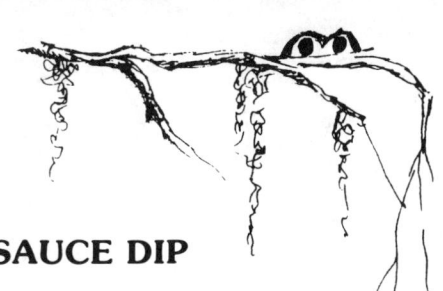

MEXICAN HOT SAUCE DIP

1 (15-ounce) can stewed tomatoes, drained
1 (12-ounce) can Rotel tomatoes, drained
1 (8-ounce) can jalapeño pepper relish, drained

1. Mix all ingredients together in blender until smooth. Serve with Doritos. Makes 1 quart. Very good on all Mexican food and as a dip.

SHRIMP DIP I

3 (8-ounce) packages Philadephia cream cheese
8 buttons of garlic or garlic salt
3 to 4 green onions or 1 package onion dip mix
3 to 4 tablespoons Worcestershire
1½ pounds cooked, clean and deveined shrimp
Vinegar and salad dressing

1. Mix cream cheese, and Worcestershire using electric mixer.
2. Using a fork, stir in garlic, onion dip and shrimp.
3. Add vinegar and salad dressing to taste.

SHRIMP DIP II

1 (8-ounce) package Philadephia cream cheese
1 (8-ounce) carton sour cream
2 cans shrimp, drained
1 teaspoon lemon juice
2 tablespoons mayonnaise
¼ bell pepper, chopped
1 onion, chopped
Salt, pepper

1. Blend cream cheese and sour cream.
2. Add lemon juice, and mayonnaise. Mix well.
3. Add shrimp, bell pepper, and onion. Mix.
4. Season and place in refrigerator until ready to serve. Garnish with paprika and tomato rose.

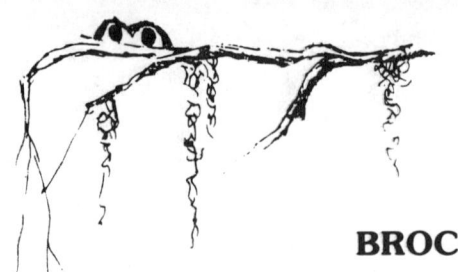

BROCCOLI DIP

1 package chopped, frozen broccoli
½ teaspoon salt
¼ cup water
1 small onion, chopped
2 tablespoons butter or margarine
1 can cream of mushroom soup
1 (6-ounce) roll garlic cheese

1 teaspoon Accent
½ teaspoon salt
⅛ teaspoon pepper
⅛ teaspoon Tabasco
1 teaspoon Worcestershire sauce
1 (4-ounce) can mushrooms, stems and pieces, drained
¾ cup slivered almonds

1. Cook broccoli with ½ teaspoon salt and ¼ cup water, drain and set aside.
2. Sauté onion in butter or margarine.
3. Add soup, cheese and seasonings; cook on medium heat until cheese melts.
4. Add broccoli and cook 1 minute longer. Stir occasionally to blend ingredients.
5. Add mushrooms and almonds. Serve hot. Use as a dip with chips or crisp crackers.

   Yields: 4 cups of dip.

ARTICHOKE DIP

2 cans Artichoke, drained
1 package Italian Dry Season Mix

1 cup mayonnaise
Tabasco

1. Combine all ingredients. Cover and place in refrigerator until ready to serve. Serve with wheat thins.

DRIED BEEF DIP

1 jar dried beef, chopped
1 (8-ounce) cream cheese
½ cup sour cream

2 tablespoons chopped fine onion
½ bell pepper, chopped
½ cup pecans, chopped

1. Mix all of the above ingredients. Cover and place in refrigerator until ready to serve. Serve in a scooped out red cabbage.

CRAB DIP

4 medium onions (size of an egg), chopped
2 packages green onions (use only half of green tails)
6 cloves garlic, chopped

1. Sauté all the above ingredients in 2 sticks of margarine.

Add:

2 cans mushroom soup
1 teaspoon red pepper
1 pound crab meat, fresh, frozen or canned
1 can mushrooms, stems and pieces, drained
1 roll jalapeño cheese or garlic cheese

2. Mix and heat thoroughly. Serve in chafing dish with garlic rounds.

BAKED CRABMEAT DIP

2 (8-ounce) packages cream cheese
1 can crab meat, picked
1/3 cup mayonnaise
3 teaspoons lemon juice
Tabasco to taste
Worcestershire sauce to taste

1. Combine ingredients. Pour into a buttered 9-inch pie plate. Garnish with paprika.
2. Bake at 300 degrees for 15 minutes. Serve cold with crackers.

VEGETABLE DIP

1/3 cup chili sauce
2 tablespoons horseradish
1 teaspoon mustard seed
1 cup mayonnaise
1 small onion chopped finely
Dash of Tabasco

1. Mix all ingredients in blender.
2. Use as a dip for cauliflower, celery, carrots, bell pepper or with shrimp.

QUICK SHRIMP DIP

1 carton Kleinpeter French onion dip
1 can shrimp, drained
Tony Chachere's seasoning to taste

Add 1 can of shrimp for each carton of onion dip.

TIP: Ranch dressing can be used as a dip for Fresh Vegetable Tray.

LAKE CHARLES DIP

½ pint sour cream
1 tablespoon mayonnaise
Juice of ½ lemon
½ tomato, chopped

1 package Good Seasons Italian
   salad dressing mix
½ avocado, chopped finely
Dash of Tabasco

1. Mix all ingredients.
2. Serve immediately or refrigerate.
3. This is delicious with chips or as a dip for raw vegetables.

SHRIMP AND MUSHROOM DIP

½ cup chopped green onion
1 onion, chopped
½ cup parsley
3 cloves garlic
1½ sticks butter
¾ pound mushrooms or 3 (4-ounce)
   cans, stems and pieces

1 pound shrimp (peeled and
   deveined)
½ cup seasoned bread crumbs
½ cup port wine (Gallo Rhine
   White Wine)

1. Sauté onions, parsley, and garlic in butter.
2. Add mushrooms and sauté 10 minutes on medium heat.
3. Add shrimp; sauté 10 minutes or until pink.
4. Add bread crumbs and mix thoroughly.
5. Add wine, simmer until heated thoroughly. Serve in a Chafing dish with garlic rounds.

BROCCOLI CHEESE DIP

1 package chopped broccoli,
   cooked and drained
3 stalks celery, chopped finely
1 medium onion, chopped finely
2 tablespoons butter

1 can cream of mushroom soup
1 roll garlic cheese
Worcestershire sauce to taste
Tabasco to taste

1. Sauté onion and celery in the butter.
2. Add cooked broccoli, mushroom soup, garlic cheese, Worcestershire sauce, and Tabasco to taste.
3. You may add ½ can of Rotel tomatoes if desired, or just use the juice.

* One pound of fresh lump crabmeat or 2 cans of crabmeat is a delicious addition also.

SPICY ITALIAN DIP

1 cup Miracle Whip salad dressing
½ cup sour cream
1 (7-ounce) package Italian salad dressing mix
½ teaspoon hot pepper sauce

1. Mix salad dressing, sour cream, salad dressing mix and pepper sauce until well blended. Chill.
2. Serve with assorted chips and/or vegetables dippers.

   Makes 1½ cups.

QUESO DIP

2 cans Hormel chili without beans
2 rolls jalapeño cheese
2 rolls garlic cheese

1. Melt cheeses together and mix with chili. Serve with corn chips.

Note: If you heat just before leaving for the game and wrap the bowl in aluminum foil, it will still be hot after you park and start to tailgate.

SALLY'S MOUNT ST. HELENA

1 can bean dip
1 container avocado dip
1 cup sour cream
¼ cup mayonnaise
1 package taco seasoning
Green onions, chopped
Tomatoes, chopped
1 large can ripe olives, sliced
Sharp Cheddar cheese

1. Spread one layer of bean dip and one layer of avocado dip in a 9 x 11-inch pan or large round platter.
2. Mix together sour cream, mayonnaise and taco seasoning; layer over the above.
3. Over that layer enough green onions to completely cover, enough chopped tomatoes to completely cover, and 1 large can of ripe olives that have been sliced.
4. Top with lots of grated sharp Cheddar cheese.

   Serve with fritos or nachos. I usually double everything.

SALAD BAR BASKET AND CHEDDAR PARTY ONIONS

Several bunches of leaf lettuce
Whole cauliflower
Red cabbage
Broccoli
Tomato
Green peppers
Carrot sticks
Cucumbers
Mushrooms
Radishes
Green onions
Your favorite dressings
Large basket
Plastic lined clay pots

1. Line a large basket with several bunches of leaf lettuce.
2. Arrange whole cauliflower; red cabbage, cut in half; broccoli stalks; tomato, cut in half; green peppers with tops and insides removed, filled with carrot sticks; cucumbers; mushrooms; and radishes over lettuce.
3. Tie groups of green onions to basket handle with clear plastic thread or florist's wire.
4. To serve, place several knives or pairs of kitchen scissors around basket allowing guests to "make" their own salads.
5. Serve your favorite dressing in plastic lined clay pots.

This clever idea could serve as an edible centerpiece for a large buffet.

Cheddar Party Onions

Green onions
Cream cheese
Cheddar cheese, shredded

1. Spread cream cheese over the bulb end of trimmed green onions.
2. Roll the onions in shredded Cheddar cheese. Make a quick and tasty hors d' oeuvre.

FRUIT YOGURT DIP

8 ounces cream cheese, softened
2 tablespoons brown sugar
16 ounces orange yogurt
1 teaspoon lemon juice
8 ounce can crushed pineapple, drained
¾ cup flaked coconut

1. Beat cream cheese at medium speed of electric mixer until fluffy.
2. Add next 3 ingredients and beat until smooth.
3. Stir in crushed pineapple and coconut.
4. Serve with assorted fresh fruit.

   Yield 3½ cups.

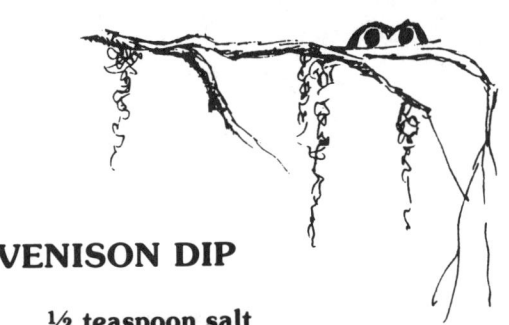

HOT BEAN-VENISON DIP

½ pound ground venison
¼ cup minced onion
1 (16-ounce) can kidney beans, mashed
1 tablespoon chili powder
½ cup catsup
½ teaspoon salt
½ teaspoon cumin
½ teaspoon cayenne pepper
1 (4-ounce) can green chilies, diced
½ pound Monterey Jack or Cheddar cheese, shredded

PREHEAT OVEN TO 350 DEGREES

1. Sauté onions in butter, then add meat and brown.
2. Add remaining ingredients, saving some of the cheese for the top, and simmer 10 to 15 minutes.
3. Pour into a casserole dish and top with the remaining cheese. Bake at 350 degrees until cheese is melted. Serve with tostadas or corn chips.

WINE PUNCH

1.5 liters Gallo Rhine wine
1 cup Karo syrup, white
Large bunch of grapes
2 lemons
1 large orange
28 ounce bottle club soda

1. Mix wine, Karo and fruit the night before; refrigerate. Cut the lemons and oranges into cartwheels, lemon twists and slices.
2. Add club soda and ice before serving. Serve in a crystal pitcher with fruit on a silver tray with wine glasses. Elegant!

PARTY PUNCH

1 (46-ounce) can unsweetened pineapple juice
1 (46-ounce) can apple juice
2 (28-ounce) bottles chilled 7up

1. Mix pineapple juice and apple juice. Freeze.
2. One hour before serving set out the frozen mixture.
3. When ready to serve place partially frozen fruit juices in punch bowl. Pour 7up over fruit juices. Garnish with lemon and orange slices, and mint leaves. Punch will be icy.

   Yield: 30 cups.

GELATIN PUNCH

2 packages fruit-flavored gelatin (cherry, raspberry or strawberry)
1 can frozen orange juice
1 can frozen lemonade
1 (46-ounce) can pineapple juice

1. Dissolve gelatin with hot water according to directions.
2. Add frozen juices diluted with amount of water required on can.
3. Add pineapple juice and mix thoroughly.
4. Add sugar if a sweeter punch is desired. Serve over ice.

   Makes over a gallon of punch. Serves 25.

CRANBERRY PUNCH

1 (12-ounce) can frozen orange juice, thawed
1 (6-ounce) can frozen lemonade, thawed
1 (20-ounce) can pineapple juice (2½ cups)
1½ quarts (6-cups) ginger ale
3 quarts (12-cups) cranberry juice cocktail

1. Prepare orange juice and lemonade according to package directions.
2. Add pineapple juice, ginger ale and cranberry juice.

   Makes 95 (4-ounce) servings or 47 (8-ounce) servings.

SPICED TEA

1 cup instant tea
1 (18-ounce) jar orange flavored instant breakfast drink
2 (3-ounce) packages lemonade mix
½ cup sugar
2 teaspoons cinnamon
2 teaspoons ground cloves

1. Mix ingredients and store in covered container.
2. To make tea, use 2 heaping teaspoons of tea mix per cup of boiling water.

CAPPUCCINO

4 teaspoons instant decaffeinated coffee granules
7 tablespoons plus 1½ teaspoons non-fat dry milk powder
4 teaspoons unsweetened cocoa powder
3 tablespoons plus 1 teaspoon sugar
½ teaspoon Imitation vanilla butter and nut flavoring

1. Process all ingredients in blender or food processor until well blended. Makes ¾ cup, 12 (1-tablespoon) servings. To serve, place 1 level tablespoon of mix in mug or cup. Add ¾ cup (6-ounce) boiling water and mix well.

FROZEN MARGARITAS

2 (6-ounce) cans frozen limeade
2 (6-ounce) cans frozen lemonade
⅓-⅔ cup Triple Sec (liqueur)
Juice of 2 limes
1-1½ cups Tequila (to taste)
6 cups water

1. Mix all ingredients in air tight plastic containers such as gallon ice cream buckets. Freeze overnight. Mixture will never freeze firm.
2. Serve in salt rimmed glasses. Will keep indefinitely in freezer.

BANANA PUNCH

2 quarts + 2½ cups water
5¼ cups sugar
8 bananas, mashed in blender
9 ounce frozen orange juice concentrate
9 ounce frozen lemonade concentrate
2 (46-ounce) cans pineapple juice
2 quarts ginger ale

1. Boil water and sugar 5 minutes.
2. Cool and add the remaining ingredients except ginger ale.
3. Freeze.
4. Remove from freezer 2 to 3 hours before serving. Mix with ginger ale.
5. May float assorted fruit in punch bowl.

   Makes 2 gallons.

MOCK CHAMPAGNE

⅔ cup chilled 7-up   ⅓ cup chilled white grape juice

Serve in punch bowl.

WINE COOLER CONCENTRATE

1 (6-ounce) can frozen cranberry juice cocktail concentrate, thawed

1 (6-ounce) can frozen orange juice concentrate, thawed

1 (6-ounce) can frozen pineapple juice concentrate, thawed

For concentrate, in a small airtight container or jar with a screw-top lid stir together all ingredients. Cover; chill up to 2 weeks.

For 1 serving: Add ⅓ cup dry white wine and ⅓ cup carbonated water to 3 tablespoons of the Wine Cooler Concentrate. Serve over ice in a tall glass. If desired, garnish glasses with an orange wedge, skewered cranberries, or pineapple chunk.

For 12 servings: In a 3-quart pitcher add 32 ounces (4 cups) each of dry white wine and carbonated water to the concentrate; mix well. Serve over ice in tall glasses. Garnish as directed above.

Makes 12 (8-ounce) servings.

Kindle the spirit of your party with this homemade wine cooler.

VODKA SLUSH

1 small orange juice, concentrated, thawed
1 large can pineapple juice
1 cup sugar

1 cup water
1 jar cherries and juice
1 (2-liter) 7-up
½ of a fifth of vodka

1. Mix and freeze.

INSTANT HOT COCOA MIX

1 box (8-quart) powdered milk
1 jar (11-ounce) Coffee Mate
1 can (16-ounce) instant chocolate (Quick)
1 box powdered sugar

1. Mix all of the above ingredients.
2. Store in an air tight container.
3. Put ⅓ cup of cocoa mix in mug. Fill with boiling water.

INSTANT SPICED TEA

1 package Kool Aid lemonade mix (5-ounce)
1 cup sugar
½ cup instant tea
7-ounce Tang
½ teaspoon cloves
½ teaspoon cinnamon

1. Combine all of the above ingredients.
2. Store in air tight container.

WASSAIL

1 quart apple cider
2 cups cranberry juice
½ cup brown sugar
3 sticks cinnamon
¼ teaspoon ground ginger
½ teaspoon allspice
¼ teaspoon ground mace
1 large orange cut into eights and pierce with whole cloves

1. Put all ingredients in large crock pot. Cover and cook for 1 hour on high, stirring occasionally.
2. Cook on low temperature for 4 hours

   Serves 12.

TIP: Serve hot food hot and cold food cold

MINTED TEA

1¾ cups sugar
2 cups water
8 regular-size tea bags
1 quart boiling water
8 sprigs fresh mint

2 quarts cold water
2 cups orange juice
¾ cup lemon juice
Fresh mint sprigs (optional)

1. Combine sugar and 2 cups water in a saucepan; stir well. Bring to a boil; boil 5 minutes.
2. Remove from heat.
3. Add tea bags and 8 sprigs fresh mint to 1 quart boiling water; cover and let stand 10 minutes. Remove tea bags and mint.
4. Combine sugar water, tea mixture, 2 quarts cold water, orange juice, and lemon juice; stir well.
5. Serve over ice. Garnish with mint sprigs, if desired.

   Yield: about 1 gallon.

BLOODY MARY A LA VIVIAN

Makes 1 gallon — keeps 10 days in refrigerator.

1 (46-ounce) can and 4 cups tomato juice
1 can Campbell's beef broth
⅓ cup Lea & Perrins
1 cup lemon juice

14 drops Tabasco
2 tablespoons celery salt
1 teaspoon black pepper
1 teaspoon salt
3 cups vodka

1. Mix all ingredients and chill several hours or overnight for flavor to develop.

TIP: To dry lemons and oranges in microwave — Take an ice pick and punch holes in lemon or orange (about 3 holes 1-inch deep). Place lemon on a folded paper towel. Microwave for 2 minutes. Take lemon out and wipe off any excess juice — microwave 2 more minutes — Repeat process until lemon is hard and dry. Excellent to use as decoration in centerpiece or topiary.

Soups
and
Gumbos

FISH CHOWDER

1 pound fillet of haddock (can use other fish)
1½ cups diced raw potato
1 cup chopped celery
½ cup chopped onions
1 bay leaf
4 cups water
1½ cups instant nonfat dry milk solid
2 tablespoons margarine
3 tablespoons flour
2 teaspoons salt
Generous dash white pepper
Chopped parsley

1. In large saucepan combine fish, potato, celery, onion, bay leaf and water. Simmer 15 minutes, until potatoes are fork tender.
2. Flake fish with fork into bite-size pieces. Remove bay leaf.
3. Strain mixture reserving liquid.
4. Stir dry milk solids into liquid.
5. Melt margarine in large saucepan. Blend in flour, salt, and pepper.
6. Gradually blend in reserved liquid.
7. Cook over medium heat, stirring constantly until mixture comes to a boil.
8. Add strained fish mixture. Heat thoroughly. Serve hot garnished with parsley.

   7 servings.

FISH CHOWDER II

1 cup chopped onion
2 tablespoons butter
1 pound frozen cod or haddock fillets (or firm white fish such as drum or grouper, or shrimp)
4 cups sliced potatoes
1 cup water
1 (4-ounce) can sliced mushrooms
1 (16-ounce) can cream-styled corn
1 (10-ounce) can cream of mushroom soup
1 (13-ounce) can evaporated milk
2 cups milk
¼ teaspoon pepper
2 teaspoons salt
2 teaspoons Cajun seasoning

1. Sauté onion in butter in large saucepan until tender. Add fish, potatoes and water.
2. Simmer, covered, for 30 minutes or until fish flakes easily and potatoes are tender.
3. Add remaining ingredients; mix well.
4. Heat to serving temperature.

   Yield: 12 servings.

   Calories: 137 per serving.

CRAB AND CORN SOUP

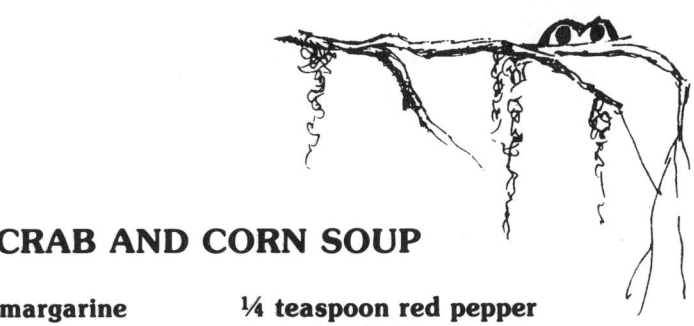

½ pound butter or margarine
3 tablespoons flour
1 large onion, chopped
1 quart milk
1 (16-ounce) can cream style corn
1 can cream of potato soup
¼ teaspoon mace
¼ teaspoon red pepper
1 pint picked crabmeat
¼ pound grated Swiss cheese
2 tablespoons snipped parsley
2 tablespoons finely chopped green onion

1. In large heavy pot, melt butter. Stir in flour until well blended, but not brown; add onions. Cook on medium heat until onions are soft, about 10 minutes.
2. Add milk, corn, potato soup, mace and red pepper. Simmer about 15 minutes. Be careful not to scorch.
3. Before serving, stir in crabmeat, cheese, parsley and green onions.

   Serves 6 to 8.

This soup is excellent using shrimp instead of crabmeat. Add 2 pounds of cleaned deveined shrimp in step 3.

SHRIMP AND CORN SOUP

⅓ cup oil
3 tablespoons flour
2 medium onions, finely chopped
1 large bell pepper, coarsely chopped
1 pound medium shrimp, peeled
2 tablespoons parsley
Salt, black pepper and red pepper to taste
1 (1-pound) can whole peeled tomatoes, undrained
1 (1-pound) can whole kernel corn (drain off ½ liquid)
1 cup water

1. Make a roux with oil and flour. When roux is golden brown, add onions. Cook for 10 to 15 minutes.
2. Add bell peppers, shrimp, parsley, salt and pepper. Simmer for 5 to 10 minutes.
3. Add tomatoes, corn, and 1 cup water. Simmer at least 1 hour adding more water gradually until desired consistency.

   Serves 6.

SEAFOOD GUMBO

1 cup bacon drippings
1 cup all-purpose flour
8 ribs celery, chopped
3 large yellow onions, chopped
1 bunch chopped green onions
1 green pepper, chopped
2 cloves garlic, minced
½ cup parsley, chopped
1 pound okra, sliced
2 tablespoons shortening
2 quarts chicken stock
2 quarts water
½ cup Worcestershire sauce
Tabasco sauce to taste
½ cup catsup
1 (16-ounce) can whole tomatoes
2 tablespoons salt
1 large slice of ham, chopped
2 bay leaves
¼ teaspoon thyme
¼ teaspoon rosemary
2 cups cooked chicken, chopped
1 pound claw crabmeat
3 to 4 pounds shrimp, peeled
1 pint oysters, optional
1 teaspoon brown sugar
Lemon juice to taste

1. Heat bacon drippings over medium heat, add flour slowly and stir constantly until roux is a chocolate-like brown. This takes a long time.
2. Add celery, onions, green pepper, garlic, parsley and cook 45 minutes to 1 hour stirring occasionally.
3. Fry okra in shortening until slightly browned. Add to first mixture and stir well for a few minutes.
4. Add chicken stock and water, Worcestershire sauce, Tabasco sauce, catsup, tomatoes with juice, salt, ham, bay leaves, thyme, rosemary.
5. Simmer 2½ hours. Add chicken, crabmeat, shrimp and simmer 30 minutes more. (If using oysters, add with seafood.) Add brown sugar and lemon juice. Serve in bowls over hot rice. Well worth the time!

Serves 20.

ITALIAN SOUP

2 cans (13¾-ounce) chicken broth
1 (28-ounce) can crushed tomatoes
1 (10-ounce) package mixed vegetables
1 (16-ounce) can white beans, drained
1 cup thin sliced cabbage
1 envelope Good Seasons Italian Salad Dressing mix
½ cup uncooked elbow macaroni
1½ cups water

1. Bring broth, water, and tomatoes to boil in large saucepan.
2. Add vegetables, beans, cabbage, salad dressing mix and macaroni. Return to boil. Reduce heat and simmer until vegetables are tender.

NOTE: I like to use frozen Italian vegetables and sometimes red kidney beans.

ADDIE McCOY'S CORN & SHRIMP SOUP

2 pounds shrimp, peeled
8 ears fresh corn (cut off kernels and scrape cob good for juice)
1 large yellow onion, chopped

¾ cup chopped celery
1 bunch green onions, chopped
1 bunch parsley, chopped
4 tablespoons tomato sauce

Roux

1 cup oil   1 cup flour

1. Make roux: Pour oil in bottom of dutch oven. Add 1 cup flour, stirring constantly until golden brown.
2. Add yellow onion and celery, sauté 1 minute, add tomato sauce, sauté 1 to 2 minutes, add green onions. Sauté 2 minutes.
3. Add corn and juice. Sauté 1 minute. Add parsley. Sauté 2 minutes. Add 4 or 5 cups of water to right consistency. Bring to a boil. Turn down to low heat. Add salt, black pepper, and Tabasco to taste. Boil slowly uncovered for 30 minutes.
4. Add shrimp. Simmer for 15 minutes (if you cook too long, shrimp will be tough.)

***Substitute for fresh corn: 1 can (17-ounce) whole kernel corn and 1 can (17-ounce) cream corn.

SHRIMP GUMBO

2 pounds shrimp
2 tablespoons oil
2 tablespoons flour
3 cups okra, chopped or 1 tablespoon filé
2 onions, chopped
2 tablespoons oil

1 can tomatoes
2 quarts water
1 bay leaf
1 teaspoon salt
3 pods garlic (optional)
Red pepper (optional)

1. Peel shrimp uncooked and devein.
2. Make roux (dark) of flour and oil.
3. Add shrimp to this for a few minutes stirring constantly. Set aside.
4. Smother okra and onions in oil. Add tomatoes when okra is nearly cooked.
5. Then add water, bay leaf, garlic, salt, and pepper. Add shrimp and roux to this.
6. Cover and cook slowly, for 30 minutes.
   If okra is not used, add gumbo filé after turning off heat. Serve with rice.

   Serves 6 to 8.

SEAFOOD GUMBO III

2 pounds shrimp
½ pint oysters
2 cans crabmeat
4 tablespoons oil
4 tablespoons flour
4 cups chopped okra
1 cup chopped onion
1 can stewed tomatoes

3 quarts water
4 garlic cloves
¼ cup chopped parsley
¼ cup shallots
1 can beer
Red pepper, black pepper and salt
   to taste

1. In heavy cast iron Dutch oven, make a dark roux. Add okra, onions, shallots, garlic and parsley. Cook over low fire until onions are clear — stir constantly to prevent sticking.
2. Add beer, water, stewed tomatoes and seasonings. Cook over medium fire for 45 minutes.
3. Add oysters, shrimp, and crabmeat. Cook 15 minutes. Serve over rice.

   6 to 8 servings.

CREAM OF PEANUT SOUP

1 medium onion, chopped
2 ribs celery, chopped
¼ cup butter
3 tablespoons all-purpose flour

2 quarts chicken stock, or canned
   chicken broth
2 cups smooth peanut butter
1¾ cups light cream
Peanuts, chopped, for garnishing

1. Sauté the onion and the celery in butter until soft, but not brown.
2. Stir in the flour until well blended.
3. Add the chicken stock, stirring constantly, and bring to a boil.
4. Remove from the heat and pureé in food processor or a blender.
5. Add the peanut butter and cream, stirring to blend thoroughly.
6. Return to low heat and heat until just hot, but do not boil.

   Serve, garnished with peanuts.

   NOTE: This soup is also good served ice cold.

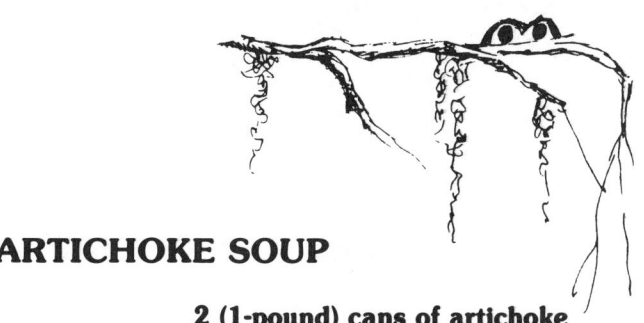

ARTICHOKE SOUP

½ cup butter
1 large onion, chopped
1 bunch green onion, chopped
2 pods garlic, pressed
2 tablespoons parsley, chopped
2 dozen oysters

2 (1-pound) cans of artichoke hearts
1 cup oyster liquor or water
1 (10¾-ounce) can cream of mushroom soup
1 bay leaf
Salt and pepper

1. Melt butter in Dutch oven.
2. Add chopped onions and cook until transparent.
3. Add garlic and parsley and cook 2 to 3 minutes.
4. Add oysters and cook 3 to 4 more minutes. Add drained, quartered artichoke hearts and cook for a few more minutes.
5. Add oyster liquor, cream of mushroom soup and bay leaf. Cook for 20 minutes. Prepare 30 minutes or so before serving to allow flavors to penetrate. Salt and pepper to taste.

Serves 4 to 6.

CHICKEN GUMBO

2 fryers
1 pound hot sausage
1 pound mild sausage
1 large package okra
2 tablespoons shortening
2 cans stew tomatoes (large)

2 large onions, chopped
1 bunch green onions, chopped
4 cloves garlic, finely chopped
3 ribs of celery, chopped
1 stick margarine
1 cup flour

1. Cook and debone chicken. Cut in bite size pieces.
2. Heat margarine over low heat, add flour slowly and stir constantly until roux is a chocolate-like brown.
3. Add onions, celery, green onions, and garlic to roux and sauté until tender
4. Fry okra in shortening.
5. Combine all ingredients. Add chicken broth and enough water to make 1½ quarts of liquid.
6. Add seasoning — salt, red pepper, black pepper and parsley. Cook for 1 hour.

CHICKEN OKRA GUMBO

1 fryer (about 2 pounds)
1½ pounds fresh okra
1 fresh tomato, chopped
1 large onion, chopped
2 tablespoons shortening

3 tablespoons shortening or bacon drippings (from that used to fry chicken)
2 tablespoons flour
3 quarts water
Salt and pepper to taste

1. Cut up chicken; dredge with flour, salt and pepper. Fry until brown.
2. Fry okra with tomato and onion in the shortening.
3. Make a roux in a heavy skillet with grease from fried chicken and flour. Brown roux.
4. Add fried chicken and the vegetables. Stir for a few minutes. Add water. Salt and pepper to taste.
5. Cook for about 2 hours.

Serves 6.

AVOCADO SOUP

1 cup chopped onion
¾ cup chopped celery
1 (5-ounce) can chicken, drained
2 cups chicken broth
1½ cups half-and-half
¾ cup sour cream

3 medium avocados, peeled and mashed
½ teaspoon hot sauce
¼ teaspoon salt
¼ teaspoon pepper
½ cup dry white wine
¼ cup chopped fresh parsley

1. Combine first 4 ingredients in a saucepan. Bring to a boil; cover, reduce heat, and simmer 20 minutes.
2. Pour half of broth mixture into container of an electric blender; process until smooth.
3. Add half each of half-and-half and sour cream.
4. Process until blended. Set aside.
5. Repeat procedure with remaining broth mixture, half-and-half, and sour cream.
6. Combine mixtures; cover and chill.
7. Stir in avocados, hot sauce, salt, pepper, and wine.
8. Chill at least 1 hour. Garnish each serving with parsley.

Yield: 7 cups.

TORTILLA SOUP

1 cup chopped onion
4 cloves garlic, minced
¼ cup vegetable oil
2 (14½-ounce) cans stewed tomatoes
2 (10-ounce) cans tomatoes and green chilies
2 (10½-ounce) cans beef bouillon
2 (10¾-ounce) cans chicken broth, undiluted
2 (10¾-ounce) cans tomato soup, undiluted
3 cups water
2 teaspoons ground cumin
2 tablespoons chopped fresh cilantro
6-8 flour tortillas, cut into ½-inch strips, divided
1 cup (4-ounce) shredded Cheddar cheese
½ teaspoon ground red chilies

1. Sauté first 2 ingredients in oil in a large Dutch oven until tender; add next 9 ingredients.
2. Bring to a boil; cover, reduce heat, and simmer 1 hour.
3. Add ¾ of tortilla strips and shredded cheese. Simmer 5 minutes.
4. Garnish with remaining tortilla strips.

   Yield: 10 cups.

This is a delicious soup to serve with Chicken Fajitas and Rolled Tortilla.

$3000 PICANTE ONION SOUP

3 cups thinly sliced onion
1 garlic clove, minced
¼ cup butter or margarine
2 cups tomato juice
1 (10½-ounce) can condensed beef broth*
1 can water
½ cup picanté sauce
1 cup unflavored croutons
1 cup (4-ounces) shredded Monterey Jack Cheese

1. In (3-quart) saucepan over medium-low heat, cook onions and garlic in butter until tender and golden brown, about 20 minutes, stirring frequently.
2. Stir in tomato juice, broth, water and picanté sauce. Bring to a boil. Reduce heat; simmer uncovered 20 minutes.
3. Ladle into soup bowls; sprinkle with croutons and cheese. Serve with additional picanté sauce.

   Makes 4 servings, about 5 cups soup.

   NOTE: 2⅔ cups single-strength beef broth may be substituted for condensed beef broth and water.

FRENCH ONION SOUP

4 large red onions
1 tablespoon olive oil
2 tablespoons butter
1 teaspoon sugar
Salt and red pepper to taste

1 quart chicken stock
Small rounds of French bread, toasted
1 package mozzarella cheese

PREHEAT OVEN TO 350 DEGREES

1. Cut onions into small pieces. Sauté onions in oil and butter until tender.
2. Add sugar, salt and red pepper. Place in 9 x 13-inch casserole and add stock.
3. Toast French bread; float it on top of soup.
4. Sprinkle cheese over soup. Bake in oven for 20 minutes.

   Serves 4 to 6.

YELLOW SQUASH SOUP

5 or 6 medium yellow squash, cubed
4 medium potatoes, peeled and cubed
1 large onion, chopped

1 stick margarine
1 can chicken broth
1 (13-ounce) can evaporated milk
Creole seasoning to taste
Salt and pepper, optional

1. Cube squash and potatoes.
2. In heavy pot, combine squash, potatoes, onion and margarine. Cover tightly and cook slowly until all vegetables are soft. Stir frequently to prevent sticking.
3. After vegetables are soft, purée in blender or food processor.
4. Return puréed vegetables to pot. Add the chicken broth and evaporated milk. Season to taste. Heat to serve but do not boil.

   Serves 6 to 8.

Salads

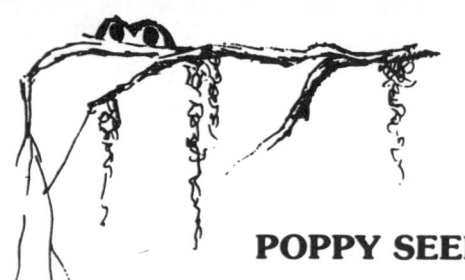

POPPY SEED DRESSING

1 cup sugar
2 teaspoons dry mustard
2 teaspoons salt
⅔ cup vinegar
3 tablespoons onion juice
3 tablespoons poppy seeds
2 cups salad oil

1. Add all ingredients and mix in mixer or shake in jar. This is better if not made in blender. Refrigerate.

    Yields 3½ cups.

THELMA'S FRESH FRUIT DIP

1 jar marshmallow cream (medium)
8 ounces cream cheese (softened)
Grated rind of 1 orange

1. Mix well and serve with fresh strawberries, bananas, pineapple, etc.

FLUFFY FRUIT DRESSING

⅓ cup sugar
1 tablespoon all-purpose flour
1 teaspoon grated lemon peel
¼ cup lemon juice
1 egg, beaten
1 cup halved marshmallows (2-ounce)
½ pint dairy sour cream (1-cup)

1. In a 1-quart saucepan, combine sugar and flour.
2. Stir in lemon peel, lemon juice and egg, mixing until smooth.
3. Add marshmallows.
4. Stir over low heat until mixture thickens slightly and marshmallows melt, 10 to 15 minutes.
5. Cool slightly.
6. Stir in sour cream. May be refrigerated several days.

    Makes 2 cups.

RUSSIAN OR THOUSAND ISLAND DRESSING

1 cup mayonnaise
⅔ cup chili sauce
2 tablespoons milk
4 tablespoons sweet pickle relish

1. Combine ingredients; chill.

CREAMY TART FRENCH DRESSING

¼ cup corn oil
¾ cup mayonnaise
¼ cup red wine vinegar
1½ tablespoons sugar

1 tablespoon paprika
1 tablespoon dry mustard
½ teaspoon salt
1 clove minced garlic

1. Gradually stir corn oil into mayonnaise. Beat until smooth.
2. Combine remaining ingredients. Add to mayonnaise mixture. Chill.

HONEY-CREAM DRESSING FOR FRUIT SALAD

1 cup mayonnaise
½ cup heavy cream, whipped
¼ teaspoon salt

1 tablespoon lemon juice
2 tablespoons honey
¼ teaspoon nutmeg

1. Combine mayonnaise with salt, lemon juice, honey and nutmeg.
2. Whip cream and fold into mayonnaise mixture.
3. Refrigerate until well chilled.
4. Combine with your favorite fruits (oranges, apples, pineapple, bananas, etc. and a small amount of coconut.) Serve on lettuce cups.

    Makes about 2 cups of dressing.

This makes quite a bit of dressing. 4 oranges, 4 apples, 4 bananas and 1 large can of pineapple chunks, drained are what I have used with this recipe.

    Serves approximately 12 to 16.

CREAMY ITALIAN DRESSING

¾ cup mayonnaise
1 tablespoon white vinegar
1 tablespoon lemon juice
1 tablespoon corn oil
1 tablespoon water

1 teaspoon Worcestershire sauce
½ teaspoon dried oregano
1 teaspoon sugar
1 small clove garlic, minced

1. Combine ingredients. Chill.

24 HOUR SALAD

1 egg
½ cup sugar
1 tablespoon cornstarch
⅛ teaspoon salt
⅓ cup orange juice

⅓ cup pineapple juice or syrup from canned pineapple tidbits
⅓ cup lemon juice
¼ teaspoon grated orange rind
½ pint whipping cream

Salad Dressing

1. Using top of double boiler or a heavy saucepan, beat the egg until thick and lemon colored.
2. Gradually beat in the combined sugar, cornstarch and salt.
3. Then stir in the fruit juice and grated peel. Cook over hot water on very low heat, stirring constantly until thickened.
4. Remove from heat. Cover. Chill.
5. Whip cream until fairly stiff.
6. Fold in the whipped cream.

Salad Mixture

2 cups fresh plums
2 cups seedless grapes
2 cups pineapple tidbits, drained

1 cup orange segments
2 cups tiny marshmallows

1. Using a salad bowl, lightly combine all fruit and marshmallows.
2. Carefully fold in liberal amount of salad dressing so that each piece of fruit and marshmallows are well coated.
3. Cover the bowl with cover, place in refrigerator to chill for at least 24 hours.

LAYERED CHICKEN SALAD

4 cups torn lettuce
1 cup sliced celery
1 (7-ounce) can small early peas, drained
3 cups cooked chicken, bite size

1 cup chopped green pepper
1 small onion, sliced
4½ ounce jar sliced mushrooms, drained

1. Layer in above order.
2. Cover top with mayonnaise.
3. Cover and refrigerate 8 hours or overnight. Top with egg and tomato wedges. Scoop to the bottom to serve.

CALIFORNIA SPINACH SALAD

5 cups torn spinach leaves (no stems)
6 slices bacon, cut in 1-inch pieces
2 cups sliced fresh mushrooms
½ cup large pieces walnuts
¼ cup pimento strips

3 tablespoons tarragon wine vinegar
1 tablespoon brown sugar, packed
1 teaspoon seasoned salt
½ teaspoon tarragon
½ teaspoon onion powder
⅛ teaspoon pepper

1. Chill spinach.
2. Cook bacon until crisp; remove and drain on paper towel.
3. Measure ¼ cup bacon drippings and discard remainder.
4. Sauté mushrooms and walnuts lightly in bacon drippings.
5. Add all remaining ingredients, stirring together until sugar is dissolved.
6. Pour over spinach, add bacon and toss until dressing coats spinach. Serve at once.

   Makes 5 to 6 servings.

POTATO SALAD

1 cup mayonnaise
¼ cup vinegar
2 tablespoons mustard
1 tablespoon salt
½ teaspoon paprika
2 quarts (4-pounds) cooked, diced potatoes (add 2 tablespoons of vinegar to water to keep potatoes from falling apart)

½ cup chopped celery
¼ cup chopped onion
1½ teaspoons celery seed
2 large pickles, diced
3 boiled eggs, diced

1. Mix together mayonnaise, vinegar, mustard, salt and paprika.
2. Toss potatoes, celery, onion, celery seeds, pickles, and egg with mayonnaise mixture until well mixed.
3. Pack into a mold and chill. Serve on a bed of lettuce.

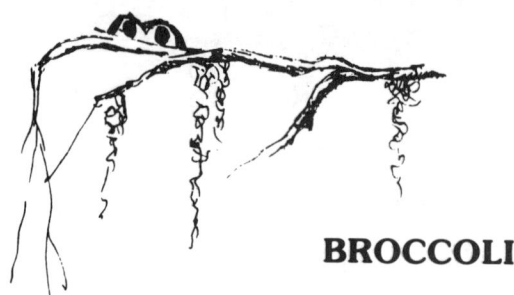

BROCCOLI SALAD

4 to 5 cups broccoli flowerettes
½ cup chopped purple onion
 (I use rings)

½ cup walnuts
½ cup raisins

Dressing:

½ cup mayonnaise
3 tablespoons sugar

1 tablespoon vinegar

1. Mix well and pour over broccoli. Chill before serving

Variations:

—Seedless grapes
—Raw sunflower seeds
—Crisp bacon or bacon bits

TEX-MEX CORNBREAD SALAD

1 (6½-ounce) package Mexican cornbread mix, prepared according to package directions
2 (15-ounce) cans pinto beans, drained
2 cups chopped tomatoes (about 2 large)
1 cup chopped green onions
½ cup chopped green pepper

¼ to ½ cup chopped and seeded jalapeño peppers
12 strips bacon, cooked and crumbled
2 cups (8-ounce) grated Monterey Jack cheese
1 cup (8-ounce) dairy sour cream
1 cup salsa
Additional sour cream and jalapeño pepper slices (optional)

1. Crumble half of prepared cornbread into bottom of large serving bowl. Top with half of beans.
2. In another bowl, combine tomatoes, onions, green pepper and jalapeño pepper; blend well. Spread half of vegetable mixture over beans. Sprinkle with half of the bacon and half of the cheese.
3. Stir together sour cream and salsa in small bowl; spread half of dressing over cheese.
4. Repeat layering procedure with remaining cornbread, beans, vegetables, bacon, cheese and dressing. Garnish with sour cream and jalapeño pepper slices, if desired. Cover tightly and chill 2 to 3 hours before serving.

   Makes 6 to 8 servings,.

LAYERED SPINACH SALAD

10 ounces fresh washed spinach leaves
Salt, pepper and sugar
6 strips of cooked bacon, crumbled
3 hard boiled eggs, sliced
Salt, pepper and sugar
1 cup sliced raw mushrooms
½ cup sliced green onions
Salt, pepper and sugar
½ cup chopped toasted pecans
1 cup homemade mayonnaise
1 cup grated Swiss cheese
Paprika, for color

1. Place dry spinach in a large Pyrex dish. Sprinkle with a small amount of salt, pepper and sugar.
2. Add the layer of bacon, then eggs and sprinkle again with the salt, pepper and sugar.
3. Add the mushroom and onion layer; sprinkle with seasonings.
4. Top with pecans, then dot mayonnaise on top.
5. Finish with a layer of Swiss cheese and sprinkle with paprika.
6. Cover and refrigerate. Make a day ahead, tossing in a large bowl before serving.

   Serves 8.

TEASIE'S COLE SLAW

5 pounds shredded cabbage
1 onion, chopped
1 cup chopped bell pepper
2 tablespoons celery seed
1 large can of pimento

1. Combine all of the ingredients in a large salad bowl.

In a saucepan combine:

1 cup vinegar
1 cup oil
1 cup sugar
Salt and pepper to taste

1. Bring to a boil and pour over shredded cabbage mixture.
2. Storage in an air tight container in the refrigerator will keep Cole Slaw for a week or two.

BEST YET SLAW

2-3 heads cabbage, shredded
4 bell peppers, chopped
3 onions, chopped
½ pound bacon, fried and chopped
2 cups mayonnaise
1 tablespoon mustard
1 teaspoon Worcestershire
½ box brown sugar

1. Combine mayonnaise, mustard, Worcestershire sauce, and brown sugar in saucepan and heat. Stir well, then cool.
2. Combine cabbage, onion, pepper, and bacon.
3. Cool bacon drippings; add mayonnaise mixture.
4. Chill dressing mixture, then combine with cabbage mixture.

Serves 10 to 15.

CREAMY FRUIT SALAD

1 can (8¾-ounce) fruit cocktail, drained
2 bananas, peeled and sliced crosswise
1 small unpared apple, diced
½ cup seedless green grapes, halved
¼ cup miniature marshmallows
5 Maraschino cherries, halved
½ cup whipping cream, whipped
Strawberries

1. In large bowl combine fruit cocktail, bananas, apples, grapes, cherries and marshmallows.
2. Fold in whipping cream; refrigerate. Just before serving, garnish with strawberries.

Makes 4 to 6 servings.

*Whipping cream can be tinted with 2 teaspoons Maraschino cherry syrup or a few drops of food color.

WATERGATE SALAD

1 (20-ounce) can crushed pineapple
1 box instant pistachio pudding mix (3¾-ounce)
1 cup miniature marshmallows
½ cup chopped pecans
1 (8-ounce) Cool Whip

1. Mix crushed pineapple with pudding mix.
2. Add all other ingredients. Mix well and chill. (Best to make up night before serving.)

FRUIT SALAD

1 (8-ounce) package cream cheese
2 teaspoons mayonnaise
Pinch salt
Juice from ½ lemon
1 large can peaches

1 can sliced pineapple
1 medium size can fruit cocktail
1 small bottle cherries
2 teaspoons sugar
1½ cups whipped cream

1. Cream the cream cheese and mayonnaise together; add salt and lemon juice.
2. Drain chopped fruit; add sugar to fruit. Add fruit to cream cheese mixture; fold in whipped cream.

FROZEN FRUIT SALAD

1 (3-ounce) package Jello-O-Mixed Fruit (strawberry, lemon, orange or pineaple
Dash of salt
1 cup boiling water
1 (8¾-ounce) can pineapple tidbits, drained
¼ cup lemon juice

⅓ cup mayonnaise
1 cup whipping cream or 2 cups sour cream
1 medium banana, sliced
½ cup seeded halved grapes
¼ cup diced Maraschino cherries
¼ cup chopped nuts

1. Dissolve Jello and salt in boiling water.
2. Drain pineapple. If necessary add water to make ½ cup of pineapple juice.
3. Stir into gelatin with lemon juice.
4. Blend in mayonnaise. Chill until very thick.
5. Whip cream. Fold fruit, nuts, whipping cream or sour cream into gelatin mixture. Pour into a 9 x 5 x 3-inch loaf pan. Freeze until frozen 3-4 hours. To serve cut in squares or slices.

   Makes 8 servings.

*Note: Fruits such as drained orange sections, crushed pineapple or drained fruit cocktail (total amount of 2 cups of fruit) may be used instead of the pineapple tidbits.

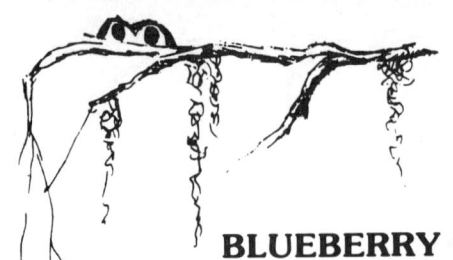

BLUEBERRY GELATIN SALAD

1 family package black cherry jello
2 cups boiling water
1 (20-ounce) can blueberries, drained

1 (20-ounce) can crushed pineapple

1. Dissolve cherry jello in 2 cups boiling water. Cool.
2. Add blueberries and pineapple with juice.
3. Pour into a 9 x 13-inch oblong Pyrex dish. Cover and place in refrigerator to gel.

Topping

1 (8-ounce) package cream cheese
1 pint sour cream

1 cup chopped pecans

1. Blend cream cheese and sour cream. Add pecans.
2. Spread on top of gelled blueberry mixture. Return to refrigerator.
3. Slice into squares and serve.

SANDRA'S SALAD DRESSING

2 cups Wesson oil
Juice of 2 lemons
6-8 garlic pods, finely minced
¼ ounce Roquefort cheese, crumbled

6 ounce Romano cheese, grated
1 teaspoon olive oil
Tabasco to taste

1. Mix all ingredients in air tight container. Keeps well in refrigerator.
2. Take out of refrigerator 1 hour before serving.

CRANBERRY SAUCE

1 cup sugar
1 cup water

1 package of fresh cranberries

1. In a saucepan mix sugar and water; stir to dissolve sugar.
2. Bring to a boil. Add cranberries and return to a boil. Reduce heat and boil gently for ten minutes.
3. Remove from heat and cool at room temperature and then refrigerate.

Makes 2¼ cups.

COCA-COLA SALAD

(Delicious and perfect for Thanksgiving or Christmas)

1 package raspberry gelatin
1 package cherry gelatin
1 can seedless Bing cherries
1 large can crushed pineapple
1 cup pecans, chopped
1 (8-ounce) package cream cheese (frozen)
2 (6-ounce) Coca-Colas (partially frozen)

1. Dissolve gelatin in juices (heated) from cherries and pineapple.
2. Then add cokes, cherries, pineapple and nuts.
3. Grate frozen cream cheese over top of molds (gives the appearance of snow). (Spray mold with Pam prior to using.)
4. Place in refrigerator to congeal. The "frozen" cokes make congealing faster.

Serves 10.

MARINATED FRUIT

1 can peach pie filling or apple pie filling
1 can drained pineapple chunks
1 (15-ounce) can drained sliced peaches
1 package frozen sliced strawberries
4 medium bananas, sliced

1. Mix all ingredients and chill.

Note: Quiche Lorraine, Marinated Fruit, and muffins or biscuits make an ideal late breakfast.

DELICIOUS FRUIT SALAD

1 can pineapple chunks
2 oranges, sectioned
2 cups small marshmallows
2 apples, diced
2 bananas, diced
½ jar small cherries
1 can drained fruit cocktail
1 cup whipping cream
½ cup sugar

1. Drain fruit cocktail and pineapple. Dice apples and add bananas; peel oranges and section them, remove all skin around each piece.
2. Whip cream and add ½ cup sugar.
3. Combine all fruits that have been well drained, marshmallows and toss lightly with whip cream and serve cold.

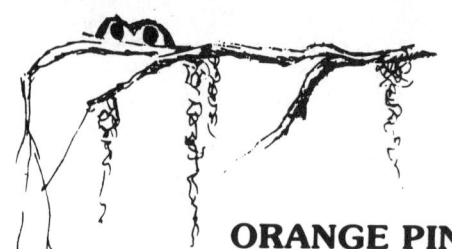

ORANGE PINEAPPLE SALAD

1 large box orange jello
1 can pineapple chunks

4 carrots, cleaned and grated

1. Dissolve jello in 2 cups boiling water.
2. Open pineapple, drain juice in measuring cup and finish filling it to the 2 cup mark.
3. Peel carrots and grate them.
4. Mix juice and water with the jello mixture and add pineapple chunks and grated carrots.
5. Chill until jelled. Serve cold on lettuce leaves.

WALDORF SALAD

6 cups chopped apples
1 cup raisins

1 cup broken walnuts
1 cup mayonnaise

1. Do not peel your apples. Combine apples, raisins and walnuts in a bowl.
2. Add mayonnaise; mix well.
3. Chill in refrigerator until serving time. Serve from a pretty bowl or spoon into lettuce cups.

STRAWBERRY SPINACH SALAD

2 bunches fresh spinach, cleaned, dried and torn
1 can mandarin orange sections, drained

1 pint fresh strawberries, cleaned, hulled and halved
1 purple onion, sliced

Dressing:

½ cup sugar
2 tablespoons sesame seed
1 tablespoon poppy seed
1½ teaspoons onion, finely minced

¼ teaspoon Worcestershire sauce
¼ teaspoon paprika
½ cup vegetable oil
¼ cup cider vinegar

1. Arrange spinach, strawberries, orange sections and onion on individual serving plates.
2. Place dressing ingredients in blender and blend until thoroughly mixed and thickened. Do not overmix.
3. Drizzle desired amount of dressing over salad and serve immediately.
4. Salad can also be placed in serving bowl and tossed gently with dressing.
5. Salad can be cut up ahead of time but add dressing just before serving.

   Serves 6 to 8.

   Delicious. A great recipe for entertaining because it's beautiful and unique.

Breads

ANGEL CORNSTICKS

1½ cups cornmeal
1 cup all-purpose flour
1 package dry yeast
1 tablespoon sugar
1 teaspoon salt

1½ teaspoons baking powder
½ teaspoon baking soda
2 eggs, beaten
2 cups buttermilk
½ cup vegetable oil

1. Combine first 7 ingredients in a large bowl.
2. Combine eggs, buttermilk, and oil, add to dry ingredients, stirring until batter is smooth.
3. Spoon the batter into well-greased cast iron cornstick pans, filling half full. Bake at 450 degrees for 12 to 15 minutes.
   Yield: 3 dozen.

DANNY'S HUSH PUPPIES

4 small onions, chopped
4 cups cornmeal (plain)
4 tablespoons flour

8 teaspoons baking powder
2 teaspoons salt
4 eggs

1. Mix dry ingredients, *scald* dry ingredients with *boiling* water. Add only enough water to make the mixture moist.
2. Add eggs and onions.
3. Mix well and carefully drop batter by level tablespoonfuls in deep hot oil (370 degrees). Cook only a few at a time, turning once.
4. Fry 3 to 5 minutes or until hush puppies are golden brown. Drain well on paper towel.
   Makes about 80 hush puppies.
   For variety — add 4 chopped bell peppers and 4 chopped tomatoes.

EDUCATED HUSH PUPPIES

1 cup corn meal
1 teaspoon baking powder
½ teaspoon sugar
Red and black pepper, to taste
1 egg
½ cup flour

1 cup water
½ teaspoon salt
½ cup green onions, finely chopped
Dash Tabasco

1. Mix all ingredients well with 1 cup of water.
2. Drop by teaspoonfuls into hot grease. Educated Hush Puppies will turn over by themselves.

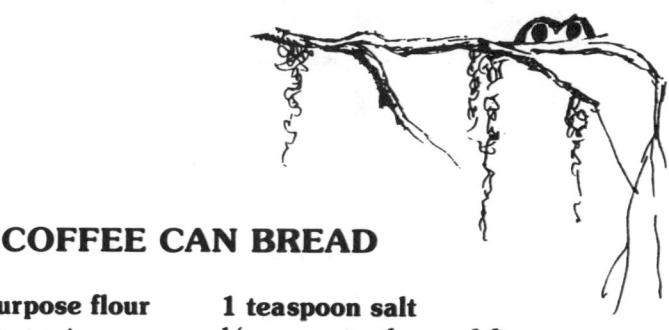

COFFEE CAN BREAD

4 cups unsifted all-purpose flour
1 package active dry yeast
½ cup water
½ cup milk
½ cup butter or margarine
¼ cup sugar

1 teaspoon salt
½ cup nuts chopped fine
½ cup chopped raisins
2 eggs, slightly beaten
2 one-pound coffee cans

PREHEAT OVEN TO 375 DEGREES

1. Mix 2 cups flour with yeast.
2. Stir water, milk, butter, sugar and salt over low heat until butter melts. Cool for about 5 minutes, add to flour and yeast.
3. Add remaining flour, nuts, fruit, and eggs. Dough will be stiff.
4. Knead on a floured board until dough is smooth and elastic and raisins are well distributed throughout.
5. Coat the inside of each coffee can, using a small amount of oil.
6. Divide dough in half, place one half in each can, cover cans with plastic tops.
7. Let rise in warm place (85 degrees) until dough reaches to approximately one inch from top. Remove plastic tops, bake at 375 degrees for about 35 minutes, or until top sounds hollow when tapped and cake tester comes out clean.

This bread can also be made using whole wheat flour for all or part of the white flour, molasses or brown sugar for the white sugar, any chopped, dried fruit in place of, or in addition to, the raisins.

STRAWBERRY NUT BREAD

2 cups margarine
3 cups sugar
2 teaspoons vanilla
½ teaspoon lemon extract
8 eggs
6 cups flour

2 teaspoons salt
2 teaspoons cream of tartar
1 teaspoon soda
2 cups strawberry preserves
1 cup sour cream
2 cups broken pecans

PREHEAT OVEN TO 350 DEGREES

1. Cream margarine, sugar, vanilla and lemon extracts thoroughly.
2. Add eggs one at a time, beating well after each addition.
3. Sift dry ingredients together.
4. Combine preserves and sour cream, add to creamed mixture alternately with flour mixture.
5. Stir in nuts, place in greased and floured loaf pans or aluminum juice cans. Bake in preheated oven at 350 degrees for 50 to 55 minutes or until done. Cool 10 minutes. Remove from pan, cool completely on wire racks.

JALAPEÑO CORNBREAD

½ cup Jalapeño peppers, chopped
3 cups cornbread mix
2½ cups milk
1½ cups grated cheese, Cheddar
1 clove garlic, pressed

3 eggs
½ cup salad oil
3 teaspoons sugar
1 large onion, finely chopped
1 cup whole corn, drained

1. Mix all ingredients together, put into greased dish and bake at 375 degrees for 20 minutes or until brown.

JALAPEÑO CORNBREAD II

2 cups yellow corn meal
1 teaspoon salt
2 tablespoons sugar
½ teaspoon soda
1 cup milk
2 eggs
2 cloves garlic, minced
1 cup finely chopped onion

¼ cup chopped pimento
3 finely chopped Jalapeño peppers (canned)
1 cup whole kernel corn
4 slices bacon, fried crisp, crumbled
2 tablespoons bacon drippings
½ pound grated cheese

PREHEAT OVEN TO 350 DEGREES

1. In large bowl, mix corn meal, salt, sugar and soda.
2. Add milk and eggs, mix well. Stir in garlic, onion, pimento, peppers, corn and bacon.
3. Beat vigorously about 1 minute.
4. Grease an 8 x 8 x 2-inch baking pan with bacon drippings and pour half of mixture into pan.
5. Sprinkle batter with cheese and add remaining mixture.
6. Bake at 350 degrees for 45 minutes or until firm.
7. Delicious served hot with ham or barbequed foods.

   Serves 12.

CAJUN CRAWFISH CORNBREAD

2 cups yellow cornmeal
1 tablespoon salt
1 teaspoon baking soda
6 eggs
2 medium onions
½ cup sliced Jalapeño peppers

16 ounces Cheddar cheese
⅔ cup oil
2 (16-ounce) cans cream style corn
2 pounds crawfish tails, lightly rinsed

PREHEAT OVEN TO 375 DEGREES

1. In a large mixing bowl, combine cornmeal, salt and soda.
2. In a medium bowl, beat eggs thoroughly.
3. Chop onions and Jalapeño peppers.
4. Grate cheese.
5. Add to beaten eggs, onions, Jalapeño peppers, cheese, oil, corn and rinsed crawfish tails. Combine this mixture with cornmeal mix and mix well.
6. Pour into greased 12 x 14-inch baking dish. Bake at 375 degrees for 55 minutes or until golden brown.

   Serves 12.

BEEFY JALAPEÑO CORNBREAD

1 cup plus 1 tablespoon yellow meal (save the 1 tablespoon)
1 cup milk
2 eggs
¾ teaspoon salt
½ teaspoon soda

½ cup bacon drippings
1 (17-ounce) corn, cream style
1½ pounds ground beef
1 large onion, chopped
8 ounces shredded cheese
4 Jalapeño peppers, chopped

PREHEAT OVEN TO 350 DEGREES

1. Combine 1 cup meal, milk, eggs, salt, soda, drippings and corn. Set aside.
2. Sauté beef until lightly browned. Drain thoroughly and set aside.
3. Sprinkle the 1 tablespoon meal in a greased 10½-inch iron skillet, pour half of batter into skillet.
4. Sprinkle evenly with beef, top with onions, then cheese. Add peppers evenly on top.
5. Pour remaining batter over top. Bake at 350 degrees for 50 minutes or until golden brown.

   Serves 6 to 8.

PANCAKES MARNEY

1 cup flour
¾ cups corn meal
3 heaping teaspoons baking powder
2 tablespoons sugar

½ teaspoon salt
2 cups milk
2 eggs
2 drops vanilla
1 stick butter or margarine, melted

1. Combine dry ingredients. Blend in eggs, milk, vanilla and butter.
2. Cook on hot griddle.

NUT ROLLS
(KALÁCS)

4 cups flour
2 sticks butter
12 egg yolks
6 tablespoons sour cream

3 tablespoons sugar
2 packages yeast dissolved in ½ cup warm milk

PREHEAT OVEN TO 350 DEGREES

1. Cut butter into flour like you would for pie dough.
2. Add sugar, egg yolks, sour cream and yeast and knead well.
3. Set in warm place to rise for about 2 hours.
4. Roll out dough and spread with nut filling.
5. Roll up like a jelly roll and let rise again until double in size. Bake in 350 degree oven for one hour.

Nut Filling

4 cups ground nuts (pecans or walnuts)
½ cup sugar

½ cup milk
1 tablespoon butter
1 teaspoon lemon juice

1. Heat milk, add sugar and nuts and stir, add butter and lemon juice and stir.
2. Cool before spreading on dough.

Paula generously shared this type of bread with her friends every Christmas.

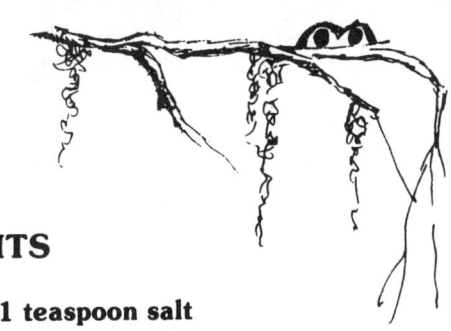

BISCUITS

2 cups flour
1 tablespoon baking powder
2 tablespoons sugar

1 teaspoon salt
⅓ cup shortening
⅔ cup sweet milk

PREHEAT OVEN TO 450 DEGREES

1. Sift dry ingredients into mixing bowl.
2. Measure shortening and cut into flour mixture with pastry blender or two knives or blending fork, until mixture looks like "meal". Stir in almost all the milk. If dough does not seem pliable, add the remaining milk.
3. Use enough milk to make a soft puffy dough easy to roll out.
4. Knead (fold dough over and press lightly with heel of hand about six times) on a lightly floured board (as lightly floured as you would powder your face). Too much handling makes tough biscuits.
5. Roll or pat out ¼-inch thick for thin crusty biscuits and ½-inch for thick soft biscuits.
6. Place on ungreased cookie sheet, close together for biscuits with soft sides, and inch apart for biscuits with crusty sides. Bake 10 to 12 minutes at 450 degrees.

   Makes about 20 2-inch biscuits.

Note: Triple this recipe when making biscuits for your freezer.
For freezing, bake about 8 minutes at 450 degrees (do not brown).
Cool, freeze on cookie sheet and then put in bags.

MRS. BUCO'S BLUEBERRY MUFFINS

1 cup milk
⅓ cup salad oil or melted margarine
1 egg (beaten)
2 cups flour
⅓ cup sugar

3 teaspoons baking powder
¼ teaspoon soda
½ teaspoon salt
1½ cups blueberries (½ cup mashed, 1 cup whole

PREHEAT OVEN TO 400 DEGREES

1. Mix milk, oil, and beaten egg.
2. In another bowl, mix flour, sugar, baking powder, soda, salt, and ½ cup mashed blueberries.
3. Pour milk mixture into flour mixture.
4. Stir quickly until flour disappears. *Do not overmix.* Fold in 1 cup whole berries. Fill muffin cups. Bake at 400 degrees for 20 to 25 minutes.

APPLE STREUSEL MUFFIN

Topping:

½ cup chopped walnuts
¼ cup all-purpose flour
3 tablespoons granulated sugar
2 tablespoons butter, at room temperature
¼ teaspoon ground cinnamon

Batter:

1½ cups all-purpose flour
½ cup granulated sugar
2 teaspoons baking powder
1 teaspoon ground cinnamon
¼ teaspoon ground all spice
¼ teaspoon baking soda
¼ teaspoon salt
2 large eggs
1 cup sour cream
¼ cup (½ stick) butter, melted
1 cup diced unpeeled apple, preferably a tart apple such as Granny Smith or Greenings

PREHEAT OVEN TO 375 DEGREES
Grease muffin cups or use foil baking cups.

1. Put streusel topping ingredients into a medium size bowl. Mix with a fork, then crumble with fingers until mixture looks like chopped walnuts.
2. To make the muffin batter, thoroughly mix flour, sugar, baking powder, cinnamon, allspice, baking soda, and salt in a large bowl.
3. Break eggs into another bowl. Add sour cream and melted butter, and whisk until well blended. Stir in diced apple.
4. Pour egg mixture over flour mixture and fold in just until dry ingredients are moistened.
5. Scoop batter into muffin cups. Top each muffin with about 2 teaspoons of the streusel topping.
6. Bake 20 to 25 minutes, or until browned. A toothpick inserted into the center should come out clean. Remove from pans and let cool at least 1 hour before serving.

Makes 18 regular muffins.

IRRESISTIBLE BISCUITS

4 cups biscuit baking mix
¾ cup club soda
8 ounces sour cream
Butter

1. Mix biscuit baking mix, club soda, and sour cream together, being careful not to overmix.
2. Flour the work surface and the rolling pin.
3. Roll dough out to about ½-inch thickness and cut with biscuit cutter.
4. Melt a little butter on the bottom of a cookie sheet. Place biscuits on sheet and bake at 450 degrees for about 15 minutes.

Makes 18 to 20 biscuits.

COUNTRY CINNAMON ROLLS

1 package active dry yeast
½ cup warm water
   (105-115 degrees)
1 tablespoon sugar
1 egg
3 cups Bisquick baking mix

2 tablespoons butter or margarine, softened
2 tablespoons sugar
2 teaspoons cinnamon
½ cup raisins
Icing

PREHEAT OVEN TO 375 DEGREES

1. Dissolve yeast in warm water. Stir in egg, 1 tablespoon sugar, and the baking mix, beat vigorously.
2. Turn dough onto well floured board. Knead until slightly blistered, about 50 times.
3. Roll dough into a rectangle, 12 x 10-inch, spread with butter. Mix sugar and the cinnamon, sprinkle over rectangle. Sprinkle raisins over sugar cinnamon mixture. Roll up tightly, beginning at wide side. Seal, cut into 1-inch slices. Place slices cut sides down in well greased muffin cups. Cover, let rise 30 minutes.
4. Heat oven to 375 degrees. Bake 12 to 15 minutes. Immediately remove from pan. Let stand 5 minutes, frost with icing. Serve warm.

   Makes one dozen.

Icing: Mix 1 cup sifted confectioner's sugar, 1 tablespoon water and ½ teaspoon almond extract until smooth.

GRANOLA MUFFINS

2 cups Bisquick baking mix
1 cup granola
2 tablespoons honey

1 egg
⅔ cup milk
⅓ cup raisins

PREHEAT OVEN TO 400 DEGREES

1. Mix all ingredients, beat vigorously ½ minute.
2. Fill 12 greased (bottoms only) medium muffin cups ⅔ full.
3. Bake about 15 minutes. Serve warm.

   Makes 1 dozen.

STEVE'S CHEESE BRAIDS

Dough

1 (8-ounce) sour cream	2 packages yeast
½ cup sugar	½ cup warm water
½ cup melted margarine	2 eggs, beaten
1 teaspoon salt	4 cups flour, sifted

1. Combine sour cream, margarine, salt and sugar in a saucepan, heat until margarine melts. Cool to lukewarm.
2. Dissolve yeast in warm water in a large bowl, let stand 5 minutes.
3. Stir in sour cream mixture and eggs using dough hooks.
4. Gradually stir in flour. Dough will be soft.
5. Cover and chill over night in refrigerator.
6. Divide dough into fourths. Knead 4 to 5 times. Roll each into a 12 x 8-inch rectangle. Spread with one fourth filling, leave ½ inch margin around edges. Roll up jelly roll fashion. Seal edges and ends using egg wash.
7. Place loaves, seam side down on greased baking sheets. Make 6 equally spaced X-shaped cuts across top of each loaf. (I use scissors for this.)
8. Cover and let rise in a warm place, free from draft, until doubled in bulk. Bake at 375 degrees for 15 to 20 minutes. Spread loaves with glaze while warm.

   Yield: Four 12-inch loaves.

Filling

3 (8-ounce) packages cream cheese, softened	1 egg
1⅛ cups sugar	3 teaspoons vanilla

1. Combine all ingredients, using an electric mixer.

Glaze

2 cups sifted powdered sugar	2 teaspoons vanilla extract
¼ cup milk	

1. Combine all ingredients, stirring well.
   Yields about ¾ cup.

Egg Wash

1 egg	2 tablespoons water

1. Stir the egg and water together.

BANANA NUT BREAD

2 cups sugar
1½ cups salad oil
3 eggs
4 bananas
3 cups flour

1 teaspoon cinnamon
1 teaspoon nutmeg
½ teaspoon salt
2 teaspoons baking soda
1 cup pecans, chopped

PREHEAT OVEN TO 350 DEGREES

1. Mix sugar and salad oil until well blended.
2. Add eggs one at a time, beating between each addition.
3. Break up bananas in chunks and add to batter.
4. Sift flour, measure, add cinnamon, nutmeg, salt, soda and sift again. Add slowly to the batter and continue beating.
5. Fold in pecans. Grease and flour two loaf pans 9¼ x 5¼ x 2¾-inches or a bundt pan. Bake for 1 hour at 350 degrees. Let cool for 30 minutes before removing from pan. Frost bread when cold. This bread may be frozen before frosting.

Frosting (Optional):

1 stick butter, softened
1 (8-ounce) package cream cheese, softened

1 box powdered sugar
1 teaspoon vanilla

1. Cream together butter and cream cheese. Add powdered sugar and vanilla and continue beating until of spreading consistency.

ROTEL CORNBREAD

¾ cup white cornmeal
¾ cup yellow cornmeal
3 tablespoons flour
¼ teaspoon soda
1½ teaspoons baking powder
1 teaspoon salt
1 teaspoon sugar

2 tablespoons vegetable shortening, melted
1 cup buttermilk
1 egg, beaten
1 finely chopped Jalapeño pepper
1 can diced Rotel tomatoes and green chilies

PREHEAT OVEN TO 425 DEGREES

1. Mix all ingredients together.
2. Pour into a greased 8 x 8 x 2-inch baking pan.
3. Bake at 425 degrees for 25 to 35 minutes.
   Serves 12.

POPPY SEED LOAF

2½ cups sugar
1½ cups milk
3 cups flour (sifted)
3 eggs, beaten
1⅛ cups Crisco oil
1½ teaspoons salt

2 teaspoons baking powder
1½ teaspoons butter flavoring
1½ teaspoons almond flavoring
1½ teaspoons vanilla flavoring
2 teaspoons poppy seeds

*Do not half recipe. Makes 2 loaves. Mix by hand.

PREHEAT OVEN TO 350 DEGREES

1. Sift and measure flour.
2. Sift flour, sugar, salt, and baking powder together. *Set aside.*
3. Mix all liquid ingredients together.
4. Pour into flour mixture and stir quickly with fork.
5. Pour into greased, floured, loaf pans, 9¼ x 5¼ x 2¾.
6. Bake at 350 degrees for 45 to 50 minutes.

Glaze:

¼ cup orange juice
¾ cup sugar
½ teaspoon butter flavoring

½ teaspoon almond flavoring
½ teaspoon vanilla flavoring

1. Combine all of the above ingredients.
2. Pour over loaves on cooling rack while hot.

ANGEL BISCUITS

5 cups flour
¼ cup sugar
3 teaspoons baking powder
1 teaspoon soda
1 teaspoon salt

2 cups buttermilk
1 cup shortening
2 tablespoons water
1 package yeast

1. Mix first 5 ingredients in a large bowl.
2. Make a well in flour, add shortening and remaining ingredients. Mix well.
3. Roll as for any type biscuits. Dip small biscuits in melted butter before placing in pan.
4. Cook at 400 degrees for 15 minutes.

MORNING GLORIA MUFFINS

2 cups all-purpose flour
2 teaspoons baking soda
2 teaspoons ground cinnamon
1½ cups finely shredded carrots
1½ cups peeled and shredded apples (1 large)
1¼ cups sugar
¾ cup coconut
½ cup snipped pitted dates
½ cup chopped pecans
3 beaten eggs
1 cup cooking oil
½ teaspoon vanilla
½ teaspoon salt

1. In a mixing bowl, combine flour, sugar, soda, cinnamon, and salt.
2. In another bowl, combine carrots, apple, coconut, dates and pecans.
3. Stir in beaten eggs, oil and vanilla to dry ingredients, stirring until moistened.
4. Add the dates, carrots, apple, and coconut mixture stirring until moistened.
5. Grease or line muffin tin with paper bake cups. Spoon batter into prepared muffin tin. Bake in 375 degree oven about 18 to 20 minutes.
6. Remove from pan, cool on wire rack. Package for giving as desired.

   Makes 24.
   Serve muffins with whipped cream cheese.

ORANGE MUFFINS

Muffins

¾ cup butter
1½ cups sugar
1½ cups sour cream
3 cups flour, sifted
1½ teaspoons baking soda
1½ teaspoons salt
1½ teaspoons orange rind

PREHEAT OVEN TO 375 DEGREES

1. Mix sugar and orange juice. Set aside for dipping after muffins are cooked.
2. Cream butter and sugar using electric mixer.
3. Combine sifted flour, baking soda, and salt in small bowl.
4. Add sour cream alternately with dry ingredients.
5. Using a fork fold in orange rind. This is a stiff batter.
6. Use well greased muffin tins that are small so these are bite sized. Bake at 375 degrees for 12 to 15 minutes. While muffins are still warm, dip them in sugar orange juice mixture. Cool on wire rack.

Sugar-Orange Juice Mixture

1½ cups sugar
¾ cups orange juice (or juice from 2 oranges)

CHRISTINE DENISE'S POTATO ROLLS

1 package dry yeast
½ cup warm water
1 cup mashed potatoes
⅔ cup shortening
⅔ cup sugar

1 teaspoon salt
1 cup scalded milk
2 eggs
4 cups flour (add more if needed)

1. Dissolve yeast in water. Scald milk.
2. Add potatoes, shortening, sugar and salt to milk. Let cool until lukewarm.
3. Add yeast.
4. Beat eggs and add to mixture.
5. Add flour (approximately 4 cups).
6. Start kneading. Knead until it shines. Place dough on floured board. Put in greased bowl, cover, and put in refrigerator until double in size. (2 hours).
7. Make into balls. Let rise double. Mash down a little. To help rise, put over pot of hot water.
8. Bake in a 13 x 9-inch pan at 400 degrees for 20 to 25 minutes or until brown.

Yield: 12 to 15 rolls.

ASPHODEL BREAD

5 cups Pioneer Biscuit Mix
½ teaspoon salt
4 eggs
2 cups warm milk

¼ cup sugar
2 envelopes yeast
¼ teaspoon cream of tartar

PREHEAT OVEN TO 350 DEGREES

1. Sift the biscuit mix, sugar and salt into a very large bowl.
2. Soften yeast in milk. Make sure milk is only warm.
3. Beat eggs until thoroughly broken up with cream of tartar.
4. Combine yeast, milk, eggs and pour into dry ingredients. Stir and set aside in warm place.
5. Cover with plastic wrap. When double in bulk, punch down. Fill 2 oiled loaf pans about ½ way, again set aside until doubled in size. Bake at 350 degrees for 30 minutes.

Makes 2 loaves.

Note: Freezes well. Allow to thaw completely before reheating.

THE BEST REFRIGERATOR ROLLS

1 cup shortening
1 cup sugar
1½ teaspoons salt
1 cup boiling water

2 eggs, beaten
2 packages dry yeast
1 cup warm water
6 cups unsifted flour

1. Pour boiling water over shortening, sugar, and salt.
2. Blend and cool.
3. Add beaten eggs.
4. Sprinkle yeast into the warm water, stir until dissolved and add to mixture.
5. Add flour. Blend well, cover and place in the refrigerator for at least 4 hours. (Dough must be in a large mixing bowl as it rises slightly, in the refrigerator).
6. This will keep a week or 10 days and may be used as needed. About 3 hours before using rolls, roll into desired shapes, using enough extra flour to make easy to handle.
7. Place in greased pan and allow to rise at room temperature for 3 hours or more until double their original size. Bake at 425 degrees for 12 to 15 minutes.

Grandma Sexton made the best yeast rolls ever
Donna

HOT HERB BREAD

1 loaf French bread
½ cup butter
1 teaspoon parsley flakes

¼ teaspoon oregano
¼ teaspoon garlic salt
Grated Parmesan cheese

PREHEAT OVEN TO 400 DEGREES

1. Slice French bread in half.
2. Blend butter, parsley, oregano and garlic salt.
3. Spread each side with herb mixture and sprinkle with cheese.
4. Wrap in foil leaving top open. Bake at 400 degrees for 10 minutes.

TIP: Slice angel cake using thread

SOUR CREAM DINNER ROLLS

1 cup sour cream
½ cup sugar
½ cup (1 stick) margarine, melted
½ cup warm water

2 packages yeast
2 eggs
1 teaspoon salt
4 cups all-purpose flour, sifted

1. Scald sour cream in melted margarine, stir in sugar, cool to lukewarm.
2. Measure warm water into large mixing bowl, on this sprinkle yeast and stir until dissolved.
3. Add sour cream mixture, eggs (unbeaten), flour, and salt, mix well. Cover with plastic wrap and refrigerate overnight.
4. To shape, turn dough out on floured board, divide into quarters.
5. Roll each quarter into a 10-inch circle. Cut each circle into 12 wedges, then shape by rolling each wedge beginning at the wide end.
6. Place on a greased baking sheet. Cover and let rise until double in bulk, about 45 minutes.
7. Bake in 375 degree oven for 15 minutes. These freeze well. (When they have been frozen, wrap in foil and heat in moderate oven before serving).

Date Nut Coffee Cake

1 stick margarine
1 cup sour cream
1 package sugar chopped dates
1½ cups chopped pecans

½ box brown sugar
1 tablespoon cinnamon
Divide ingredients into 5 parts
(⅕ for each ball of dough)

Use Sour Cream Dinner Roll Dough . . . divide dough into 5 balls of equal size. Roll dough in rectangular shape, brush with melted margarine mixed with sour cream. Sprinkle with brown sugar and cinnamon. Cut dates in small pieces and place on top of sugar and cinnamon. Break pecans into small pieces and sprinkle over dough. Roll up like jelly roll. Pinch ends to seal.

Place on greased cookie sheet, brush with melted margarine. With a sharp knife cut slits across top of roll. Let rise 45 minutes or until almost double in size. Bake in 350 degree oven 15 to 20 minutes or until brown. Remove from oven and place on cooling rack. *While warm brush with confectioner Icing as follows:*

1 box confectioner sugar
1 teaspoon vanilla extract

Warm water (small amount or enough to make a thin frosting)

This will frost 5 coffee cakes.

YEAST ROLLS

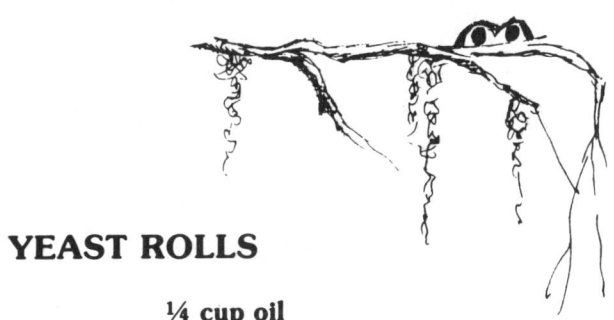

⅓ cup powdered milk
1 envelope yeast
1 cup lukewarm water
1 egg

¼ cup oil
1 teaspoon salt
½ cup sugar
3 cups flour

PREHEAT OVEN TO 350 DEGREES

1. Put first 3 ingredients in blender container and let stand 5 minutes, then blend at medium speed for 20 seconds.
2. Add all but flour and blend 10 seconds.
3. Add to flour in a large bowl and mix well.
4. Let rise till double in bulk (2 hours).
5. Dump onto well floured surface and work flour in until no sticky surface appears.
6. Roll out to ½-inch thickness and cut with biscuit cutter.
7. Dip rolls in melted butter and place in buttered pan almost touching. Let rise till double (1 hour). Bake at 350 degrees for 20 minutes or until brown.

   Makes 1½ dozen.

Variation to make cinnamon rolls:

1. Roll dough out thin into long rectangles and brush with melted butter.
2. Sprinkle generously with powdered sugar, cinnamon and chopped pecans (Optional).
3. Roll jelly roll fashion and seal edges.
4. Slice 1-inch thick and place in buttered pan almost touching. (Use a thread to slice rolls). Let rise. Bake at 350 degrees for 20 minutes. Glaze.

Glaze:

½ cup melted margarine
1 cup powdered sugar

½ teaspoon vanilla
Milk to thin

1. Combine all the above ingredients. Add milk to glaze mixture for proper consistency.

TIP: Cream cheese — to soften, roll and mash in hands before you take off the wrapper

JOE KELLY BREAD

French bread, 1 loaf sliced vertically 1-inch thick
1 stick butter melted
Garlic powder (not garlic salt)
½ pound bacon, fried crisp and crumbled
Dry parsley

1. Spray with Pam one side of foil large enough to completely cover bread.
2. Place bread on foil — between each piece:
    1. sprinkle garlic
    2. crumbled bacon
    3. parsley
    4. Pour butter, reserve enough to pour over top of bread.
3. Seal foil air tight.
4. Bake at 350 degrees for 20 minutes.

* 1 average loaf yields 10 to 12 slices.

** May also add 1 slice of mozzarella cheese between each slice before baking.

SWEET POTATO BREAD

3 cups sugar
½ teaspoon cinnamon
1 can sweet potatoes, drained and mashed
1 teaspoon soda
4 eggs
½ teaspoon salt
3 cups flour
1 cup nuts, chopped
1 cup oil
½ teaspoon nutmeg
¾ cup water

1. Cream together sugar and oil. Add eggs and cream again. Add other ingredients.
2. Bake at 350 degrees in a greased loaf pan for about 45 to 60 minutes.

TIPS: A purple cabbage hulled out makes a beautiful holder for dips, especially in the center of a colorful vegetable tray.

Using a small round bowl, turn the bowl on top of cabbage and mark. Take a sharp knife and hull out the cabbage.

FRENCH BREAD

Makes 2 (18-inch Baguettes)

2 packages dry yeast
2½ cups lukewarm water
  (85 to 105 degrees F.)
6 cups white flour
2 teaspoons salt

2 teaspoons water
Cornmeal
Vegetable shortening
1 egg white
1 tablespoon water

Step 1 In a large bowl sprinkle yeast over warm water and stir with a wooden spoon until yeast becomes creamy, about 3 minutes. Add 4 cups of the flour (1 cup at a time) mixing thoroughly between additions. Beat mixture with spoon about 100 times, turning the bowl ¼ turn after each 25 whips. Add salt and water mixture and continue beating until combined. Add more flour ¼ cup at a time until dough starts leaving the sides of the bowl and forms a ball. Remove from bowl and knead on a floured surface adding more flour as needed. Place dough in a large greased bowl, cover tightly with plastic wrap and place on a shelf in oven with oven light as only source of heat for 1½ hours.

Step 2 Turn back plastic wrap, return dough to floured surface, punch down and knead for 2 or 3 minutes. Return to bowl, recover and let rise again for 1 hour.

Step 3 Turn dough out of bowl. Punch down. Cut the dough into two (2) pieces of equal size, forming each into a ball and let rest for 5 minutes before shaping. Shape baguettes and put into pans prepared with shortening and sprinkled generously with cornmeal. Cover loaves with a loosely woven cloth and let rise until loaves have doubled in size.

Step 4 Preheat oven to 450 degrees F. Cut diagonal slits in top of loaves. Brush tops with egg white, beaten with a fork in 1 tablespoon water. Bake for 30 minutes on middle shelf of oven.

Step 5 Turn loaves upside down, either in pans or directly onto oven shelf, and bake an additional 5 minutes. Remove to rack and cool.

ZUCCHINI BREAD

3 eggs
2 cups sugar
1 cup Wesson oil
2 teaspoons vanilla
3 cups flour
1 teaspoon cinnamon
¾ teaspoon salt

¼ teaspoon baking powder
1 teaspoon baking soda
½ cup chopped walnuts or pecans
½ cup raisins
¾ cups coconut
2 cups zucchini, peeled and grated

1. Beat eggs until foamy. Add sugar, oil, vanilla and mix. Sift together the flour, cinnamon, salt, baking powder, baking soda and fold into above mixture. Add the chopped walnuts or pecans, raisins, coconut and zucchini.
2. Turn finished mixture into 2 greased and floured (9 x 5-inch) or 3 (8 x 4-inch) pans. Bake at 350 degrees for 1 hour in large pans; 45 to 50 minutes in smaller pans.

POGACSA BISCUITS

8 ounces cream cheese
8 ounces margarine
8 ounces (about 1⅔ cups) flour

½ teaspoon salt
1 egg

1. Mix first four ingredients by hand. If too sticky, add more flour a little at a time. Refrigerate for 20 to 30 minutes.
2. Roll out dough about ¾-inch thick. Decorate dough by scoring top with a table knife.
3. Using a small 1½-inch round cookie cutter, cut out biscuits. Place on a greased 10 x 5-inch baking sheet. Brush biscuit tops with egg that has been beaten with a fork.
4. Preheat oven to 500 degrees. Put biscuits in oven and immediately lower heat to 400 degrees. Bake about 20 minutes or until a light golden brown color. Don't overbake or the biscuits will be dry.
5. Serve while warm. Biscuits can be kept in a resealable plastic bag until serving time. Reheat in the broiler for 2 to 3 minutes.

Makes about 80 cocktail-sized biscuits, which are especially good for serving with alcoholic drink.

Eggs, Cheese, Pasta

FRENCH OMELET

6 eggs
¼ cup milk or cream
¼ teaspoon salt
¼ teaspoon black pepper
3 tablespoons butter

¼ cup grated cheese
2 slices ham (cut in strips) julienne
1 tablespoon green onion
1 tablespoon parsley

1. Beat eggs until fluffy, add milk, add salt and pepper.
2. Pour into sizzling butter in skillet over low heat. (Electric skillet — 300 degrees.
3. Cook slowly — keeping heat low. As undersurface becomes set, start lifting it slightly with spatula to let uncooked portion flow underneath and cook.
4. Sprinkle green onions, parsley, cheese and ham over top of eggs.
5. As soon as mixture seems set, fold or roll it.
6. Serve immediately.

PESTO

½ cup fresh basil leaves
½ cup pine nuts
2 garlic cloves
Salt

Cooked pasta
½ cup grated Parmesan cheese
(1½-ounces)
½ cup olive oil

1. Put basil leaves, pine nuts, garlic and salt in a blender or food processor.
2. Process until mixture forms a paste.
3. Add Parmesan cheese to basil mixture; process until well blended. Add oil, a little at a time; process until sauce has a creamy consistency.

   Makes 4 to 6 servings.

Variation:

When fresh basil leaves are unavailable, a version of pesto may be made with fresh parsley. Use walnuts instead of pine nuts.

NOT: Pesto is used as a sauce for pasta, and is also added to dishes such as minestrone soup to give added flavor.

EGGS BENEDICT

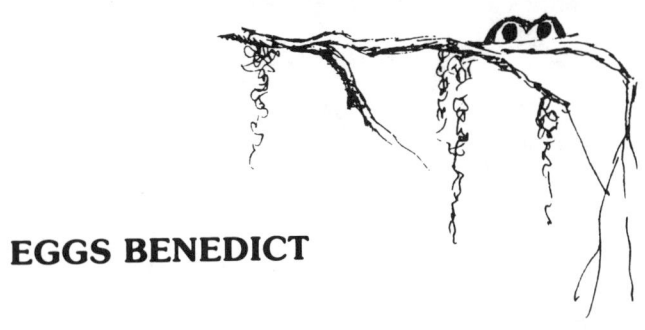

Eggs Benedict

4 rounds English muffins
4 slices lean ham
4 thin slices tomato

4 poached eggs
Hollandaise sauce
Paprika

1. Heat muffins in oven.
2. Top with slice of ham, then tomato, then poached egg. Cover this with hollandaise sauce and sprinkle with paprika.

   Serves 4.

Hollandaise sauce:

½ cup butter (divided into 4 parts)
4 egg yolks, beaten
¼ cup lemon juice

White pepper, salt and red pepper to taste

1. In top of double boiler (do not let water boil or touch bottom of pan) place egg yolks and beat in lemon juice slowly and add ¼ of the butter. Stir with wooden spoon until butter is melted.
2. Add second amount of butter and continue this process, stirring constantly, until all butter is used. When well mixed, remove pan from heat and continue stirring until thick and creamy. Add white pepper, salt and red pepper. Use immediately. If the mixture should curdle, beat in 1 tablespoon of boiling water or cream, beating constantly in order to rebind. (This may be repeated several times.)

Quickie: Substitute undiluted mushroom soup for hollandaise.

RICE PATTIES

2 beaten eggs
2 cups cold cooked rice
4 slices bacon, cooked and crumbled
⅓ cup chopped green pepper

¼ cup grated Parmesan cheese
2 tablespoons chopped onion
Salt and pepper to taste
2 tablespoons oil

1. Combine eggs, rice, bacon, green pepper, cheese, onion, salt, and pepper. Cover and chill one hour.
2. Shape ⅓ cup mixture into patties.
3. Fry over medium heat till brown.

DELICATE GRITS

1 quart milk
½ cup butter
1 cup of 3-minute grits
1 cup grated Swiss cheese
Salt and pepper to taste
⅓ cup grated Parmesan cheese

PREHEAT OVEN TO 375 DEGREES

1. Bring milk and butter to slow boil and stir in grits slowly. Stir often, until mixture looks like farina.
2. Put in large bowl and beat with electric mixer until grits become creamy, about 5 minutes.
3. Add grated cheese and salt and pepper.
4. Mix well with a wooden spoon. Pour mixture into a greased 2-quart casserole. Put a large piece of butter on top and sprinkle with Parmesan cheese.
5. Bake at 375 degrees for 35 to 40 minutes. This is excellent served with grillades or game.

   Serves 6 to 8.

GARLIC CHEESE GRITS

1 cup grits, uncooked
4 cups water
1 teaspoon salt or to taste
1 stick butter or margarine
1 roll garlic cheese
½ pound sharp cheese
2 tablespoons Worcestershire sauce
Tabasco or cayenne pepper to taste

PREHEAT OVEN TO 350 DEGREES

1. Cook the grits in salted water.
2. When cooked add the butter, garlic cheese, sharp cheese and Worcestershire sauce.
3. Stir until the butter and cheese have melted.
4. Put in greased casserole, and sprinkle with paprika. Bake in preheat 350 degree oven for 15 to 20 minutes.

   Serves 8 to 10.

   Use as a main supper dish or starch.

SARAH'S HAM AND CHEESE ROLLS

1 package dinner rolls (small rolls in foil pan)
2½ slices of ham
2½ slices of Swiss cheese
3 tablespoons poppy seeds
1 stick melted margarine
3 tablespoon Kraft mustard

PREHEAT OVEN TO 350 DEGREES

1. Slice rolls in half — lift off top.
2. Mix poppy seeds, margarine and mustard together.
3. Spread both halves with poppy seed mixture.
4. Place ham and cheese on bottom side of rolls.
5. Place tops on.
6. Bake at 350 degrees for 13 minutes. Slice the rolls. Serve hot.

QUICHE LORRAINE WITH HAM

4 thin slices onion
1 tablespoon margarine
10-inch pie shell, partially baked
4 slices crisp bacon, chopped
8 paper-thin slices ham, shredded
8 paper-thin slices imported Swiss cheese
3 eggs
¼ teaspoon dry mustard
1 cup light cream, heated
Garlic powder to taste
Nutmeg to taste

PREHEAT OVEN TO 400 DEGREES

Prebake Pie Shell 10 Minutes In 400 Degree Oven

1. Sauté onion in margarine until soft.
2. Sprinkle drained onions and bacon over bottom of pie crust.
3. Add half the ham, then 4 slices of cheese.
4. Repeat layer using remaining ham and cheese.
5. Beat eggs and mustard together.
6. Add heated cream to eggs and continue beating.
7. Pour over pie and let stand 10 minutes.
8. Sprinkle tiny bit of garlic powder and nutmeg on top.
9. Bake in 375 degree oven 25 to 30 minutes or until custard is set.

   Serves 6.

Variation: Use 1 to 1½ cups lump crabmeat instead of ham.

SPINACH QUICHE

1 roll Jimmy Dean's hot pork sausage
1 container Stouffer's Spinach soufflé (in frozen food section)
1 unbaked pie shell
1 small jar sliced mushrooms, drained
8 ounces Swiss cheese
3 eggs
2 tablespoons milk

PREHEAT OVEN TO 425 DEGREES

1. Brown sausage and drain. (Use a fork to break up the sausage to brown.
2. Add spinach soufflé and stir until melted.
3. Add mushrooms and cheese.
4. Cook until melted.
5. Beat eggs and milk together. Add to mixture.
6. Pour into pie shell and bake at 425 degrees for 25 minutes.

BRUNCH CASSEROLE

6 slices bread, decrusted
6 eggs
1 teaspoon salt
1 teaspoon prepared (ground) mustard
Black pepper to taste
4 cups Cheddar cheese, grated
1 pound bulk breakfast sausage (hot)
1 pint half-and-half cream
2 tablespoons chopped onion
1 teaspoon margarine

1. Sauté onion in 1 teaspoon margarine.
2. Place decrusted bread on bottom of 9 x 13-inch casserole dish, top with onions.
3. Fry sausage, use a fork to break up bulk sausage, drain, place on bread. Place grated cheese on top.
4. Mix eggs, half-and-half, salt, pepper and mustard in a bowl.
5. Mix well. Pour over cheese and sausage.
6. Refrigerate over night or can be frozen and thawed out later when ready to use.
7. Bake at 350 degrees for 40 minute.

   Serves 12.

Delicious served with poppy seed bread, and marinated fruit. Your husband or wife will love you for cooking this dish.

FETTUCCINE ALFREDO

8 ounces uncooked fettuccine
½ cup whipping cream
¼ teaspoon white pepper
½ cup butter

¾ cup grated Parmesan cheese
2 tablespoons chopped parsley (fresh)

1. Cook fettuccine according to package directions, omitting salt. Drain well; place in a large bowl.
2. Combine butter and whipping cream in a small saucepan; cook over low heat until butter melts.
3. Stir in cheese, pepper and parsley.
4. Pour mixture over fettuccine, toss until fettuccine is coated.

   Yield: 4 servings.

TORTELLINI SALAD

17-ounce package frozen cheese tortellini or 3½-ounces (2 cups) dried cheese tortellini
1 small red sweet pepper, cut into thin bite-size strips
¾ cup broccoli flowerets
1 small carrot, thinly sliced
⅓ cup sliced pimento
⅓ cup stuffed olives or sliced pitted ripe olives
¾ cup mayonnaise or salad dressing

⅓ cup purchased pesto sauce
¼ cup milk
2 tablespoons grated Parmesan cheese
1 tablespoon olive oil or cooking oil
1 teaspoon vinegar
½ teaspoon pepper
1 clove garlic, minced (optional)
Fresh spinach leaves

1. Cook tortellini according to package directions; drain.
2. Rinse with cold water; drain well.
3. In a large mixing bowl combine cooked tortellini, sweet pepper, broccoli, carrot, pimento and olives.
4. For dressing: In a small mixing bowl, stir together mayonnaise or salad dressing, pesto sauce, milk, cheese, oil, vinegar, pepper, and garlic.
5. Pour dressing over salad and chill at least 5 hours.
6. Serve in a spinach lined bowl. Makes 8 side-dish servings.

TRI COLOR CHEESE SURPRISE

3 tablespoons olive oil
¾ cup shallots or onion, finely diced
1 pound (2-cups) ricotta cheese
½ pound (8-ounces) cream cheese
½ teaspoon garlic powder
1 teaspoon salt, optional
1 (4-ounce) jar sliced pimentos, drained and pureed
½ teaspoon ground cumin seed
¼ cup pinenuts or slivered almonds, toasted and chopped
4 teaspoons dried cilantro (or ¼ cup fresh, chopped)
½ teaspoon dried jalapeño peppers (or 1 tablespoon canned, chopped)
Cilantro and pinenuts for garnish

1. In skillet, heat olive oil and sauté shallots until soft but not brown.
2. In medium bowl, beat together ricotta cheese, cream cheese, garlic powder, and salt just until blended. Stir in the shallots. Divide mixture evenly into three small bowls.
3. In first bowl, stir in pureed pimentos and cumin. Into second bowl, stir in pinenuts. Into third bowl, stir in cilantro and jalapeño peppers.
4. To prepare mold, smoothly line a straight-sided plain mold such as a clean (6-inch) clay flower pot or (5-6 cup) loaf pan, terrine or charlotte mold with two layers of moistened cheesecloth or plastic wrap. With a rubber spatula, carefully place the cilantro mixture into the mold, spreading it evenly to the sides of the mold. Repeat with the white pinenut mixture, ending with the pimento mixture. Fold ends of cheesecloth or plastic over filling and press down lightly to compact. Chill overnight.
5. Just before serving, invert mold onto a platter. Gently remove cheesecloth or plastic wrap. Garnish top with cilantro and toasted pinenuts. Serve with corn tortilla chips and fresh vegetables.

Makes 1 (2-pound) appetizer.

BECKY'S PASTA AND CRAWFISH CASSEROLE

1 (16-ounce) bag spiral noodles
1 to 2-pounds crawfish tails
1 (8-ounce) jar jalapeño Cheez-Whiz (slightly melted)
1 can cream of mushroom soup
1 (4-ounce) can mushrooms (pieces and stems)
2 cups grated Cheddar cheese
1 large onion, chopped
½ cup celery, chopped
1 bell pepper, chopped
1 stick butter
Tony's seasoning

PREHEAT OVEN TO 350 DEGREES

1. Cook noodles as directed on package.
2. Sauté onions, celery and peppers in butter. Add crawfish tails and season with Tony's. Sauté until crawfish is tender.
3. Combine noodles, crawfish tail mixture, Cheez-Whiz, soup, mushrooms, and 1 cup Cheddar cheese. Pour into casserole. Top with Cheddar cheese. Bake for 10-12 minutes.

Meats

Beef
Pork
Poultry
Game

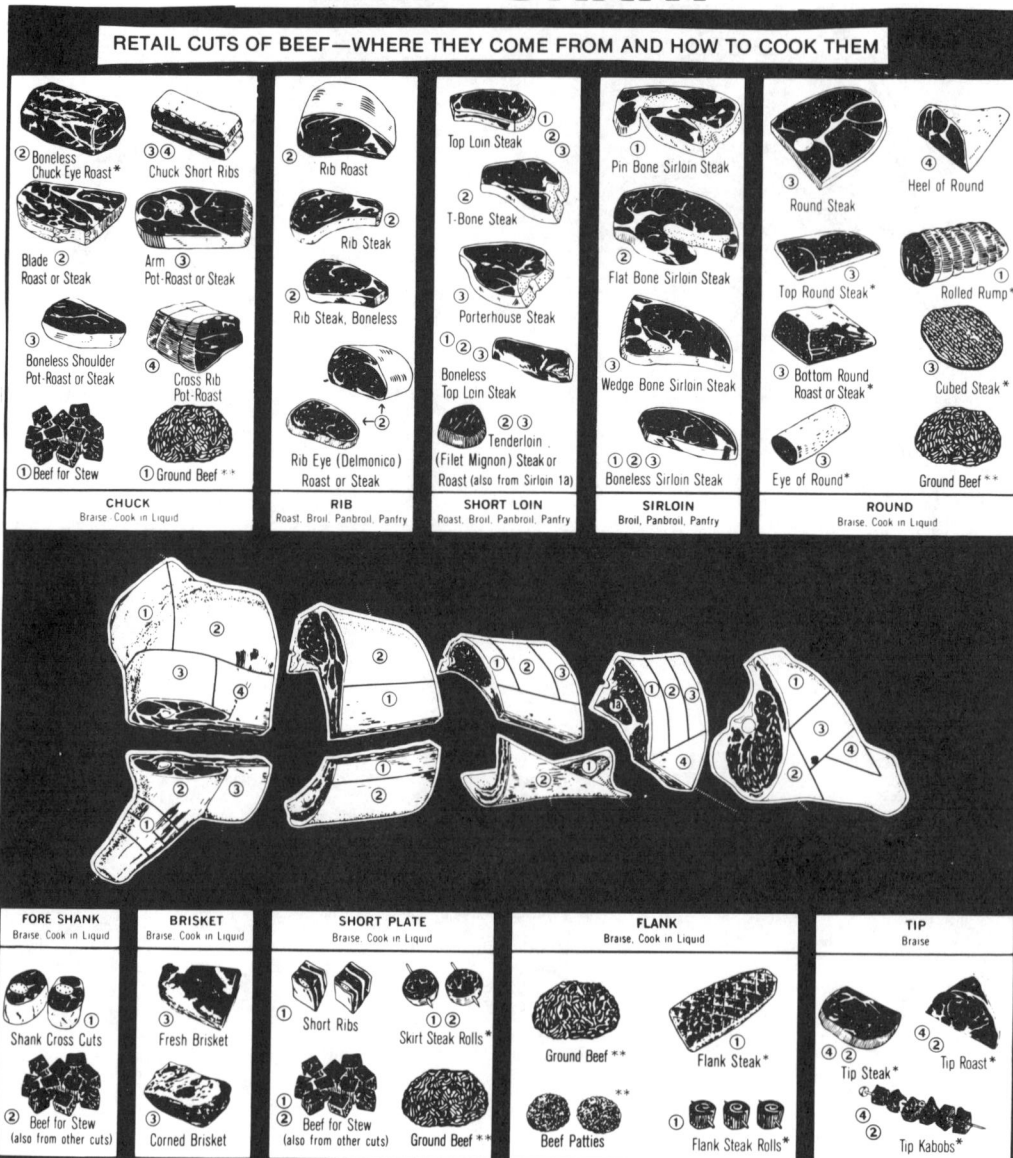

BARBECUED BRISKET

1 (8 to 10-pound) Beef Brisket (flat cut), trimmed
3 ounce liquid smoke
Celery salt
Garlic salt

Onion salt
Worcestershire sauce
Salt and pepper
18 ounce Bullseye BBQ Sauce

1. Place brisket in oblong baking dish; sprinkle with liquid smoke and salts.
2. Cover and refrigerate overnight. When ready to bake, sprinkle with Worcestershire sauce, salt and pepper
3. Seal pan with foil. Bake at 350 degrees for one hour. Reduce heat to 225 degrees and bake 6 hours.
4. Remove foil, pour off excess liquid and cover with BBQ sauce.
5. Bake uncovered at 225 degrees for 30 minutes.
6. Slice across grain with electric knife.

   Serves 10.

MARINATED BRISKET

7 or 8 pounds beef brisket
2 bottles liquid smoke
1 large onion, sliced
Garlic salt

Celery salt
Salt, black and red pepper
¼ cup Worcestershire sauce
1 can sliced mushrooms, drained

1. Sprinkle brisket with salts and peppers.
2. Combine liquid smoke, Worcestershire sauce, and sliced onion and pour over brisket.
3. Marinate in refrigerator for 24 hours.
4. Cover brisket and marinade with foil. Bake at 325 degrees for 6 hours.
5. Drain juice into pan and wrap meat in foil and place in refrigerator.
6. Trim all fat from brisket. Slice thinly across grain.
7. Defat broth and reserve 1 cup. Make a brown gravy and add 1 can of sliced mushrooms, drained.
8. Pour 1 cup of broth over brisket. Heat for 45 minutes in a covered dish.

MARINATED EYE OF THE ROUND

1 (5-pound) eye of the round roast
¼ cup salad oil
2 tablespoons lemon-pepper seasoning
½ cup wine vinegar
½ cup lemon juice
½ cup soy sauce
½ cup Worcestershire sauce

1. Marinate roast in mixture of next 6 ingredients for 1-3 days (in refrigerator) turning at least once a day.
2. Cook uncovered with marinade in a Dutch oven at 250 degrees for 3 hours.
3. Refrigerate overnight. Slice thin and serve with heated marinade. Garnish with parsley and cherry tomatoes.

   This is delicious for a buffet supper. Freezes well.

   Serves 10 to 15.

RUMP ROAST

1 (5 to 6-pound) rump roast
1 tablespoon salt
1¼ teaspoons black pepper
½ teaspoon red pepper
2 tablespoons cooking oil
5 cloves garlic (cut into halves)
½ cup flour

1. Cut slits in roast using the point of your knife (about 1-inch deep) and stuff with garlic.
2. Stir together flour, salt, black pepper and red pepper; rub mixture on meat.
3. Heat cooking oil in large skillet, brown (sear) roast on all sides.
4. Wrap in foil. Roast at 350 degrees, 30 minutes per pound.

SURPRISE ROAST

Rib-eye roast or sirloin tip
Onion powder
Garlic powder
Red pepper
Salt and pepper

PREHEAT OVEN TO 500 DEGREES

1. Rub roast with onion powder, garlic powder, red pepper, salt and pepper.
2. Place roast in an open pan in 500 degree oven.
3. Cook 5 minutes per pound
4. Turn the oven off. **Do not open oven door until oven is completely cold.** Delicious!

GRILLED STEAKS

Rib eye steaks
Meat tenderizer

Garlic powder
Liquid smoke

1. Sprinkle steaks lightly with meat tenderizer on both sides, piercing steak with fork.
2. Sprinkle heavily with garlic powder.
3. Place steak in casserole and marinate 2 hours with liquid smoke. (At room temperature).
4. Place steaks on hot grill — for a ¾-inch steak grill 5 minutes on one side, turn and grill 4 minutes on the other side. If you like your steak rare descrease your cooking time by 1½ minutes for each side.

For a real treat:

Saute' 1 stick butter and 1 box of mushrooms washed and sliced, add 2 tablespoons parsley and 1 tablespoon dried onion. Saute' until golden brown; season with Tony Chachere's seasoning while they are cooking. Serve piping hot on steak.

KATHY'S VEAL PARMIGIANA

1 cup Italian style bread crumbs
¼ cup Parmesan cheese
Salt and pepper
4 to 6 thin veal cutlets
1 egg, slightly beaten or 2 if using more veal
5 tablespoons olive oil
2 tablespoons butter
1 cup chopped onion

1 clove garlic, crushed
2 (8-ounce) cans tomato sauce
⅓ cup dry red wine
½ teaspoon oregano
Salt and pepper
Pinch of basil or thyme
1 (8-ounce) package sliced mozzarella cheese
½ cup Parmesan cheese

PREHEAT OVEN TO 350 DEGREES

1. Mix bread crumbs and ¼ cup Parmesan cheese in shallow plate.
2. Salt and pepper veal. Dip in beaten egg, then in crumbs.
3. Brown in 2 tablespoons olive oil and 2 tablespoons butter. When lightly browned, set aside.
4. In saucepan saute' onions and garlic in 3 tablespoons olive oil until soft.
5. Add tomato sauce, red wine, oregano, salt and pepper and basil or thyme.
6. Cover and simmer for 15 minutes.
7. Arrange overlapping layers of mozzarella cheese and veal in baking dish.
8. Spoon sauce over veal and cheese.
9. Sprinkle with ½ cup Parmesan cheese. Bake 20 to 25 minutes, uncovered. The mozzarella cheese should cover each piece of veal when arranging it.

   Serve 4 to 6.

ROASTED TENDERLOIN IN CANE SYRUP

1 special trimmed beef tenderloin or pork tenderloin
½ cup port wine
1 cup Louisiana cane syrup
½ cup cracked black pepper
1 tablespoon salt
1 tablespoon thyme
1 tablespoon basil
1 tablespoon tarragon

PREHEAT OVEN TO 400 DEGREES

1. In a baking pan with 1-inch lip, place tenderloin and cover with port wine, rubbing well into the meat. Allow excess wine to remain in bottom of baking pan. Using the same technique, add the cane syrup, making sure the beef is well coated.
2. Season meat completely using all of the remaining ingredients. Allow to set at room temperature for one hour.
3. Place baking pan in center of oven and cook uncovered approximately 25 minutes for medium rare. For accuracy, a meat thermometer may be used. This dish may be served hot or cold. For variation, grill or smoke meat on an outdoor pit and top roasted tenderloin with a Marchand De Vin sauce.

Serves 6.

Marchand de Vin:

¼ cup butter
¼ cup finely minced ham
½ cup finely sliced green onions
¼ cup finely minced garlic
2 tablespoons finely minced onion
½ cup dry red wine
1 cup demi-glace (see recipe)
1 teaspoon salt
¼ teaspoon cayenne pepper
Pinch of cracked black pepper

1. In a heavy bottom sauté pan, melt butter over medium high heat. Sauté minced ham, green onions, garlic and onions three to five minutes or until vegetables are wilted.
2. Deglaze with red wine and reduce to one half volume.
3. Add demi-glaze and return mixture to a simmer. Season to taste using salt, cayenne pepper and cracked black pepper.
4. Continue to reduce until sauce is slightly thickened and all flavors are well incorporated. This sauce is best served over any sauted or grilled meat or veal.

Makes 2 cups.

(recipe continued on page 83)

Demi-Glaze:

2 quarts beef, veal or game stock
½ cup light roux

1 ounce tomato sauce

1. Equally divide the stock into two heavy bottom sauce pans and bring to a boil.
2. Using a wire whisk, add ½ cup light roux into one of the sauce pans, stirring constantly as mixture thickens. Into the thickened mixture, blend tomato sauce. What you have just created is known in classical cooking as an espagnole sauce. If this sauce is not full-flavored, you may wish to add a mirepoix or bouquet garni. Continue simmering while skimming all impurities that rise to the surface.
3. As the espagnole sauce reduces, replace the volume with the stock from the second pot until all has been incorporated.
4. Strain through cheese cloth or fine strainer. You may wish to add an ounce of sherry or brandy to add flavor.

   Makes 1 quart.

GROUND MEAT CASSEROLE

1 large onion, chopped
1 tablespoon margarine
1½ pounds ground meat (beef)
1 (8-ounce) can tomato sauce
1½ cups water

1 package of noodles
1 can cream of mushroom soup
1 can Mexican style corn
½ cup grated Cheddar cheese (mild)

PREHEAT OVEN TO 350 DEGREES

1. Sauté 1 onion in a large pot with 1 tablespoon of margarine. Add ground meat and brown.
2. Add 1 can tomato sauce, 1½ cups water, package of noodles, and cook for 20 minutes (covered).
3. Remove from fire. Add 1 can cream of mushroom soup and 1 can of corn (Mexican style).
4. Put in casserole dish — 1 layer of meat and ¼ cup grated cheese, 1 layer of meat and ¼ cup grated cheese (4 layers).
5. Bake at 350 degrees until cheese melts.

LASAGNA I

3 pounds ground meat
4 chopped onions
3 pods garlic
4 tablespoons dry parsley flakes
2 tablespoons basil
2 (8-ounce) cans tomato sauce
1 #2 can whole tomatoes

1. Brown ground meat — drain off fat.
2. Add onions, garlic, parsley and basil to meat and sauté.
3. Add tomato sauce and tomatoes.
4. Cook slowly 2 hours.
5. Cool.

Cook lasagna noodles — 1 box — according to directions on box.

Mix in a bowl:

2 (12-ounce) boxes creamed cottage cheese
2 raw eggs
2 tablespoons parsley
1 cup grated Romano and Parmesan cheese
3 (6-ounce) packages mozzarella cheese

1. Lay boiled drained lasagna noodles in a 9 x 13-inch casserole dish 1 layer deep, then 1 layer of meat sauce, mozzarella cheese, cream cheese mixture and repeat. End with layer of meat sauce on top. Bake at 350 degrees for 20 minutes.

   Freezes well. 24 servings. Serve with Hot Herb Bread.

JERRY'S MEXICAN PIE

1 prepared pie shell
1 can refried beans with chili peppers
1 can green chile peppers, mild
1 pound ground meat
1 (3¼-ounce) can chopped ripe olives
1 large onion, chopped
1 package taco seasoning
½ cup Monterey Jack cheese, grated
½ cup Cheddar cheese, grated
Sour cream for topping

1. Put beans in pie shell. Layer green chilies over the beans. Sauté meat and onions together. Drain off fat.
2. Add the ripe olives and taco seasonings. Mix well and put over beans and peppers.
3. Cover with grated cheeses and bake at 350 degrees for approximately 30 minutes. Slice and serve with a dollop of sour cream.

LASAGNA II

Sauce:

1 pound sweet Italian sausage
½ pound ground beef
½ cup chopped onion
2 cloves garlic, crushed
2 tablespoons sugar
1½ teaspoons salt
1½ teaspoon dried basil leaves
¼ teaspoon pepper
¼ cup chopped parsley
4 cups canned tomatoes
2 cans (6-ounce) tomato paste
½ cup water

1. Brown together first 4 ingredients and drain.
2. Add rest of ingredients and bring to a boil. Reduce heat and simmer about 1½ hours.

Noodles:

12 curly lasagna noodles

Boil a few at a time in salted water; drain, rinse and pat dry.

Cheese:

15 ounce ricotta cheese
¾ cup grated Parmesan cheese
¾ pound grated mozzarella cheese
1 egg
½ teaspoon salt
2 tablespoons parsley

Combine ricotta, egg, parsley and salt.

PREHEAT OVEN TO 350 DEGREES

Assembly:

1. Spoon 1½ cups sauce in 13 x 9 x 2-inch baking dish.
2. Layer with 6 lasagna noodles overlapping to cover.
3. Spread with ½ of ricotta mixture.
4. Top with ½ mozzarella.
5. Spoon 1½ cups sauce over cheese.
6. Sprinkle with Parmesan.
7. Repeat starting with 6 lasagna noodles and ending with 1½ cups sauce sprinkled with Parmesan. Spread with remaining sauce. Top with rest of mozzarella and Parmesan.

Baking:

Cover with foil tucking around edges. Bake at 350 degrees for 25 minutes. Remove foil and bake uncovered 25 minutes longer. Cool 15 minutes before serving.

GLORIA'S EASY LASAGNA

Sauce:

1 pound ground turkey
1 (32-ounce) jar spaghetti sauce
1 (12-ounce) V8 juice (spicy hot)

1. Brown meat - add spaghetti sauce and V8 juice.
2. Simmer 10 minutes.

Cheese Filling:

Mix together:

1 (16-ounce) small curd low fat cottage cheese
3 cups (12-ounce) grated mozzarella cheese
2 beaten eggs or ½ cup egg beaters
¼ teaspoon pepper

Noodles:

8 ounce lasagna noodles, uncooked.

PREHEAT OVEN TO 350 DEGREES

1. Pour 1 cup sauce on bottom of 13 x 9 x 2-inch baking dish.
2. Layer 3 pieces of uncooked lasagna over sauce.
3. Cover with 1½ cups sauce.
4. Spread ½ of cheese filling over sauce.
5. Repeat layers of lasagna, sauce and filling. Top with layer of lasagna noodles and remaining sauce. Cover with foil tightly and bake at 350 degrees for 1 hour. Remove foil and continue baking for 10 minutes. Let stand 10 minutes before cutting.

SPAGHETTI SAUCE

1 pound ground turkey
1 large onion, chopped
3 cloves garlic, minced
2 (1-pound) cans tomatoes, cut up
1 (8-ounce) can tomato sauce
1 (12-ounce) can tomato paste
1 teaspoon beef bouillion in ½ cup water
2 tablespoons minced parsley
1 tablespoon brown sugar
1 teaspoon oregano leaves, dried
1 teaspoon basil leaves, dried
1 teaspoon salt
¼ teaspoon pepper

1. Brown turkey with onions and garlic in skillet. Drain fat.
2. Add other ingredients to pot with meat mixture.
3. Cover and cook at a low temperature for 1 hour.

Makes 8 serving.

HOT TAMALE PIE

2 pounds cooked ground meat (chuck or rump - venison also may be used)
Several cloves of garlic, minced
2 large onions, chopped
1 (8-ounce) can tomato sauce
½ (6-ounce) can tomato paste
8 tablespoons chili powder (more if desired)
1 cup pimento-stuffed olives
½ cup chopped parsley
½ cup chopped green onions
1 tablespoon sugar
3¾ cups stock from roast (seasoned with bay leaf, onion, and celery)
1 teaspoon salt
2 cups cornmeal
Cold water
2 tablespoons butter
Garlic salt, salt and red pepper, and Worcestershire sauce to taste
Paprika

1. Chop cooked roast in a food processor or meat grinder. Sauté garlic and onions in small amount of oil and add chopped meat. Mix in the tomato sauce, tomato paste, chili powder, and olives. Use about ½ cup to ¾ cup stock to make mixture a nice consistency. Then add parsley and green onions. Set aside the meat mixture.
2. Prepare the mush by adding a little cold water to the cornmeal, stirring it in gradually. Then gradually stir in 3 cups of the hot, boiling stock from the roast, stirring constantly to keep it from lumping. In about 5 minutes it should be thick and ready to use.
3. Add sugar and seasonings to meat mixture. Mix well. In a deep, greased, ovenproof dish, put a layer of the cornmeal mush on the bottom, follow with half of the meat mixture. Top it with a layer of the mush and then cover with the other half of the meat mixture. End with a final layer of the cornmeal mush and put the butter on top of it, plus a little paprika.
4. The dish may be frozen or refrigerated ahead. When ready to serve, bake in preheated 350 degree oven for 25 minutes, covered with foil. Bake the last 5 minutes, uncovered. The top should be soft and not like a crust. If shallow casserole dish is used, use only two layers of cornmeal mixture, one on the bottom and one on the top with all the meat mixture in between.

Serves 8.

BEEF BURGUNDY STROGANOFF

½ pound fresh mushrooms, sliced
¼ cup chopped onion
1 clove garlic, minced
¼ cup butter or margarine, melted
1 pound boneless sirloin, cut into 3 x ½ x ¼-inch strips
2 tablespoons all-purpose flour
1 (10½-ounce) can consomme, undiluted
3 tablespoons lemon juice
3 tablespoons Burgundy
¼ teaspoon pepper
1 cup commercial sour cream
Hot cooked noodles

1. Sauté mushrooms, onion, and garlic in butter until onion is tender.
2. Add beef; cook, stirring constantly, until browned.
3. Stir in next 5 ingredients; bring to a boil. Reduce heat, and simmer 15 minutes, stirring occasionally.
4. Stir in sour cream; cook until thoroughly heated (do not boil). Serve over hot cooked noodles.

Yield: 4 servings.

NELL'S HUSBAND'S DELIGHT

1 package narrow-size noodles
2 pounds ground chuck
1 bell pepper, chopped
1 clove garlic
1 tablespoon brown sugar
Salt and pepper
2 (8-ounce) cans tomato sauce
2 (3-ounce) packages cream cheese
1 carton sour cream
1 bunch green onions
2 cups grated cheese

1. Cook noodles and set aside. (Cook while meat simmers).
2. Cook meat in small amount of shortening; drain off fat.
3. Add bell pepper, garlic, brown sugar, salt and pepper.
4. Add the tomato sauce; simmer together for 15 to 20 minutes.
5. Meanwhile mix sour cream and cream cheese; add green onions and tops.
6. Grease casserole dish.
7. Arrange casserole by putting one layer of noodles, layer of hamburger mixture, layer of sour cream mixture; repeat layers, ending with a layer of noodles on top.
8. Baked covered at 350 degrees for 25 minutes. Uncover, sprinkle with grated cheese, bake for approximately 5 minutes longer or until cheese melts.

Serves about 8.

TAMALES

Blend in Blender or Food Processor:

- 2 medium onions
- 4 cloves garlic
- 3 seeded jalapeño peppers (excess may be frozen)
- 1 can drained Rotel tomatoes
- 1 small can tomato sauce
- 1 teaspoon salt
- 2 tablespoons chili mix
- 6 tablespoons chili powder
- 2 tablespoons cumin (comino)
- ½ cup water

Add To:

- ½ cup white self-rising cornmeal
- 2 pounds ground meat (½ beef and ½ pork)

Roll meat into cylinder shapes and roll in cornmeal twice. Wrap in wet papers and stand upright in pot.

Blend Together:

- 1 can Rotel tomatoes
- 1 small can tomato sauce
- 1 to 3 teaspoons salt (to taste)
- 2 tablespoons chili mix
- 2 tablespoons chili powder

Pour over tamales and add water to cover. Bring to boil-reduce heat and simmer 1½ hours. (Put corn shucks on bottom and top of tamales in pot to improve flavor.)

Makes 50 to 60 tamales

Tamale Papers May Be Ordered From:
Rainbow Paper Co.
P.O. Box 9985
New Iberia, LA 70562-9985
1/318/369-9007

NATCHITOCHES MEAT PIES

1½ pounds ground beef
1½ pounds ground pork
1 cup chopped onions
2 green onions, chopped
1 bell pepper, chopped
1 tablespoon salt
1 teaspoon coarse ground black pepper
1 teaspoon coarse ground red pepper
1 tablespoon chili powder
½ cup all-purpose flour
¼ cup sherry

Crust:

2 cups self-rising flour
⅓ heaping cup Crisco, not melted
1 egg, beaten
⅔ cup milk.

1. Combine ground beef, ground pork, onions, bell pepper and seasonings in large Dutch oven. Cook over medium heat, stirring often until meat loses its red color. Do not overcook the meat.
2. Sift the flour over the meat mixture, stirring often, until well combined with meat.
3. Remove from heat and cool to room temperature.
4. Place meat in a large colander to drain off excess grease and juice. Add sherry.

Crust:

5. Sift flour and cut shortening into flour.
6. Add beaten egg and milk.
7. Form dough into a ball. Roll about ⅓ of the dough at a time on a lightly floured board. Cut dough into 5 to 5½-inch circles. (I use the top of an old coffee pot, which is exactly the right size. I find it easier to cut out all of the circles for the pies and place them on a cookie sheet, separated by waxed paper.

To Assemble:

1. Place a heaping tablespoon of filling on one side of the pastry round.
2. Dampen edge of pies containing meat with fingertips, fold top over meat and crimp with fork dipped in water. Prick with fork twice on top.

To Fry:

1. Fry in deep fat fryer at 350 degrees until golden brown. These meat pies freeze beautifully if enclosed in plastic sandwich bags. When frying frozen meat pies, do not thaw before frying. Cocktail meat pies may be made the same way, using a biscuit cutter and 1 teaspoon of meat filling.

   Makes 26 to 28, 5 to 5-inch pies.

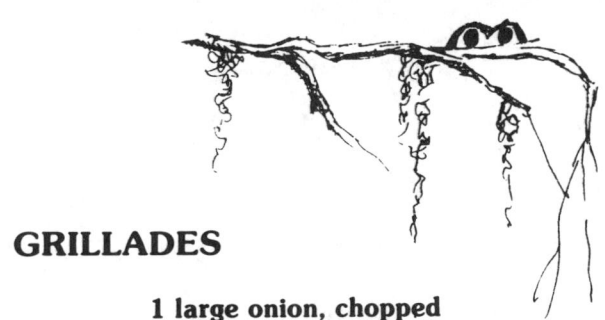

GRILLADES

1 round steak
Salt and pepper
3 tablespoons flour
3 tablespoons shortening or oil

1 large onion, chopped
2 tomatoes, chopped
1½ to 2 cups water
½ teaspoon vinegar

1. Pound round steak well and cut into 4-inch pieces.
2. Salt and pepper well and dust lightly with flour. Brown in shortening and set aside.
3. In the same skillet, make a roux of flour and shortening.
4. Add chopped onion, tomatoes and their juice, water and vinegar. Place browned steak on top.
5. Cover and simmer slowly for 45 minutes to 1 hour

   Serves 4.

Very nice with grits for a morning brunch.

CHILI POT

1 onion, chopped
2 tablespoons margarine
1 pound lean ground beef
1 (14-ounce) bottle ketchup
1 can dark kidney beans
2 teaspoons chili powder
2 tablespoons Worcestershire sauce

1 tablespoon sugar
1 can hot tamales
1 can cream style corn
1 or 2 onions thinly sliced for topping
1 cup grated cheese

1. Brown onion in margarine. Add the ground beef. Cook until beef is no longer pink.
2. Add bottle of ketchup, kidney beans, chili powder, Worcestershire sauce and sugar. Check for seasoning. Do not oversalt because you will serve over Fritos. You may need to add pepper. Simmer for about 10 minutes.
3. Spray casserole with non-stick coating. Layer chili mixture, hot tamales, and the corn.
4. Slice thin onion rings and place them over corn. Cover with grated cheese.
5. Heat in 325 degree oven for ½ hour or until piping hot.
6. Serve over Fritos.

   Serves 6.

BAKED MANICOTTI WITH CHEESE FILLING

Manicotti Shells:

1 cup milk
2 eggs
1 cup flour

1. Combine all ingredients and stir lightly.
2. Grease a small (6-inch) black iron skillet.
3. Pour 1 spoonful of mixture in greased skillet.
4. Cook on low heat till firm.
5. Flip shell out of pan and place on waxpaper.

   Makes 17 shells.

Sauce:

1 large can tomato pureé
1 (6-ounce) can tomato paste
1 teaspoon salt
1 teaspoon sugar
3 tablespoons olive oil
1/8 teaspoon cinnamon
1/4 teaspoon black pepper
1 teaspoon oregano
2 teaspoons minced garlic

1. In a large pot, put 3 tablespoons olive oil and garlic. Sauté.
2. Add all other ingredients and cook for 1½ to 2 hours.

PREHEAT OVEN TO 325 DEGREES

Cheese Filling:

1 pound ricotta cheese
3 eggs
1 tablespoon chopped parsley
1 (8-ounce) package of mozzarella cheese

1. Mix all the above ingredients in large bowl.

To assemble:

I. Place in middle of each shell, 1 heaping tablespoon of cheese filling.
II. Roll up. Place in baking dish seams down.
III. Place sauce on top and sprinkle with Parmesan cheese.

Bake in 325 degree oven, covered with foil for 15 to 20 minutes or until bubbly. Take out of oven and let set for 5 minutes before serving.

MANICOTTI WITH FLORENTINE FILLING

***Spaghetti Sauce:* 4 cups**

(In a hurry I use a large jar of Prego; if I have at least four hours for it to cook, I make my own.)

1 package manicotti noodles (14 pieces)

Cook for 10 minutes in a large pot of salty water. Drain.

Filling:

- 1 pound ground beef
- 1 medium onion, minced
- 1 (10-ounce) package frozen spinach (thawed)
- 2 to 4 tablespoons Parmesan cheese
- 1 cup soft bread crumbs
- 1 tablespoon olive oil
- 3 eggs, slightly beaten
- 1½ teaspoons salt
- ¼ teaspoon pepper
- ¼ teaspoon red pepper
- 1 tablespoon parsley
- 2 cloves garlic, chopped

(If you like cottage cheese, you can add ½-carton to the filling, but it may be necessary to add an extra egg.)

PREHEAT OVEN TO 375 DEGREES

1. Brown beef and onion in oil (preferably olive oil) for 5 minutes.
2. Blend together meat, spinach, and remaining ingredients, except the sauce.
3. Cover bottom of baking dish with 1 cup sauce.
4. Fill cooked manicotti noodles with filling. Any left-over filling can be blended in with the sauce.
5. Arrange stuffed noodles in a single layer in a baking dish. Leave space between noodles for expansion.
6. Cover with the remaining sauce and add ½ cup water.
7. Cover with aluminum foil and bake for 1 hour at 375 degrees.
8. Before serving sprinkle with Parmesan cheese.

BARBECUE SAUCE

- 1 cup vinegar
- 1 cup water
- 2 onions
- ¼ cup Real Lemon
- ¼ bottle Lea & Perrins
- 1 stick margarine
- 2 teaspoons brown sugar
- ½ teaspoon mustard (dry)
- Salt and pepper

1. Mix ingredients together in saucepan and simmer for 30 minutes. Stores well.

   This sauce is excellent to marinate steaks.

SKILLET PIZZA

No stick cooking spray
1½ cups biscuit mix
¾ cup milk
1 cup pizza sauce

1 (4-ounce) can mushrooms, stems and pieces
1 (6-ounce) package mozzarella cheese, sliced
¼ cup grated Parmesan cheese

1. Spray cold large electric skillet with no stick cooking spray.
2. Slightly blend biscuit mix and milk together.
3. Spread dough evenly in skillet.
4. Spread pizza sauce evenly over dough.
5. Arrange drained mushrooms and cheese slices on top.
6. Sprinkle with Parmesan cheese.
7. Cover and close vent.
8. Set heat at 325 degrees and bake about 20 minutes.
9. Serve hot.

Serves 4 to 6.

Variations:

May add ground beef, sliced pepperoni, pork sausage, olives, or fresh vegetables.

Season ground meat with red pepper, black pepper, salt or Tony's seasoning. Mix and roll into balls the size of a marble. Place on top of pizza.

REUBEN SANDWICHES

12 slices rye bread
3 tablespoons prepared mustard
¾ cup sauerkraut

¼ cup butter or margarine, melted
12 slices (1-pound) corned beef
12 slices Swiss cheese

PREHEAT GRILL TO 350 DEGREES

1. Spread 6 slices bread with mustard, allowing ½ tablespoon for each.
2. Cover each slice with 2 tablespoons sauerkraut, 2 slices corned beef and 2 slices Swiss cheese (do not allow cheese to extend over edge of bread).
3. Top each with a slice of bread. Brush both outer sides of each sandwich with melted butter.
4. Brown sandwiches on one side about 3 minutes. Turn and repeat 3 minutes. Serve immediatlely.

Makes 6 sandwiches.

SANDRA'S HOT PEPPER SANDWICHES

1 loaf French bread (slice in half lengthwise)
1 jar Cheese Whiz with jalapeño peppers
1 pound ground beef
3 large jalapeño peppers (may be omitted if too hot)
15 ounce can tomato sauce
1½ teaspoons oregano
4 ounce can of chopped mushrooms
¾ cup chopped onions
4 tablespoons oil
5 ounces Parmesan cheese (or mozzarella)

PREHEAT OVEN TO 325 DEGREES

1. Cover cookie sheet with foil. Spread Cheese Whiz on sliced bread and place on cookie sheet.
2. Brown hamburger meat and drain off excess fat. Add peppers if desired. Add ½ of the can of tomato sauce. Simmer 5 minutes. Add salt to taste and oregano. Cook 2 minutes more.
3. Spread meat mixture on bread. Top with mushrooms and onions. Spoon on the rest of tomato sauce (sometimes all remaining is too much).
4. Drizzle oil on top to prevent drying out. Top with cheese.
5. Bake at 325 degrees for 20 minutes.

RED BEANS AND RICE WITH TASSO

1 pound red beans (preferable Camillia brand)
¼ teaspoon sugar
¼ pound piece of tasso or 1 big ham bone or 1½ pounds hot sausage, or 1½ pounds Andouille, or any combination of the above
3 onions, finely chopped
3 to 4 tablespoons bacon grease
3 bay leaves
2 tablespoons thyme
5 cloves garlic, mashed
Salt to taste
Cooked rice

1. Soak the red beans overnight or at least 3 hours in cold water.
2. Drain off the water and put in a large pot and cover with water.
3. In a skillet, brown the onions in the bacon grease. Adding the sprinkle of sugar will assist in the browning.
4. Add the onions and the remaining ingredients to the red beans and bring to a boil, then reduce to a simmer and cook for 2½ to 3 hours until creamy.
5. Serve with cooked rice and Tabasco sauce.

Serve with cole slaw and cornbread for a delicious, nutritious, inexpensive meal.

GIBLET GRAVY

1 stick margarine
½ cup flour
2 cups milk
2 hard cooked eggs, chopped

Chopped giblets and broth from turkey (reserve ½ of giblets from turkey)

1. Melt margarine and stir in flour (Do not brown).
2. Slowly add milk and stir until you have a smooth sauce. (This is a white sauce.)
3. Add eggs and chopped giblets
4. Cook for 15 minutes. Use broth from turkey to thin to desired consistency.

BROWN SAUCE OR GRAVY
(For all meat and game)

Pan drippings
1 tablespoon chopped green scallions (onion tops)
1 tablespoon parsley
Flour (enough to thicken)

1. Use pan drippings (remove excess fat) of meat or game.
2. To this add scallions, parsley and enough flour and water to the mixture to thicken.
3. Cook about 5 minutes.

If desired add mushrooms and if you like gravy on the sweet side, add 1 tablespoon currant jelly.

VIVIAN'S BARBEQUE SAUCE

½ quart vinegar
½ quart water
3 onions, chopped
½ cup Real Lemon
½ bottle Lea & Perrins

2 sticks margarine
1 tablespoon brown sugar
1 teaspoon mustard
Salt and pepper

1. Mix all of the above ingredients.
2. Bring to boil. Reduce heat and simmer 10 minutes.
3. Use mixture to baste meats on grill.

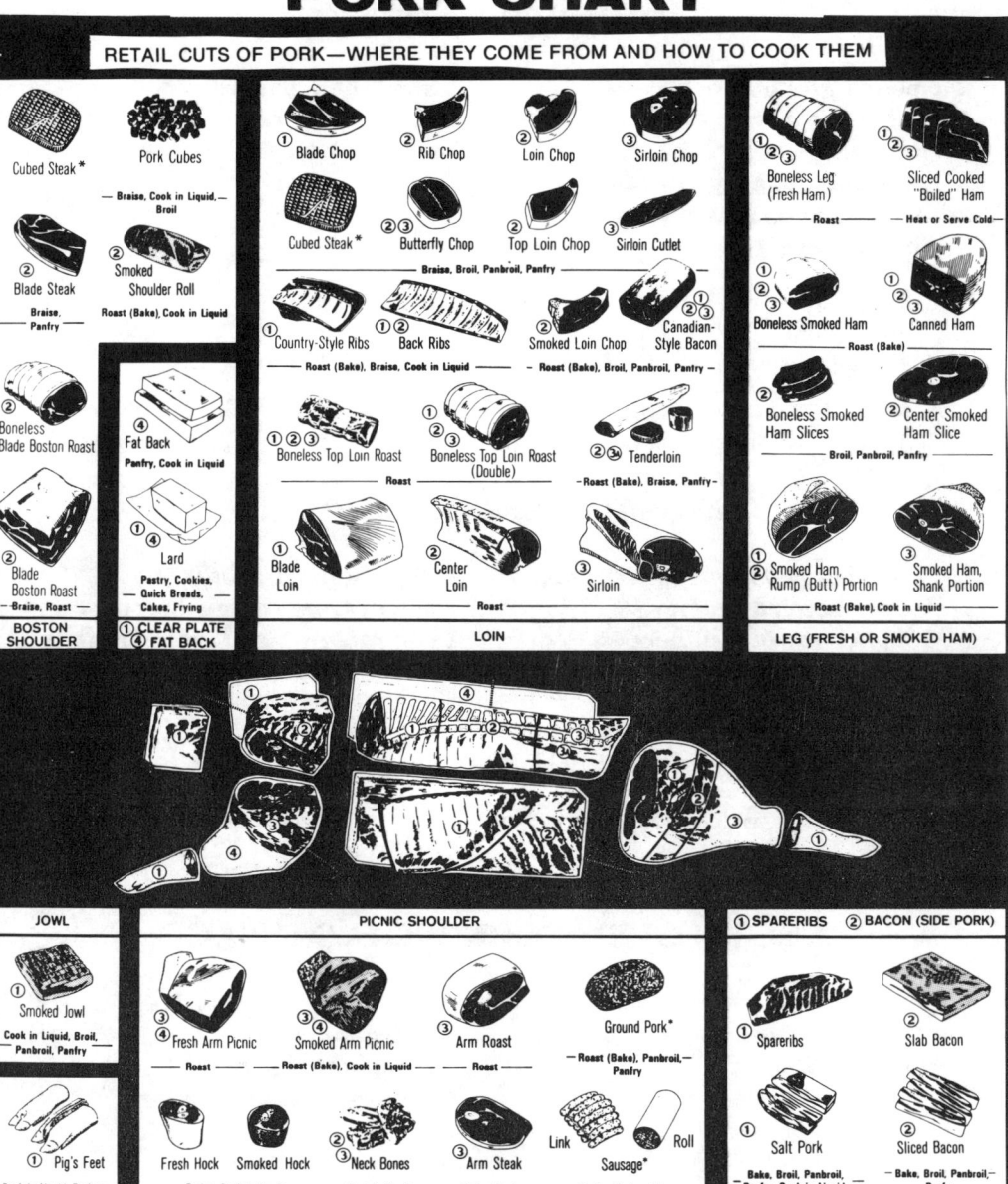

JOHNNY'S MARZETTI

1 pound ground pork
1 large onion, chopped
½ green pepper, chopped
1 (8-ounce) package noodles or shells, cooked as directed on package
1 small can mushrooms
1 can tomato soup
½ pound Velvetta cheese
Salt and pepper

1. Brown pork; add onions and pepper. Cook a little longer.
2. Add cooked noodles, mushrooms, soup and cheese. Mix all together.
3. Place in baking dish. Cover and cook 1 hour at 350 degrees.

Note: I like to double this recipe. I use shells and sometimes add 3 cans of tomato soup when I double the recipe. You can also use spaghetti sauce.

SAUSAGE AND RICE PILAF

1 pound of *Hot* fresh pork sausage
½ cup chopped onion
½ cup chopped bell pepper
1 cup chopped celery
1 can of cream of mushroom soup
1 cup raw rice, cooked separately

1. Cook sausage over low heat in large skillet, pouring off grease now and then. Stir to crumble the meat.
2. Add onions, green pepper, and celery and cook for 5 minutes.
3. Stir in soup and cooked rice.
4. Pour into a casserole dish. *Cover* and bake at 350 degrees for 30 minutes.

Serves 8.

ESCALLOPED CORN WITH SAUSAGE

1½ pounds bulk pork sausage
2 (1-pound) cans cream style corn
⅔ cup milk
2 eggs
2 tablespoons margarine
½ teaspoon salt
⅛ teaspoon pepper
1½ cups cracker crumbs

PREHEAT OVEN TO 350 DEGREES

1. Slice sausage, fry on low fire, drain.
2. Mix corn with milk, eggs, cracker crumbs and seasonings. Put mixture into buttered baking dish, alternating with sausage.
3. Dot top with margarine and cover with additional cracker crumbs. Bake 1 hour in 350 degree oven. (45 minutes covered, 15 minutes uncovered.)

STUFFED PORK CHOPS

8 pork rib chops (12-ounces ea.) about 1½-inches thick
1 (6-ounce) package original long grain and wild rice mix
¼ cup wild rice
1 cup water
½ cup raisins
1 teaspoon arrowroot
⅛ teaspoon ground cinnamon
½ cup firmly-packed brown sugar
⅛ teaspoon ground coriander
1 cup finely chopped apple
¼ cup grated fresh ginger root
2 teaspoons powdered thyme
½ cup butter or margarine
¼ cup lemon juice

1. Prepare long grain and wild rice mix according to package directions, adding ¼ cup additional wild rice when rice packet is called for in preparation.
2. Combine 1 cup water, raisins, arrowroot, cinnamon and coriander in a large saucepan. Cook over medium heat, stirring constantly until thickened. Remove from heat; add apples and prepared rice mixing well.
3. Cut an opening in each chop from the rib side, widening the pocket, without cutting through the other edge of the chop. Stuff with rice stuffing; close pockets with wooden picks. Rub chops with ginger root and thyme.
4. Melt butter in a small saucepan; add brown sugar and lemon juice. Bring to a boil over low heat, stirring until sugar dissolves.
5. Place chops on grill approximately 6-inches above medium coals. Grill 15 to 20 minutes on each side. Baste with brown sugar glaze and continue grilling 15 to 20 minutes, turning and basting frequently with glaze.

Serves 8.

STUFFED PORK LOIN

Blade loin or center loin roast
1 bell pepper, seeded, sliced
1 large onion, peeled, sliced thick
6 to 8 toes garlic, peeled, sliced thick
Cajun seasoning mix
Garlic powder

NOTE: Roast: Have butcher crack the bone between each rib, cut into separate chops, and tie all chops back together.

1. Stuff 1 slice of bell pepper, 1 slice of onion, and 2-3 slices of garlic between each chop.
2. Sprinkle outside of loin heavily with cajun seasoning mix and garlic powder.
3. Place loin bone side down on a rack in a roasting pan.
4. Bake at 350 degrees until inserted meat thermometer registers 185 degrees. Be sure inserted meat thermometer does not touch bone.

NOTE: May be grilled by browning on both sides over very hot coals then moving to the other end of the grill to cook slowly for approximately 2-2½ hours.

TEXAS BARBECUED PORK CHOPS

6 center cut pork chops (16-ounce) each about 2-inches thick
Salt
Freshly ground black pepper
½ cup butter or margarine
½ cup tomato juice
½ cup ketchup
¼ cup tomato sauce
1 (1½-ounce) package chili quick instant chili mix or chili mix seasoning
2½ tablespoon vinegar
1 tablespoon lemon juice
1 tablespoon mustard with horseradish
1 tablespoon hot sauce
1 tablespoon Worcestershire sauce
1 (20-ounce) can pineapple slices, drained

1. Season pork chops with salt and pepper. Cover and refrigerate for 1 to 2 hours.
2. Melt butter in a medium saucepan. Add tomato juice, ketchup, tomato sauce, vinegar, lemon juice, mustard, hot sauce, Worcestershire sauce, and chili mix. Cook over medium heat stirring constantly, until well combined and heated thoroughly.
3. Place chops on grill approximately 6-inches above medium coals. Grill 30 to 40 minutes. Remove chops and place on heavy-duty foil. Top each with 1 to 2 pineapple slices, and a small amount of sauce. Wrap, and return to grill. Cook over low heat about an hour. Serve with remaining sauce, if desired.

Serves 6.

STUFFED PORK CHOPS

4 to 5 large pork chops (1-inch) thick
2 cups soft bread crumbs
¼ teaspoon celery salt
½ cup chopped onion
½ teaspoon poultry seasoning
½ teaspoon sage
1 teaspoon salt
¼ teaspoon pepper
⅓ cup melted butter

1. Slit pockets in chops. Combine all ingredients with just enough water to moisten. Mix lightly
2. Stuff each chop with part of mixture. Fasten pockets with toothpicks.
3. Season chops with a dash of salt and pepper and brown on both sides in a skillet in a small amount of fat.
4. Place chops in an 8 x 8-inch roasting pan; place additional stuffing over chops. Cover with aluminum foil. Bake at 350 degrees for 1 hour. Uncover the last 10 to 15 minutes of baking.

BRAISED STUFFED PORK CHOPS

2 boneless butterfly pork chops (about ½-pound each)
1 tablespoon butter or margarine, melted
2 tablespoons diced onion
2 tablespoons diced celery
1 tablespoon butter or margarine, melted
½ cup commercial herb stuffing mix
1 teaspoon minced fresh parsley
¼ teaspoon paprika
⅛ teaspoon salt
⅛ teaspoon pepper
3 tablespoons milk
1 cup beef broth
1 tablespoon cornstarch

1. Lightly brown pork chops in 1 tablespoon butter, and set aside.
2. Sauté onion and celery in 1 tablespoon butter until vegetables are crisp-tender. Remove from heat.
3. Add stuffing mix and next 4 ingredients; mix well.
4. Stir in milk.
5. Stuff pork chops with stuffing mixture, and secure with wooden picks.
6. Place pork chops in a lightly greased 8 x 8-inch baking dish. Pour beef broth over pork chops.
7. Cover and bake at 350 degrees for 1 hour or until done; baste occasionally. Transfer pork chops to serving dish.
8. Stir cornstarch into ¼ cup water until dissolved; add to pan drippings. Add more water to pan drippings, if necessary, to make 1 cup.
9. Cook in heavy saucepan over medium heat until mixture begins to bubble, and boil 1 minute, stirring constantly. Serve with pork chops.
    Yield: 2 servings.

CHICKEN CASSEROLE

3 pounds chicken
1 can condensed cream of chicken soup
4 ounce can chopped green chilies or ¼ cup Salsa
⅛ teaspoon garlic powder
¼ teaspoon black pepper
1 cup chicken broth
8 ounces sharp Cheddar cheese, grated
1 can condensed cream of mushroom soup
1 can mushrooms
1 teaspoon chili powder
4 teaspoons minced onion
¼ teaspoon Tabasco sauce
4 cups Dorito chips

PREHEAT OVEN TO 350 DEGREES

1. Cook and debone chicken, reserve 1 cup broth.
2. Combine soups, mushrooms, green chilies, spices, Tabasco and broth.
3. Cover bottom of dish with 2 cups Doritos.
4. Spread ½-chicken, ½-sauce, ½-cheese. Repeat ending with cheese. Bake in 350 degree oven for 30 to 40 minutes.

CHICKEN SAUSAGE JAMBALAYA

1 broiler-fryer (about 3-pounds) cut up
1 pound smoked pork sausage (hot)
2 cups rice
2 can beef consommé
6 green onions, chopped
1 large onion, chopped
4 ribs celery, chopped
4 cloves garlic, chopped
1 green pepper, chopped
1 stick margarine
Salt and pepper to taste
Hot pepper sauce, if desired
¼ cup chicken broth
2 tablespoons parsley

1. Put chicken in a large saucepan with 3 cups water, 1 teaspoon salt, and a few peppercorns or black pepper. Bring to boiling, lower heat, cover. Simmer 45-60 minutes or until chicken is tender.
2. Drain, debone, cut meat into bite-size pieces. You should have about 2 cups.
3. Place uncut sausage in oven at 350 degrees for 10 minutes. Remove and slice into bite-size pieces.
4. Sauté onions, garlic, celery, green pepper in margarine.
5. Combine chicken, sausage, rice, consommé and all other ingredients in a heavy pot with tight fitting cover.
6. Bring to boiling; lower heat; cover. Simmer at lowest heat for 1 hour. *Do not remove cover at any time during cooking.*
   Serves 6 to 10.

Hint for today: Use food processor with chopping blade. Chop garlic first, then put in cubed onion (process only long enough for onion to be very coarse.) Remove blade; replace with slicing blade and slice four large ribs of celery. Sorry, pepper will have to be chopped by hand. Hold clean green onions in a bunch in your hand and cut with scissors.

CHICKEN TORTILLA CASSEROLE

1 (3-pound fryer)
1 (8-ounce) sour cream
2 cans cream of mushroom or cream of chicken soup
1 small can green chili pepper
Monterey Jack cheese
Tortilla

1. Cook and debone 1 large fryer. Chop in large pieces.
2. Add sour cream, soup and green chili pepper.
3. Mix well.
4. Heat tortilla on each side for 15 seconds.
5. Fill tortilla with mixture and fold.
6. Put in casserole. Sprinkle with Monterey Jack cheese. Cook for 30 minutes at 325 degrees.

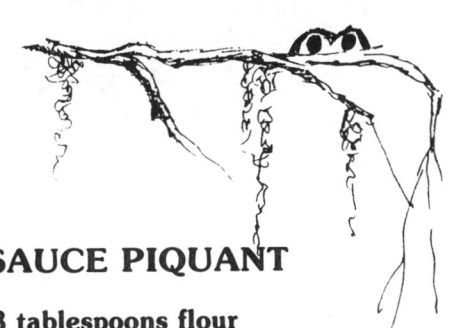

KATHY'S CHICKEN SAUCE PIQUANT

1 stewing hen (about 4-pounds) cooked and deboned
1 pound hot smoked sausage
Salt, black pepper and cayenne to taste
¼ cup oil
3 medium onions, chopped
1 cup chopped bell pepper
1 cup chopped celery
4 cloves garlic
3 tablespoons flour
1 can Rotel tomatoes
1 pound can tomatoes*
4½ to 5 cups water
1 tablespoon sugar
1 can (4-ounce) sliced mushrooms
½ cup onion tops
½ cup parsley
½ cup Sauterne wine

1. Cut chicken into pieces. Cut sausage into bite-size pieces.
2. Season chicken with the salt, black pepper and cayenne, leaning heavily on the cayenne to give the sting (which is the piquant). Put oil into large heavy pot, add chicken and sausage and brown well. Remove meat and set aside.
3. Add to pan the vegetables (onions, bell pepper, celery and garlic) and cook until wilted.
4. Sprinkle in flour and stir well. Add tomatoes and water. Cook over medium heat for about 25 minutes (if oil floats to top, remove).
5. Add chicken and sausage, mushrooms and sugar. Add additional seasonings to individual taste. Cook about 30 minutes longer. Add green onions, wine and parsley. Serve over steamed rice.

    Serves 8.

*Tomato juice or V-8 juice may be used instead of tomatoes.

CHICKEN IN MUSTARD SAUCE

8 breasts and thighs, deboned
3 to 4 tablespoons Dijon mustard
2 tablespoons peanut oil
3 tablespoons butter
1 medium size onion, chopped
1 cup stock
1 cup whipping cream
4 garlic cloves
¼ cup vinegar or dry wine

1. Dry chicken. Sprinkle with flour. Heat butter and oil. Sauté chicken pieces on both sides till golden.
2. Remove chicken to a baking pan.
3. Deglaze pan with vinegar. Reduce for a few minutes by boiling.
4. Add garlic, stock, cream and mustard. Cook till slightly thickened. Pour over chicken. Cook at 375 degrees for 25 minutes or until tender. Delicious served with white wine, green beans and rice.

CHICKEN FAJITAS

2 tablespoon lemon juice
½ teaspoon salt
¼ teaspoon coarsely ground pepper
¼ teaspoon garlic powder
½ teaspoon liquid smoke
3 chicken breast halves, skinned, boned and cut into strips

6 (6-inch) flour tortillas
2 tablespoons vegetable oil
1 green or sweet red pepper, cut into strips
1 medium onion, sliced and separated into rings

1. Combine first 5 ingredients in a small bowl.* Add chicken; stir to coat.
2. Cover and chill at least 30 minutes. Drain chicken, reserving marinade.
3. Wrap tortillas in aluminum foil; bake at 350 degrees for 15 minutes.
4. Heat oil in a heavy skillet. Add chicken; cook 2 to 3 minutes, stirring constantly.
5. Add marinade, pepper, and onion; sauté until vegetables are crisp-tender. Remove from heat. Divide mixture evenly and spoon a portion onto each tortilla. If desired, top with any of the following: chopped tomato, green onions, lettuce, guacamole, grated cheese, and picante sauce, then wrap.

   Yield: 3 servings.

* If short on time, use ½-cup of Italian dressing and 1 tablespoon liquid smoke to marinate chicken.

FAJITAS

2½ or 3 pounds chicken breast or fajitas meat (beef skirt steak)

Marinade:

½ medium onion, minced
1 clove garlic, minced
1 small jalapeño pepper, minced
½ cup olive oil
½ cup red wine vinegar

½ teaspoon pepper, freshly ground
1 teaspoon sugar
½ teaspoon salt
½ teaspoon paprika

1. Lightly brown onion, garlic and pepper in oil; add remaining ingredients and bring to a boil.
2. Reduce heat and simmer for 5 to 10 minutes. Cool.
3. Slice meat across grain. Pour marinade over strips.
4. Marinate three hours to overnight in refrigerator.
5. Remove meat from marinade.
6. Stir-fry meat on medium high until cooked. Serve hot, wrapped in a soft flour tortilla with picante sauce or Pico de Gallo.

   Serves 4 to 5.

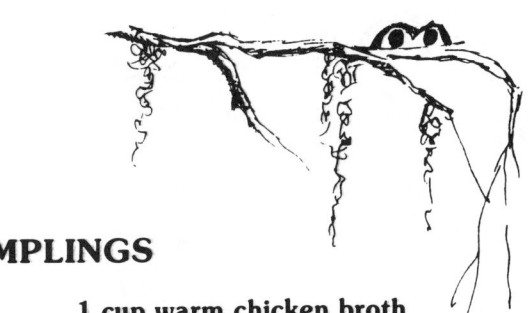

DUMPLINGS

3 cups self-rising flour
1 egg
2 tablespoons shortening

1 cup warm chicken broth
Salt and pepper

1. Start with 3 cups self rising flour in a large bowl. Make a well in the flour, like making biscuits.
2. Add one whole egg, and 2 tablespoons shortening if broth is not rich. Gradually add 1 cup warm chicken broth, mixing with fork or fingers till you have a nice soft dough.
3. Roll out on floured board separating dough into about 3 balls. Roll balls out fairly thin and then cut into squares and sprinkle with flour.
4. Drop into hot boiling broth (3-4 quarts) and cook fast until you have all the dumplings into pot.
5. Reduce heat to low and cook about 20 minutes longer with lid on. Add salt and pepper.

   Optional: You may add ½ stick of butter or margarine and about ½ cup milk if desired for richness.

FLUFFY DUMPLINGS

1½ cups flour
⅔ teaspoon salt
Black pepper to taste
4 teaspoons baking powder
1 egg

1 tablespoon melted shortening or oil
⅔ cup milk
1 teaspoon thyme
1 teaspoon basil

1. Sift flour, salt, and baking powder into mixture of beaten eggs, shortening, and milk. (For richness use 1 small can Pet milk.)
2. When ready to serve, drop by teaspoonsful into boiling gravy (about 4 cups), cover, and cook gently for 8 to 10 minutes or until done.

MOM'S CHICKEN FLAMBEAU

8 chicken breasts
2 envelopes onion soup
1 bottle Russian dressing

4 ounces Apricot preserve
Salt and pepper to taste
Dash garlic powder

PREHEAT OVEN TO 300 DEGREES

1. Arrange chicken in casserole.
2. Mix ingredients together; pour over chicken. Bake in 300 degree oven for 2 hours.

MAKE YOUR FAVORITE DRESSING

½ pound lean pork, ground
½ pound lean beef, ground
1 pound gizzards, ground
2 sticks margarine
2 large onions, chopped fine
4 sticks celery, chopped fine
2 cloves garlic, chopped fine
1 can chicken bouillon
1 tablespoon Worcestershire sauce
Salt and pepper to taste

1. Melt 1 stick margarine and fry meat until brown, about 20 minutes.
2. Add onions, celery and garlic; stir and cook until soft.
3. Add Worcestershire sauce, bouillon and 1 stick margarine. Stir well, bring to a boil and simmer for about 2 hours. Season to taste with salt and pepper.

Serves 12.

Variations:

(1) For **Dirty Rice:** Add about 6 cups of cooked rice. Sauté ½ cup chopped green onion tops and ½ cup minced parsley in ¼-stick margarine. Mix well with rice.

(2) For **Corn Bread Dressing:** Add 6 cups crumbled corn bread combined with sautéd onion and parsley as above.

(3) For **Bread Dressing:** Add 6 cups torn bread and sautéd onions and parsley as above.

DIRTY RICE

Mrs. Turner, this one is for you

6 cups cooked rice
2 pints chicken liver, cooked and chopped
1 cup chopped onions
10 green onions, chopped
4 cloves garlic, chopped
1 cup chopped celery
2 tablespoons parsley (dried) or ¼ cup fresh parsley
2 tablespoons butter + 2 tablespoons bacon drippings
½ pound fried bacon, crumbled
Red pepper, black pepper, and salt to taste

1. Cook chicken livers in 2 cups water and 1 teaspoon salt until tender.
2. Place chicken livers in food processor and blend.
3. Sauté onions, green onions, garlic, celery, and parsley in butter and bacon drippings.
4. Mix rice, sauté vegetables, chicken livers, bacon crumbs, and salt, red pepper and black pepper to taste
5. Pour into a buttered casserole, dot with butter, cover and bake at least 350 degrees for 20 minutes.

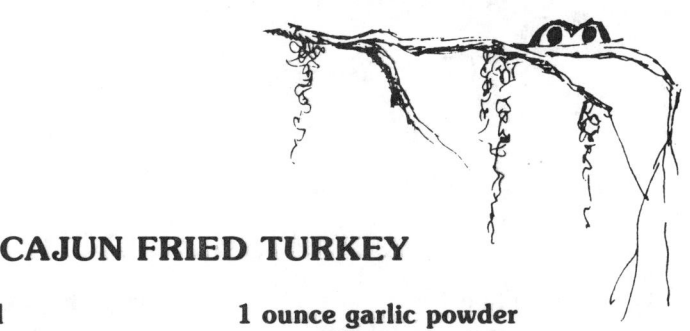

CAJUN FRIED TURKEY

5 gallons peanut oil
1 (12 to 14-pound) turkey
1 cup salad oil
Hot pepper sauce to taste
½ ounce cayenne pepper
1 ounce onion powder
¼ cup vinegar
1 ounce garlic powder
1 ounce paprika
1 ounce Cajun spice mix
Salt and pepper to taste
½ cup Italian salad dressing
2 tablespoons liquid crab boil

1. Coat entire turkey with salad oil and hot pepper sauce. Combine dry spices and Cajun spice mix, and cover turkey with mixture.
2. Strain salad dressing and mix with crab boil. Fill large cook's syringe with mixture and inject into turkey in different places. Let stand overnight in refrigerator.
3. Preheat peanut oil and vinegar to 350 degrees.
4. Immerse turkey in hot oil and cook approximately 3 minutes per pound, turning every 5 minutes. Remove and drain before serving.

Yield: 12 portions.

TIP: ¼ cup vinegar will keep turkey from absorbing the fat.

TURKEY SHOOT UP A LA JOHNNY

2 tablespoons salt
2 teaspoons garlic juice
2 teaspoons onion juice
1 stick margarine
3 tablespoons Lea & Perrin
3 tablespoons soy sauce
2 tablespoons Tabasco
¾ cup white sherry (sweet wine)

1. Mix all ingredients and inject into a large turkey before roasting, smoking, or frying whole.
2. Cover turkey with Tony Chachere's seasoning after injecting.
3. Roast or smoke turkey as desired. Especially good for deep frying a turkey.

TURKEY SHOOT UP A LA RONNIE

3 bottles liquid garlic
3 bottles liquid onion
1 cup butter flavored oil
1 stick margarine, melted
Salt, red pepper to taste

For large turkey use full recipe. For small turkey or breast of turkey use a ½ recipe.

Use syringe to inject mixture into a turkey before smoking or roasting.

CHICKEN AND SPAGHETTI

1 (4-pound) hen
8 ounce package spaghetti
1 cup chopped celery
1 cup chopped onions
½ cup pimento
1 cup chopped ripe olives
1 cup chopped green peppers
Salt and pepper to taste
1 can cream of mushroom soup
½ stick of butter or margarine

PREHEAT OVEN TO 350 DEGREES

1. Boil hen until tender; debone and cut into small pieces.
2. Cook spaghetti in broth until tender; set aside.
3. Mix together onions, celery, and pepper in pan with small amount of butter or margarine, cook until tender.
4. Mix this mixture with spaghetti and chicken. Add olives and pimento
5. Put in casserole dish and spread mushroom soup over and bake until it bubbles.

CHICKEN AND DUMPLINGS #2

1 (3-pound) chicken or 3 pounds chicken pieces
4 (8-inch) flour tortillas torn into small pieces

1. Cook chicken in enough water to cover in large saucepan.
2. Add salt and simmer until chicken is very tender.
3. Remove and discard chicken bones. Strain broth. Combine chicken and broth in deep saucepan.
4. Bring broth to simmering point over low heat. Drop tortilla pieces several at a time into broth. Be sure broth keeps on simmering.
5. Simmer, covered for 15 minutes or until tortillas are very tender.

Yields: 4 servings. *Note:* Try the dumpling recipe on the Bisquick box.

DORIS' CHICKEN

6 deboned chicken breast
1 jar dried beef
1 pound bacon-cut strip of bacon in half
1 can golden mushroom soup
1 cup sour cream

1. Grease baking dish and debone chicken breast.
2. Roll each piece, wrap chip beef around, then wrap this with ½ slice bacon. Secure with picks. Place seam side down in baking dish. Cover with golden mushroom soup, mixed with 1 cup sour cream.
3. Cook uncovered at 275 degrees for 3 hours.

I bake 12 breast halves and double the soup and sour cream. Serve with rice and a gelatin salad.

CHICKEN JAMBALAYA

3 cups long grain rice
1 large fryer
6 medium size onions, chopped
1 clove garlic, finely chopped
1 tablespoon bell pepper (chopped small)
1 tablespoon celery (chopped small)
½ pound hot smoked sausage
Salt
Black pepper
Cayenne pepper
1 cup cooking oil

1. Cut up chicken, wash and season with salt and both peppers. Fry until golden brown in cooking oil over hot fire.
2. Lower heat and add all chopped seasoning except garlic. Cook until all seasoning is clear or onions, bell pepper and celery are tender. Here's where you may add the hot sausage. I think this makes a better jambalaya.
3. Add rice, salt and pepper to chicken and seasoning. Cook slowly for about 15 minutes over low heat, stirring often.
4. Add 4 cups water and chopped garlic, stir and cover. *Do not stir anymore.* Simmer over low flame for about 1 hour, or until rice is done. Keep covered.

   Serves 8.

Variations: This same recipe may be used with pork, duck, squirrel, rabbit, sausage or beef.

CHICKEN TETRAZZINI

2 fryers
2 bell peppers, chopped
2 onions, chopped
2 sticks butter
2 pound package spaghetti
2 pounds Velvetta cheese
1 can Rotel tomatoes, drained

1. Cook fryers until tender. Debone. Be sure and save chicken broth.
2. Sauté bell peppers, onions in 2 sticks of butter.
3. Cook 2 pounds spaghetti in chicken broth until tender.
4. Salt and pepper to taste.
5. Mix sautéed mixture with deboned chicken, spaghetti, and cheese. Add drained Rotel tomatoes.
6. Place in casserole — heat until bubbly at 350 degrees.

   Serves 20.

An excellent recipe to divide up into 3 casserole dishes and freeze.

CHICKEN AND RICE

1 or 2 fryers (cut into pieces)
2 cups rice
1 can cream of mushroom soup
1 can bouillon
1 can onion soup
1 can cream of chicken soup
1 stick butter
Red pepper and paprika to taste

1. Grease baking dish.
2. Put rice in baking dish. Combine mushroom, cream of chicken, onion and bouillon soups. Pour ½ of soup mixture over rice; stir.
3. Place chicken on top of rice mixture. Pour remainder of soup mixture over chicken. Dot with butter. Garnish with paprika and red pepper.
4. Cover air tight. Cook for 1 hour at 350 degrees. *Do not open lid!*

CHICKEN WITH ARTICHOKES

1 large fryer, cut up
¼ teaspoon salt
¼ teaspoon pepper
¼ teaspoon paprika
¼ teaspoon onion salt
½ cup flour
1 cup olive or vegetable oil
2 medium onions, chopped
4 green onion, chopped
3 stalks celery, chopped
1 clove garlic, minced
¼ cup parsley
1 medium green pepper, chopped
1 (4-ounce) can mushroom stems and pieces, drained with liquid reserved
1 (6-ounce) jar marinated artichoke hearts, drained with oil reserved
¼ teaspoon Italian seasoning
¼ to ½ cup white wine

1. Perpare chicken for frying. In paper bag combine salt, pepper, paprika, garlic, onion salt and flour.
2. Place chicken, one or two pieces at a time, in paper bag. Shake until chicken is coated.
3. Heat oil in a heavy Dutch oven or pot. Fry chicken until brown. Remove and drain on brown paper.
4. Pour off part of oil, leaving enough to cover bottom of pot. Sauté onions, celery, garlic, parsley and green pepper in remaining oil.
5. Add juice from can of mushrooms and oil from jar of artichokes to sautéed mixture.
6. Return chicken to pot and simmer until chicken is tender, about 20 minutes.
7. Add Italian seasoning, mushrooms, artichokes and wine to chicken; heat for a few minutes and serve over rice or wild rice.

Serves 6.

MARY'S LEMON CHICKEN

4 chicken breasts
1 stick butter
2 teaspoons dry tarragon
¼ cup flour
3 tablespoons *Coleman* dry mustard
Dash of black pepper

2 tablespoons Instant Chicken Bouillon
1½ cups hot water
1½ tablespoons fresh lemon juice
1 large can drained whole mushrooms (fresh is fine, but sauté them with butter)
1 tablespoon parsley

1. Cut chicken into bite-size chunks. Mix dry ingredients together and dredge chicken.
2. Melt butter in large heavy skillet. Sauté chicken until brown all over.
3. Add mushrooms just as chicken is done. Remove chicken and mushrooms from skillet (keep warm).
4. With flour mixture left, put into skillet and slightly brown.
5. Add lemon juice and chicken bouillon and water into mixture and make gravy. Add chicken and serve in chafing dish with toothpicks on side or serve over angel pasta with Banana Nut Bread and Fruit Salad.

CHICKEN DIVAN

1 (3-pound) fryer, split
1 bunch broccoli (or 2 packages frozen)
2 tablespoons butter
3 tablespoons flour

2 cups broth
Salt and pepper to taste
3 tablespoons sherry wine
¼ pound grated Parmesan cheese

PREHEAT OVEN TO 400 DEGREES

1. Boil chicken in seasoned water until tender. Save broth. Debone the chicken in large pieces, then slice.
2. Cook broccoli until just tender, drain, and place in casserole dish.
3. Melt butter in top of a double boiler and blend in the flour.
4. Measure the chicken broth. If there is not enough to make 2 cups, add milk to make up the difference.
5. Add the broth to the butter and flour, stirring until thickened. Add salt, pepper, and sherry.
6. Cover the broccoli in the casserole dish with a layer of chicken, then add the sauce. Sprinkle with grated cheese. Bake in 400 degree oven for about 12 minutes.

   Serves 4.

CORNISH HENS

6 cornish hens (14 to 16-ounces)
1 stick butter or margarine
1 cup chicken broth
½ cup basic vegetable mixture
  (1½ teaspoons onions, 1½
  tablespoon celery,
  1 tablespoon parsley)
3 strips bacon
8 ounce can mushrooms, stems, pieces
1 tablespoon Worcestershire sauce
½ cup chopped green onion tops and parsley
1 tablespoon (heaping) flour
2 heaping tablespoons currant jelly
3 tablespoons Tony's seasoning

PREHEAT OVEN TO 325 DEGREES

1. Season inside and out the cornish hens generously with Tony's seasoning.
2. Stuff inside birds with equal parts margarine and vegetable mixture.
3. Place in baking dish breast side up.
4. Layer with bacon slices.
5. Pour 1 cup chicken broth in pan with birds. Cover pan with aluminum foil and bake in preheated 325 degree oven for at least 1½ hours until birds are tender.
6. Remove foil, pour off pan juices into skillet on top of stove.
7. Replace birds in oven. Raise oven temperature to 500 degrees and watch closely until brown.
8. To the pan juices in skillet, add onion tops, and parsley.
9. Add mushrooms and mixture to skillet juices, also currant jelly. Cook and stir about 5 minutes until gravy thickens.
10. Pour gravy over each bird and serve. Serve with petit pois, cornbread dressing, broccoli casserole, green salad, and French bread.

CHICKEN SALAD

3 cups cooked chicken, or 3 cans drained
3 hard cooked eggs, diced
¼ teaspoon salt
⅛ cup chopped onions
3 sweet pickles, chopped
1 apple, diced
Mayonnaise or salad dressing

1. Mix chicken, diced apple, onions, eggs, pickles and salt.
2. Moisten with salad dressing. Serve in large lettuce cups or stuffed into tomatoes.

SAVORY CORNISH HENS

2 cornish hens
Salt
Pepper
2 tablespoons olive oil
1 clove garlic
3 tablespoons finely chopped celery, including a few leaves
2 tablespoons finely chopped shallots, tops and bottoms
2 tablespoons finely chopped parsley
3 tablespoons Sauterne
1¾ cups water
1 cup raw rice

1. Use dutch oven. Lightly salt and pepper hens.
2. Heat oil and add garlic. Slowly brown hens on all sides. When brown, remove and set aside.
3. Add celery, shallots, parsley and cook slowly until tender, about 5 minutes.
4. Add wine and simmer about 1 minute. Add rice and water. Stir thoroughly.
5. Set cornish hens on top of rice and cover Dutch oven with tight-fitting lid. Cook slowly for 30-35 minutes, or until rice is done.

CHICKEN CURRY

1 tablespoon butter
1 cup finely chopped pared apple
1 cup celery
½ cup chopped onions
1 clove garlic, minced
2 tablespoons cornstarch
1 teaspoon curry powder
¾ teaspoon salt
¾ cup cold chicken broth
¼ teaspoon red pepper
2 cups milk
2 cups diced cooked chicken
Black pepper
1 (3-ounce) can sliced mushrooms, drained
Hot cooked rice
Curry condiments: coconut, raisins, peanuts (chopped)

1. In saucepan melt butter; add apple, celery, onion and garlic. Cook until onion is tender.
2. Combine cornstarch, curry, salt and broth. Stir into onion mixture.
3. Add milk; cook and stir until mixture thickens and bubbles.
4. Stir in chicken and mushrooms. Heat thoroughly.
5. Serve curry chicken over hot rice. Sprinkle coconut, peanuts and raisins on top.!

   Delicious!

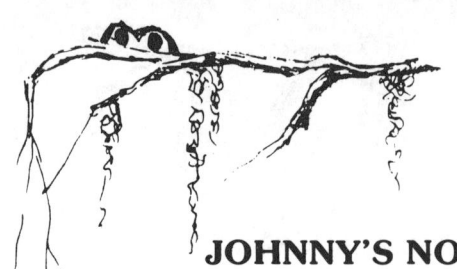

JOHNNY'S NO WORK CHICKEN

4 chicken breasts
¼ cup Dijon style mustard
½ cup honey
1 teaspoon curry powder
2 tablespoons soy sauce

PREHEAT OVEN TO 325 DEGREES

1. Place chicken snugly, skin side down in baking dish in one layer.
2. Mix mustard, honey, curry powder and soy sauce. Pour over chicken
3. Marinate 6 hours in refrigerator.
4. When ready to bake, turn chicken over. Cover dish with foil and bake at 350 degrees for 1 hour.
5. Remove foil, baste well and bake uncovered for 15 minutes.
6. Spoon sauce over chicken and serve with rice.

Rice:

1 tablespoon butter
1 envelope onion soup
1½ cups water
1 cup rice
1 can stems and pieces mushrooms
Red pepper to taste
2 tablespoons parsley

1. Cook rice, water, onion soup, mushrooms, parsley, red pepper and butter in 1½-quart saucepan with a tight fitting lid on a regular 6-inch surface unit. Turn switch to high until steaming freely (leaving cover off utensil), then immediately cover and turn to lowest heat position and cook 30 minutes.
2. Do not remove cover during cooking.

CHICKEN ENCHILADAS

4 chicken breasts, boiled, deboned and chopped (2-cups)
1 onion, chopped
1 pound yellow cheese, grated
1 can green chilies, chopped
1 can cream of mushroom soup
1 can cream of celery soup
1 package tortillas (find them in the dairy case)

1. Steam tortillas for just a few minutes. (This is necessary to make them pliable and able to roll.)
2. Combine chicken, onion and cheese and place small amount in each tortilla. Roll and put folded edge on bottom of dish.
3. Mix soups and green chilies. Pour over top and bake in 350 degree oven for about 20 minutes.

MRS. CRUMP'S CORNBREAD DRESSING

Cornbread (see recipe below)
6 to 8 pieces light bread
4 hard cooked eggs, peeled and diced
1 medium size onion, chopped
1 bunch green onions, chopped
2 ribs celery, chopped
½ cup fresh parsley, chopped
1 delicious apple, peeled and chopped
½ stick margarine
½ teaspoon black pepper
¼ teaspoon red pepper
2 teaspoons instant chicken bouillon
Salt to taste
Giblets — neck, gizzard and liver from turkey
¼ box chicken livers (frozen), optional

1. In a saucepan with lid, simmer gizzard and neck in a quart of water until tender. Add liver and cook a few minutes more until done.
2. Chop all giblets fine for dressing.
3. Sauté celery, parsley, green onions and onions in margarine until tender, but not brown, add seasoning, more or less than amounts suggested to suit taste. Do not add salt until last. Chicken bouillon is very salty.
4. Crumble cornbread and white bread into large mixing bowl. Combine sautéed vegetables, chicken bouillon, diced eggs, apple and sufficient amount of broth from baked turkey or hen to make a moist dressing. If you don't have enough broth use enough milk to make a moist dressing. Place in buttered casserole.
5. Bake at 350 degrees for 15 to 20 minutes or stuff turkey.

This is truly the best dressing I have ever made!

Golden Cornbread:

1 cup yellow cornmeal
¾ cup all-purpose flour
4 teaspoons baking powder
¾ teaspoon salt
1 slightly beaten egg
1 cup milk
2 tablespoons melted shortening

1. Sift dry ingredients into bowl and add the slightly beaten egg, milk and melted shortening. Beat thoroughly.
2. Pour into greased shallow pan. Bake in a 450 degree oven for 15 minutes or until golden brown.

HOT CHICKEN SALAD

4 chicken breasts (hot), cut up
4 hard boiled eggs, diced
1½ cups mayonnaise
1 cup diced celery
2 tablespoons lemon juice
½ cup almonds
¼ cup pimento
1 teaspoon salt
½ teaspoon Accent
1 tablespoon onion
1 cup grated Cheddar cheese (sharp)
1½ cups potato chips (crushed fine)

1. Mix all except Cheddar cheese and potato chips and let stand at least 12 hours.
2. When ready to bake, add cheese and potato chips and mix well.
3. Bake 30 minutes at 375 degrees.

VENISON MARINADE

½ cup soy sauce
3 tablespoons vegetable oil
2 cloves garlic, minced
1 tablespoon grated ginger or
¾ teaspoon ground ginger
3 tablespoons honey

1. Combine all ingredients. Place venison in a glass, enamel or stainless steel dish and marinate several hours, turning occasionally. Broil or grill venison.

SMOKED DUCK

4 ducks
Seasoned salt to taste
Cayenne pepper to taste
Red wine and water
1 cup cola
½ cup dark brown sugar

1. Season ducks generously inside and out with seasoned salt and cayenne pepper.
2. Mix the sugar and cola in a bowl for basting.
3. Fill the pan of the smoker with two parts water to one part wine, and smoke the duck with pecan or cherry wood.
4. Smoke about 5 hours, basting the ducks whenever they look dry. Cook until medium rare. Do not overcook!

CROCKPOT VENISON CHILI

1 pound ground venison
2 onions, chopped
1 clove garlic, minced
1 tablespoon Worcestershire sauce
2 bell peppers, chopped
1½ tablespoons chili powder
1 (8-ounce) can tomato sauce
1 (6-ounce) can tomato paste
1 to 3 cups water
2 (16-ounce) cans red kidney beans

1. Brown meat, onions and garlic in oil in an iron skillet.
2. Put into crockpot with all ingredients except beans.
3. Cook on low for 8 to 10 hours, adding beans the last hour.

BAYOU BENGAL BACKSTRAP

1 venison backstrap
3 ounces Bayon Bengal Cajunpeppa sauce
1 cup brown sugar
Salt and course ground black pepper to taste

1. Mix brown sugar with Cajunpeppa sauce to make a thick sauce.
2. Marinate backstrap in this mixture 2 hours at room temperature.
3. Season meat with salt and course ground black pepper.
4. Grill over a very hot, close fire about 1½ minutes on each side, or until meat is almost black and the sugar caramelized. It should be rare inside. If you prefer your meat less rare, move it off the direct fire and continue to cook until it reaches the desired degree of doneness.

DUCK IN ORANGE MUSTARD SAUCE

8 ounces Hot Orange Sauterne Mustard
6 duck breasts
1¼ cups chicken broth
⅓ cup soy sauce
1 clove garlic
1 teaspoon fresh grated ginger
½ cup orange juice
½ cup brown sugar
1 teaspoon salt
1 cup sauterne wine
2 sliced oranges

PREHEAT OVEN TO 350 DEGREES

1. Mix together all ingredients except oranges.
2. Place breasts in large baking dish and pour mixture over them.
3. Cover and bake at 350 degrees for 1½ hours. Baste every 15 minutes.
4. Arrange orange slices over breasts and continue baking (uncovered) for ½ hour or until there is a golden glaze. Superb!

You can use chicken breasts as well...cut down the cooking time by about 45 minutes.

VENISON ROAST WITH SAUSAGE

1 large venison roast
1 link of hot rope sausage
4 cloves garlic
Salt, pepper and red pepper to taste
3 tablespoons shortening
3 tablespoons flour
1 cup water
2 cups black coffee
1 packet onion-mushroom soup mix

1. Freeze the link of sausage straight.
2. Cut a hole in the roast big enough to push the sausage through it, then insert the sausage.
3. Peel and cut the garlic lengthwise and stuff in slits in the roast. Season with salt, pepper and red pepper to taste.
4. In a large pot, brown the roast, using as little shortening as possible, about 3 tablespoons. Remove the roast and brown 3 tablespoons flour in the oil.
5. Add 1 cup water and stir to make a gravy. Add 2 cups black coffee, 1 packet onion-mushroom soup mix and more hot pepper if desired. Return roast to pot and simmer 3 to 4 hours or until tender. Baste the roast frequently with the gravy while cooking.

BAKED DUCK WITH ORANGE CURRANT SAUCE

Clean ducks thoroughly. Put salt into duck cavity. Also put ¼ orange, apple and turnip into cavity. Place ducks in pan and cover with strips of bacon. Surround with celery, onions, and little water. Bake 3 hours. Start in hot oven 450 degrees and turn down to moderate 350 degrees.

Sauce for duck to be served at table.

ORANGE CURRANT SAUCE

6 tablespoons currant jelly
Grated rind of 1 orange
3 tablespoons water

1. Combine the above and beat 3 minutes with rotary beater.

Add:

2 tablespoons port wine
2 tablespoons orange juice
Dash red pepper
2 tablespoons lemon juice
¼ teaspoon salt

Stir well. Serve room temperature.

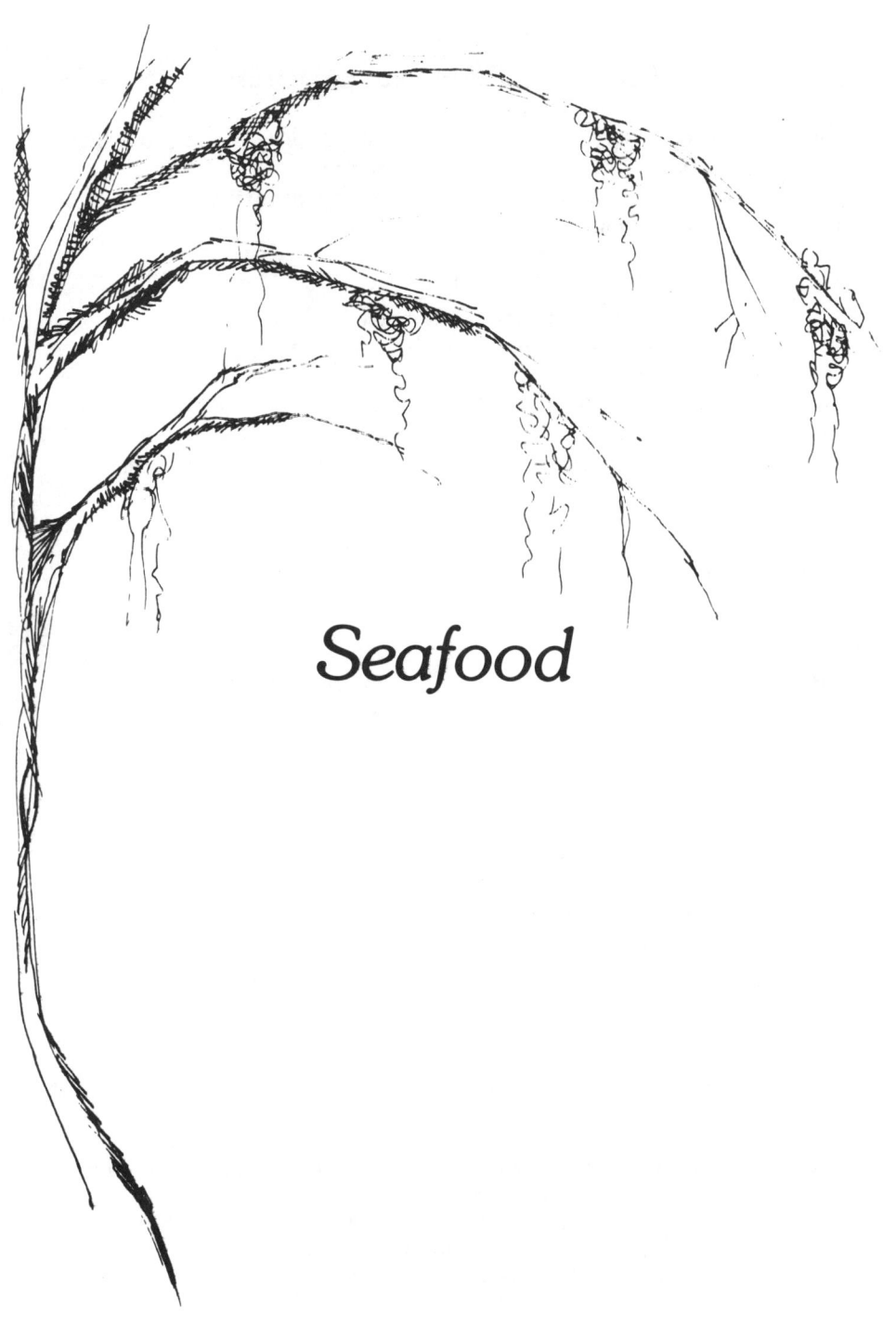

Seafood

KIM'S BAR-B-QUE SHRIMP

1 pound shrimp
Juice of 1 lemon
½ teaspoon garlic powder
3 to 4 dashes Tabasco

3 tablespoons Worcestershire sauce
1 stick margarine

PREHEAT OVEN TO 450-500 DEGREES

1. Wash and drain shrimp leaving shells on.
2. Place in pan (15x1-inch) deep enough to hold sauce.
3. Sprinkle with salt and pepper or pepper corns, juice of one lemon, ½ teaspoon garlic powder, and 3-4 dashes Tabasco.
4. Bake at 450-500 degrees for 20 minutes, stirring occasionally. Recipe doubles or triples well. Serve with French bread for dipping into sauce.

BARBECUED SHRIMP

8 to 10 pounds large shrimp (heads and shells on)

Sauce

1 pound margarine
1 tablespoon black pepper
1 teaspoon ground rosemary
4 lemons, sliced
3 cloves garlic

1 pound butter
6 ounces Worcestershire sauce
1 teaspoon Tabasco
4 teaspoons salt

PREHEAT OVEN TO 400 DEGREES

1. Melt butter and margarine in saucepan. Add Worcestershire sauce, pepper, rosemary, Tabasco, lemons, salt and garlic. Mix well.
2. Divide shrimp between two large shallow pans and pour hot sauce over each. Stir well, until shrimp is well coated with sauce.
3. Cook in 400 degree oven for 15 to 20 minutes, turning once. Shells will be pink and meat white, not translucent.

   Serves 8.

Treat yourself or your guests to this delicious shrimp dish — large whole shrimp cooked in a well-seasoned butter sauce.

The secret to serving good shrimp is to cook them only a short time. They are done when firm and a reddish pink color. Avoid overcooking because this shrinks as well as toughens the shrimp.

Do not shell the shrimp. They are cooked with the head and shell on. The hot buttery sauce is poured over the shrimp and then is baked in the oven.

Hot slices of French bread, a good green salad and Barbequed Shrimp are perfect go-togethers.

SHRIMP CREOLE

¼ cup margarine
1 large onion, chopped
½ cup chopped green pepper
3 cloves garlic
1 teaspoon black pepper

⅛ teaspoon paprika
2 cups canned tomatoes
1 pound cooked, cleaned shrimp or
   3 (5-ounce) cans of canned
   shrimp (drained)

1. Saute' onion, green pepper and garlic in margarine until tender.
2. Add salt, pepper, paprika and tomatoes. Bring to boil.
3. Reduce heat and simmer 15 minutes.
4. Add shrimp, heat thoroughly. Serve on hot, fluffy rice.

   Makes 4 servings.

BAR-B-QUED SHRIMP

1 pound shrimp
Olive oil
Cracked black pepper
Salt

Lemon juice
Tabasco
Lea & Perrins
Butter

1. Place whole shrimp, keep shells on, in single layer in oven proof dish. Drizzle olive oil on top of shrimp. Pepper shrimp until they are black. When you think you have enough pepper, add more. Add lots of salt, lemon juice, Tabasco and Lea & Perrins. Remember you are seasoning through the shells. Cut up butter on top of shrimp and broil until shrimp are cooked, 15 to 20 minutes.
2. Be sure to taste to see if they are done. Serve these with newspaper on the table and lots of napkins. Have French bread to sop up the oil. With cold beer and green salad, you have the makings of a great informal party.

   Base the amount of shrimp on the number of guests.

FRIED SHRIMP (For 4)

2 eggs
1 cup milk
1 pound large shrimp (uncooked)
1 cup flour

1½ teaspoons garlic salt
36 saltines, smashed with the
   fingers

1. Beat the eggs and add the milk.
2. Clean the shrimp and split down the back to "butterfly".
3. Dip in the seasoned flour, then the egg and milk, then in the smashed saltines.
4. Fry in deep fat until golden brown.
5. Serve with a good cocktail sauce or Remoulade. The smashed saltines give them a rough pretty appearance, and somehow they "eat" better.

SEAFOOD SQUASH

½ cup chopped onion
2 or 3 yellow squash, sliced
½ to 1 pound shrimp meat
Dash of black or red pepper
Salt to taste
½ stick butter

1. Sauté onions in butter.
2. Slice squash thinly, similar to cucumber slices in thickness.
3. Add shrimp to onions, then add squash. Stir. Cook over medium low heat for approximately five to seven minutes, or until squash is cooked to taste.
4. Season with red pepper and salt. (May substitute crab meat for shrimp.)
   Serves 4 to 6.

BAKED SHRIMP AND ARTICHOKES

2 pounds medium-large shrimp
⅓ cup butter or margarine
4 to 5 cloves garlic, minced
Salt, freshly ground pepper
2 (6-ounce) or 1 (14-ounce) jar marinated artichoke hearts
3 teaspoons lemon juice
¼ cup dry white wine
Chopped parsley
Lemon wedges

1. Shell shrimp, leaving last segment on tail. Devein, rinse and drain on paper towels.
2. In large skillet, combine butter and garlic over medium heat until sizzling.
3. Add shrimp, turning to coat all sides. Sprinkle lightly with salt and pepper. Bake at 400 degrees for 5 minutes, just until shrimp begin to turn pink.
4. Add artichoke hearts with half the marinade, the lemon juice and wine.
5. Return to oven and bake until shrimp are done and artichokes are heated through, about 5 minutes longer.
6. Turn into serving dish. Sprinkle with parsley. Serve with lemon.
   Serves 6.

CRABMEAT AU GRATIN

½ pound onions (1 large white, some green)
3 ribs celery
½ pound butter
4 tablespoons flour
1 large and 1 small can Carnation milk
2 egg yolks
2 pounds fresh white crabmnt
10 ounces yellow cheese, grated

PREHEAT OVEN TO 350 DEGREES

1. Sauté onions and celery in butter until soft.
2. Add flour and blend. Add milk and blend.
3. Remove from heat, add egg yolks, crabmeat, salt, pepper, and grated cheese.
4. Put in casserole with cheese on top, and bake. Bake until Au Gratin is bubbly.
   Serves 6 to 8.

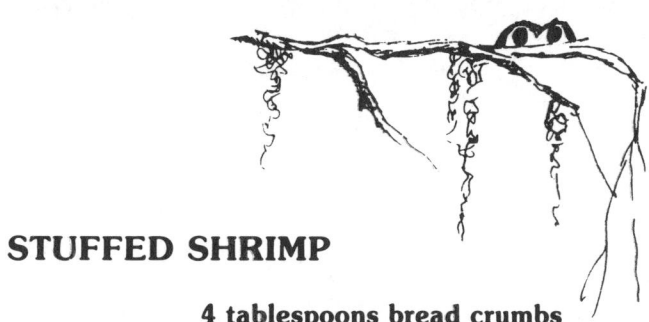

STUFFED SHRIMP

1 tablespoon butter
1 tablespoon chopped onion
1 tablespoon chopped celery
1 tablespoon chopped green pepper
1 tablespoon flour
1 cup milk

4 tablespoons bread crumbs
½ cup cooked crab meat
¾ teaspoon Worcestershire sauce
¼ teaspoon parsley
⅛ teaspoon salt
⅛ teaspoon pepper
1½ dozen large shrimp

1. Melt butter in skillet, sauté onion, celery, and green pepper, using medium heat.
2. Stir in flour, and milk, stirring constantly until thick.
3. Add bread crumbs, crabmeat, Worcestershire sauce, chopped parsley, salt and pepper.
4. Mix well.
5. Remove shell and vein from shrimp leaving tails on.
6. Slit back of shrimp, put two shrimp together with crab stuffing.
7. Hold together with toothpicks.
8. Chill in refrigerator until ready to cook.
9. Place shrimp in broiler pan, 5-inches from broiler unit.
10. Baste occasionally with butter.
11. Broil about 5 minutes on each side.

SHRIMP AND PORK EGG ROLLS

2 tablespoons oil
3 cups finely chopped celery
1 can mushrooms
½ pound raw shrimp, (cleaned, deveined, and finely chopped)
1 cup finely chopped bean sprouts
1 cup lean cooked pork

1 tablespoon soy sauce
1 tablespoon sherry
1 teaspoon salt
1 teaspoon sugar
1 tablespoon cornstarch (dissolved in 2 tablespoons water)

1. Heat oil in wok.
2. Add celery, and mushrooms. Stir fry about one minute.
3. Add shrimp and continue to stir fry until shrimp are firm and pink. Add bean sprouts and cooked pork. Stir to blend.
4. Stir in soy sauce, Sherry, salt, sugar and dissolved cornstarch.
5. To assemble the egg rolls, place 2 tablespoons of filling on the center of each egg roll skin. Fold 2 sides over edge of filling and roll up. Seal with flour paste. Fry in hot oil until golden brown.

Makes 18 to 20 rolls.

SHRIMP ST. JOHN

½ stick margarine
1 onion, chopped
3 ribs celery, chopped
3 cloves garlic, chopped
2 tablespoons parsley
1 can mushrooms, drained
1 or 2 pounds deveined shrimp
Salt, pepper and red pepper to taste
1 can cream of mushroom soup
1 cup sour cream

1. Sauté all of the above ingredients in margarine except shrimp, soup and sour cream.
2. Add shrimp and sauté until tender.
3. Add Cream of Mushroom soup, sour cream, and seasonings.
4. Simmer for 2 minutes. Serve hot over rice or pasta.

SHRIMP OR CRAWFISH THERMIDOR

¼ cup chopped onion
¼ cup chopped green pepper
2 tablespoons margarine
1 can (10¾-ounce) condensed cream of potato soup
¾ cup evaporated milk
¼ teaspoon red pepper flakes
1 pound crawfish tails or deveined shrimp
2 tablespoons lemon juice
½ cup mozzarella cheese, shredded

1. Cook onion and green pepper in margarine in a medium size saucepan or frying pan until tender.
2. Add the soup, milk and red pepper flakes. Cook slowly until it comes to a boil.
3. Add the shrimp or crawfish, lemon juice and cheese. Heat only until the cheese melts.
4. Serve over rice. Add Tabasco to taste.
   Serves 4 to 6.

BOILED SHRIMP

15 pounds shrimp with heads
4 bags crab boil
4 ribs of celery
2 lemons, sliced
6 cloves garlic
Red potatoes, new
Corn on cob, frozen
Salt to taste

1. Wash and drain shrimp. Set aside.
2. Bring water to a boil in a large pot. Add salt, lemons, garlic, crab boil and celery.
3. Drop potatoes into boiling mixture. Cook for 15 minutes.
4. Add shrimp and corn. Bring back to boiling point and cook for 5 minutes.
5. Remove from heat, let stand for 20 minutes. Drain and serve hot.

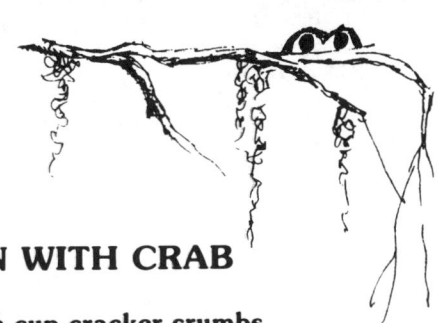

STUFFED CHICKEN WITH CRAB

2 tablespoons butter or margarine
¼ cup all-purpose flour
¾ cup milk
¾ cup chicken broth
⅓ cup Chablis or other dry white wine
⅓ cup chopped green onions
1 tablespoon butter or margarine, melted
1 (6-ounce) package frozen crabmeat thawed and drained
1 (4-ounce) can mushroom stems and pieces, drained and chopped
½ cup cracker crumbs
1 tablespoon parsley, fresh and chopped
¼ teaspoon salt
½ teaspoon pepper
8 chicken breast halves, boned and skinned
1 cup (4-ounce) shredded Swiss cheese
1 teaspoon paprika
Hot cooked rice

1. Melt 2 tablespoons butter in heavy saucepan over low heat; add flour, stirring until smooth. Cook one minute, stirring constantly.
2. Combine milk, broth, and wine; gradually add to flour mixture. Cook over medium heat, stirring constantly, until thickened and bubbly. Set sauce aside.
3. Sauté green onions in 1 tablespoon melted butter until tender.
4. Stir in crabmeat, mushrooms, cracker crumbs, parsley, salt and pepper. Stir in 2 tablespoons sauce.
5. Place each chicken breast half on a sheet of waxed paper. Flatten chicken to ¼-inch thickness, using a meat mallet or rolling pin.
6. Spoon ¼ cup crabmeat mixture in center of each chicken breast half. Fold opposite ends over and place, seam side down, in a greased 13 x 9 x 2-inch baking dish. Pour remaining sauce over the chicken.
7. Cover dish, and bake at 350 degrees for 1 hour.
8. Sprinkle with cheese and paprika; bake an additional minute or until cheese melts. Serve over hot cooked rice.
   Yield: 8 servings.

CRABMEAT MORNAY

1 stick butter
1 small bunch green onions, chopped
½ cup finely chopped parsley
2 tablespoons flour
1 pint breakfast cream
½ pound grated Swiss cheese
1 tablespoon sherry wine
Red pepper to taste
Salt to taste
1 pound white crab meat

1. Melt butter in heavy pot and sauté onions and parsley. Blend in flour, cream, and cheese, until cheese is melted.
2. Add other ingredients and gently fold in crab meat. This may be served in a chafing dish with Melba toast or in patty shells.

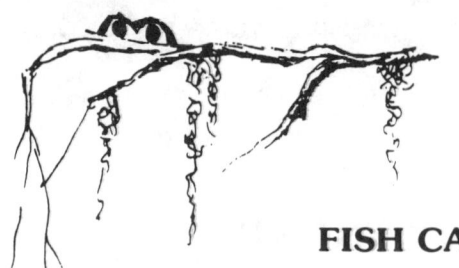

FISH CASSEROLE

Bass filets (enough to cover bottom of flat 2-quart casserole)
Milk, to cover fish
Flour
1 stick butter
1 bell pepper, minced
¼ cup minced celery
1 tablespoon minced parsley
1 tablespoon minced green onions

2 cans shrimp soup
1 small can shrimp
1 can sliced mushrooms
Juice of one lemon
½ cup milk
Salt
Red pepper
Worcestershire

1. Soak filets in milk 2 to 3 hours. Season well. Dip in flour and brown in butter.
2. Place in baking dish.
3. Sauté bell pepper, celery, parsley and green onions in butter until limp. Add soup, shrimp, mushrooms, lemon juice, milk and seasonings to taste.
4. Pour over filets and bake at 350 degrees for 30 to 40 minutes.

Serves 6.

FROG LEGS

24 frog legs

Marinade:

1 egg
½ cup mustard
2 cups milk
1 red onion, chopped

1 bell pepper, chopped
2-3 tablespoons Worcestershire sauce
Tabasco sauce, generously to taste

1. Mix all marinade ingredients well. Pour over frog legs. Add more milk if necessary to cover frog legs with liquid. Marinate at least 2 hours.

Breading

1 box seasoned Zatarain fish fry
1 teaspoon baking powder
4 teaspoons garlic powder

¼ cup parsley flakes
¼ cup cayenne pepper
½ cup flour

1. Mix all breading ingredients well and put in plastic bag large enough to shake several frog legs at one time.
2. Heat grease to moderately hot. Bread frog legs just before frying by shaking in bag. Legs are done when they float and breading is golden. Don't overcook.

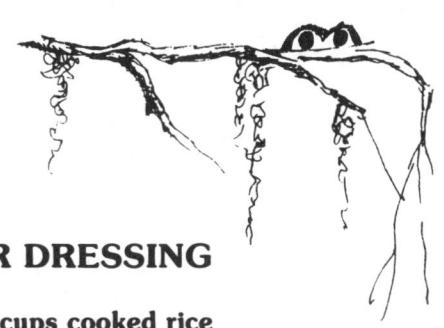

RICE AND OYSTER DRESSING

½ cup butter or margarine
10 to 12 chopped green onions
1 white onion, chopped
1 cup chopped celery
2 small green peppers, chopped
1 quart oysters
Cooked giblets, chopped (1 box of frozen chicken livers)
3 cups cooked rice
½ cup chopped parsley
Red and black pepper
½ cup onion blades
1 teaspoon minced garlic
1 teaspoon onion salt
1 teaspoon Accent
1 teaspoon celery salt

1. Melt butter in skillet, add onions, celery and green peppers.
2. Cook until slightly tender, but not brown.
3. Add oysters and giblets. Cook until edge of oyster curls.
4. Pour over rice, add parsley and onion blades. Mix well. Stir in salts and pepper and other seasonings.
5. If dressing is too dry, add some of liquid in which giblets were cooked. Bake in a shallow pan at 375 degrees for 45 to 50 minutes.

CRAB AND EGGPLANT DRESSING

4 large eggplants
2 tablespoons bacon fat
Salt and red pepper to taste
2 large onions
1 large bell pepper
2 stalks celery, chopped
2 pounds (lump) crabmeat or substitute fresh shrimp
Seasoned bread crumbs
½ cup freshly grated Romano cheese

1. Peel and cube eggplants. Soak in cold salted water. Drain and cook in large Dutch oven in bacon fat.
2. Cook over medium heat about 1 hour, then add salt, red pepper and celery. Continue cooking until thoroughly done. (A potato masher can be used to break eggplant up while cooking.)
3. Now add crabmeat, stir in without cooking. (If shrimp is used, cook another 10 minutes.)
4. Add enough seasoned bread crumbs to absorb liquid.
5. Stir in the Romano cheese.
6. Place in buttered 2-quart casserole and top lightly with more bread crumbs and cheese.
7. Bake at 350 degrees for 30 minutes.

Serves 8 to 10.

SHRIMP AND CORN CHOWDER

½ pound bacon fried crisp
3 tablespoons bacon fat
2 cups onions, chopped fine
1 cup celery, chopped fine
½ cup bell pepper, chopped fine
½ cup grated carrots
½ bay leaf, crumbled
2 cups of potatoes, diced
¼ cup of water
2 tablespoons flour
4 cups shrimp stock
2 (6½-ounce) cans cream style corn
1 (16½-ounce) can whole corn
1 (13-ounce) can low fat evaporated milk
2 pounds of shrimp cooked and deveined
1 tablespoon salt
½ teaspoon cayenne pepper
½ teaspoon black pepper
1 (8-ounce) can of mushroom and stems
Tabasco to taste

1. Fry bacon, crumble and set aside. Reserve bacon fat.
2. Sauté onions, celery, bell pepper and carrots in bacon fat.
3. Add bay leaf, potatoes and water. Cook for 5-10 minutes.
4. Sprinkle flour over mixture, stir well and add shrimp stock. Bring to boil. Add corn, milk, mushrooms, shrimp, salt, pepper, and Tabasco (Optional).
5. Simmer over low fire for approximately 30 minutes.

Serves 8 to 10.

SHRIMP WITH TOMATO AND FETA

½ cup chopped onion
2 tablespoons olive oil
1 (28-ounce) can Italian style plum tomatoes, drained, cut up
⅓ cup dry white wine
2 teaspoons dried oregano leaves
¾ pound medium shrimp, cleaned
¾ cup (4-ounces) crumbled feta cheese
2 tablespoons chopped fresh parsley

1. Cook and stir onion in oil in large skillet over medium heat 3 minutes.
2. Add tomatoes, wine and oregano. Reduce heat to low; simmer 5 minutes or until thickened.
3. Add shrimp. Cook 3 minutes, stirring frequently, until shrimp are pink.
4. Sprinkle with feta cheese and parsley; simmer 1 minute.

Serve over rice, if desired.

Makes 4 servings.

CRABMEAT QUICHE

½ pound white and green onions, mixed
3 ribs celery
½ pound butter
2 egg yolks
2 unbaked pie shells

4 tablespoons flour
2 pounds white crab meat
1 small and 1 large can evaporated milk
1 pound sharp Cheddar cheese, grated

PREHEAT OVEN TO 375 DEGREES

1. Chop onions and celery.
2. Saute' in butter until soft. Add flour and blend well. Slowly add milk, stir in and blend. Remove from heat.
3. Add the egg yolks, which have been beaten. Stir well.
4. Add crab meat, salt to taste, white pepper to taste, and ¾ of the grated cheese.
5. Put in prepared unbaked pie shells. Bake at 375 degrees until pastry is brown. Check about 20 minutes into baking, sprinkle remaining cheese on top. Fills 2 (10-inch) pie shells generously.

    Each will serve 6 to 8.

HALLELUJAH CRABS

Per person:

2 soft-shell crabs
4-ounces seafood stuffing

1 quart egg wash (egg whites and water
1 pound self-rising flour

Seafood stuffing:

½ onion, diced
½ bell pepper, diced
1 teaspoon minced garlic
4-ounces small shrimp

4-ounces white crabmeat
4-ounces crawfish tails
6-ounces bread crumbs

1. Saute' onion, bell pepper and garlic in one ounce butter until tender. Add shrimp and cook until done. Add white crabmeat and crawfish tails. Simmer 5 minutes, remove from heat, and add bread crumbs. Cool completely before stuffing crabs.
2. Place stuffing between body and upper shell. Then submerge in egg wash and roll in flour. Repeat this process a second time. Deep fry in hot oil 340 degrees for 10 minutes until golden. Present standing on end with claws in air for a dramatic effect.
3. Serve with baby new potatoes cut in shape of mushrooms and parslied, pecan rice, and broccoli with Hollandaise sauce.

BAKED SEAFOOD CASSEROLE

2 (6-ounce) cans crab meat or 1 large can fresh crab meat
2 cans shrimp or 1 pound fresh, cooked shrimp
1 small can mushrooms
½ green pepper, chopped fine
½ cup chopped onion
½ can pimiento, chopped
1 cup chopped celery

II

1 cup salad dressing (mayonnaise can be used, but makes it very rich)
½ teaspoon salt
1 cup top milk
⅛ teaspoon pepper
1 tablespoon Worcestershire sauce
½ to 1 cup raw rice, cooked
½ teaspoon red pepper
Paprika to taste

1. Mix all ingredients in each of the two groups, then blend together.
2. Place in 2 quart buttered casserole. Sprinkle with bread crumbs and bake 30 minutes at 375 degrees, though it does not seem to affect it to stay in the oven longer. Amounts of pepper, onion, pimiento, and mushrooms may be increased if desired.

   Makes 8 large servings.

DEEP FRIED FROG LEGS

Frog legs
Vinegar
Sliced onions
Minced garlic, to taste
1 egg, beaten
1 cup all-purpose flour
½ cup milk
¼ teaspoon cayenne pepper
1 teaspoon salt

1. Marinate clean frog legs in vinegar seasoned with onions and garlic for at least 3 hours.
2. Prepare batter by mixing remaining ingredients. Drain frog legs well and dip in batter.
3. Fry in deep fat at 375 degrees until golden brown.

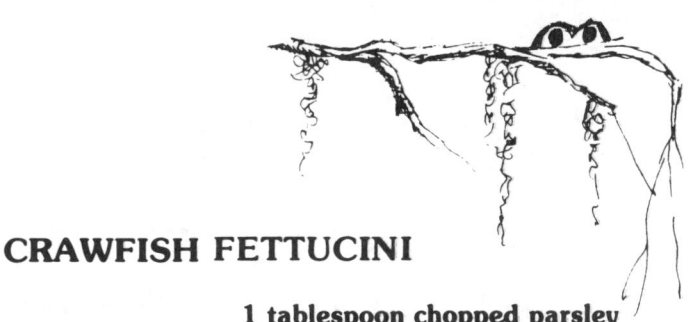

CRAWFISH FETTUCINI

- 3 sticks butter
- 3 onions, chopped
- 2 green bell peppers, chopped
- 3 ribs celery, chopped
- 3 pounds crawfish tails
- 3 cloves garlic, minced
- 1 tablespoon chopped parsley
- ½ cup flour
- 1 pint half-n-half
- 1 pound Kraft Jalapeno cheese, cubed
- 12 ounces fettucini

PREHEAT OVEN TO 300 DEGREES

1. In a saucepan, melt butter and sauté onion, bell pepper, and celery until tender.
2. Add crawfish and simmer 10 minutes, stirring occasionally.
3. Add garlic, parsley, flour and half-n-half and mix well. Simmer on low heat for 30 minutes, stirring occasionally.
4. Add cheese and stir until melted.
5. Meanwhile, cook noodles, drain, and cool.
6. Combine noodles and sauce. Pour into a greased 6 quart casserole or two greased 3 quart casseroles.
7. Bake uncovered in a 300 degree oven for 20 minutes or until heated thoroughly. Freezes well.

     12 servings.   *A delicious first course.*

CRAWFISH FETTUCINI II

- 1 bell pepper
- 1 large onion
- Whites of 1 bunch of green onions
- 3 garlic cloves
- 1 can cream of shrimp soup
- 1 stick butter
- 1 pint half-n-half
- 1 pound Velveeta cheese
- 1½ pound flat egg noodles
- 1 pound crawfish

1. Boil noodles; drain and set aside.
2. Sauté bell pepper, onions and garlic in butter until tender over low heat in large saucepan. Cut cheese into small pieces and melt in pan over low heat with previous ingredients.
3. Add soup and crawfish and mix well. Add noodles and ½ of half-n-half milk.
4. Simmer on low for approximately 20 minutes. Add remaining half-n-half prior to serving.
5. Salt and pepper to taste. One to two teaspoons liquid crab boil may be used for a spicier dish.
6. Shrimp may be used in place of crawfish.

     Makes 6 to 8 large servings.

CRAWFISH "TOUT ETOUFFE"

3 pounds peeled crawfish tails
Creole seasoning
1 cup vegetable oil
¾ cup flour
2 large onions, chopped
1 green bell pepper, chopped
1 stalk celery, chopped

4 green onion tops, chopped
12 sprigs parsley, chopped
1 clove garlic, chopped
2 dashes hot pepper sauce
1 (8-ounce) package cream cheese
2 tablespoons cornstarch
2 cups water

1. Sprinkle crawfish with Creole seasoning.
2. In an aluminum pot, make a roux with oil and flour by cooking over medium-low heat, stirring constantly, until the color of peanut butter.
3. Add onions, bell pepper, celery, green onions, parsley, garlic, and hot pepper sauce and sauté until vegetables are tender.
4. Add crawfish and cook 5 minutes. Add cream cheese and stir until melted.
5. Mix cornstarch with water and add to crawfish.
6. Cook on low heat for 15 to 20 minutes.

   12 main course servings.

   This is wonderful in so many ways — as a dip in a chafing dish, over pasta or rice, or simply on patty shells — like name says "Crawfish Everything".

CRAWFISH ETOUFFEE

2 pounds peeled crawfish tails
1 stick butter
1 cup chopped onions
1 cup chopped celery
1 cup chopped green pepper

2 cloves garlic, chopped
⅛ cup parsley
1 can cream of mushroom soup
1 can cream of celery soup
½ teaspoon liquid crab boil

1. In a saucepan melt butter and sauté onions, celery, green pepper, and garlic until tender.
2. Add cream of celery soup, cream of mushroom soup, and crawfish. Cook for 10 to 15 minutes, stirring occasionally.
3. Add ½ teaspoon liquid crab boil and parsley. Serve over rice.

CRAWFISH (OR SHRIMP) SQUASH DRESSING

6 cups sliced squash (about 2 pounds)
2 cups water
1 large onion, chopped
1 bell pepper, chopped
1 cup chopped celery
1 clove garlic, minced
½ cup butter or margarine, melted
1 egg, slightly beaten
1 cup Italian-seasoned bread crumbs
⅓ cup grated Parmesan or Romano cheese
1 teaspoon Beau Monde seasoning
½ teaspoon salt
¼ to ½ teaspoon black pepper
¼ teaspoon thyme
⅛ teaspoon red pepper
⅛ teaspoon hot sauce
1 pound crawfish tails or shrimp

1. Combine squash and water in Dutch oven; cook until tender. Drain well.
2. Sauté onion, bell pepper, celery and garlic in butter until tender.
3. Add vegetables and egg to squash, stir in remaining ingredients.
4. Spoon mixture into greased (12 x 8 x 2-inch) baking dish.
5. Bake in 350 degree oven for 30 minutes.

   Serves 8.

PECAN RICE DRESSING

3 tablespoons butter
1 cup onions
½ cup celery
Black pepper, salt to taste
2 to 3 tablespoons garlic
3 tablespoons bell pepper
½ pound ground beef
½ pound ground pork

1. Cook all the above ingredients in a heavy black skillet for 30 minutes.
   Add:

1 pound crawfish tails
¼ cup red bell pepper and yellow pepper
½ cup chopped green onions
½ cup chopped pecans

1. Cook until crawfish is tender.
2. Add equal amounts of cooked rice. Mix well and heat. Garnish with parsley on top.

FAYE'S CRAWFISH ETOUFFEE

1 stick butter
⅓ cup all-purpose flour
1 cup chopped onions
1 cup chopped celery
1 cup chopped green peppers
2 cloves garlic, minced
1 pound crawfish tails
1 (8-ounce) can tomato sauce
1½ cups water
2 teaspoons instant chicken bouillon
¼ cup fresh parsley (2 tablespoons dried)
1 teaspoon salt
⅛ teaspoon each ground black and red pepper
3 cups hot cooked rice

1. Melt butter in large skillet or electric skillet, 350 degrees.
2. Blend flour and stir over medium low heat or 300 degrees, until roux is dark brown, 10 to 15 minutes.
3. Add onions, celery, green peppers, and garlic, cook until tender 2 to 3 minutes. Add crawfish and sauté.
4. Stir in remaining ingredients except rice.
5. Simmer 20 minutes.
6. Ladle etouffee into soup bowls. Top each serving with ½ cup fluffy rice.

    Makes 6 to 8 servings.

DEVILED OYSTERS

1 quart oysters
1 cup margarine or cooking oil
¾ cup chopped celery
¾ cup chopped green pepper
½ cup chopped onion
½ cup chopped green onion and tops
1 clove minced garlic
6 tablespoons flour
2 teaspoons salt
½ teaspoon black pepper
1½ cups oyster liquor
1 tablespoon Worcestershire sauce
½ teaspoon lemon juice
½ teaspoon liquid hot pepper sauce
Pastry shells

1. Cook oysters in natural liquor for 4 to 5 minutes or until done. Drain well, reserving 1½ cups liquor. Chop oysters.
2. Cook celery, green pepper, onion, green onions, and garlic in margarine until vegetables are tender. Blend flour, salt and pepper into vegetable mixture.
3. Stir in oyster liquor gradually and cook over low heat until sauce is thick.
4. Add oysters, Worcestershire sauce, lemon juice, and liquid hot pepper sauce. Heat. Serve hot in pastry shells.

    Makes approximately 5 cups.

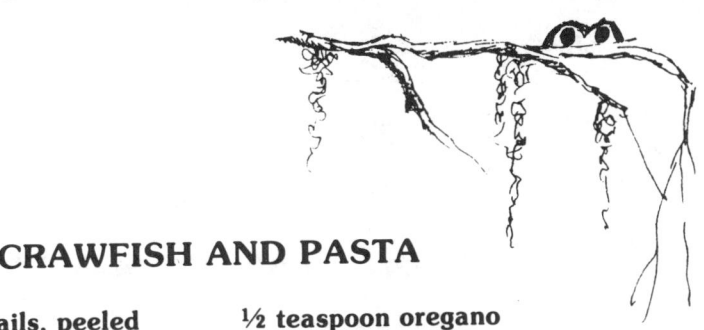

CRAWFISH AND PASTA

1 pound crawfish tails, peeled
½ cup white onion, chopped
½ cup purple onion, chopped
1 cup green onion tops, chopped
¼ cup red bell pepper, chopped
3 cloves garlic, pressed or minced
¼ cup butter
¼ cup tasso, sliced thinly
1 teaspoon Cajun Chef hot sauce
1 teaspoon whole black pepper, cracked
½ teaspoon oregano
1 teaspoon basil
¼ teaspoon thyme
Salt, cayenne and white pepper to taste
½ cup dry white wine or vermouth
½ pint whipping cream or pet milk
¼ cup Romano cheese
1 (9-ounce) package fresh spaghetti

1. Melt butter in a large, heavy saucepan. Add onions, green onion, red bell pepper, garlic and tasso and sauté over high heat being careful not to burn, stirring often. Add the seasonings and continue cooking, scraping the bottom of the pan.
2. As the vegetables begin to stick, add the wine or vermouth in small amounts to deglaze the skillet. Scrape the bottom of the skillet and continue cooking adding more liquid as needed.
3. Add the crawfish and continue sautéing for three minutes. Add the whipping cream and Romano cheese until ingredients are just barely covered. Continue cooking the sauce over high heat until the sauce thickens slightly and is golden in color.
4. Serve over hot cooked pasta.

Serves 4.

CRAWFISH RICE CASSEROLE

1 pound crawfish tails
½ stick butter
1 large onion, chopped
¼ cup parsley
1 can onion soup
1 can cream of shrimp soup
½ cup chopped mushrooms
1 can Rotel tomatoes
1 bell pepper
½ cup green onions
1½ cups uncooked rice

1. Rinse and drain rice.
2. In Dutch oven sauté onion, peppers, and parsley.
3. Add mushrooms, crawfish, all soups, tomatoes and ½ can of water. Add salt and pepper. Stir in rice.
4. Bake *(covered)* at 350 degrees for 1 hour. Stir lightly after 15 minutes.

CREOLE SEAFOOD SEASONING

⅓ cup plus 1 teaspoon salt
2 tablespoons oregano
¼ cup granulated sugar
¼ cup black pepper

⅓ cup cayenne pepper
2 tablespoons thyme
⅓ cup plus 1 tablespoon paprika
3 tablespoons granulated onion

1. Combine all ingredients and mix thoroughly. Makes 2 cups of seasoning, which can be stored indefinitely in a covered glass jar in the refrigerator.

GRANNY'S SEASON-ALL

2 cups salt
2 tablespoons sugar
1 tablespoon garlic powder
1 tablespoon curry
1 tablespoon chili powder
1 teaspoon cayenne pepper
1 teaspoon onion powder
1 teaspoon allspice

6 tablespoons paprika
1 tablespoon accent
1 tablespoon celery salt
1 tablespoon dry mustard
2 tablespoons black pepper
1 teaspoon ginger
1 teaspoon nutmeg

1. Mix thoroughly. Store in covered container.
   Makes 3 cups.

BASIC ROUX

The basis for all stews and gumbos

1 cup all-purpose flour

1 cup cooking oil, your favorite brand (I use margarine)

1. Heat oil in heavy pot or Dutch oven. When oil is hot, gradually add flour, stirring continuously until well mixed.
2. Lower flame and continue stirring until chocolate brown.
3. When roux is chocolate brown, remove from pot and set aside. If roux remains in the pot it will continue to cook and get too dark.

   Always use warm water to dissolve the roux.

   While you are at it, make more than enough as it keeps well in or out of the refrigerator.

SEAFOOD PASTA

1 pound crawfish tails, peeled
1 pound small shrimp
1 pound crabmeat
4 bunches green onions
1½ bunches curley parsley, chopped
1½ pints half-and-half
4 sticks butter or margarine
12 tablespoons flour
Salt
Cayenne pepper

1. Sauté the shrimp and crawfish tails in skillet with one stick of margarine, approximately 3 to 5 minutes. Be sure not to overcook or meat will get hard. Set aside.
2. In large deep skillet or Dutch oven, put 2½ sticks margarine with parsley and green onions and sauté until soft.
3. Add flour, stirring constantly. When flour is thoroughly combined, add the shrimp, crawfish and crabmeat, mixing well.
4. Season with salt and cayenne pepper to taste. If the mixture appears too thick, add a little more half-and-half. Serve over angel hair pasta.

   Serves 10 to 14 people.

CRAWFISH ELEGANTE

1 pint half-and-half
1½ sticks butter
1 large onion, chopped
Tony Chachere's seasoning
¼ cup flour
1 tablespoon parsley
1 pound crawfish tails

1. Sauté onion in 1 stick of butter. Add flour and stir.
2. Add half-and-half, cook until thick.
3. In another skillet add:

   ½ stick butter
   1 pound crawfish

   (a) Sauté until tender. Season with Tony Chachere's seasoning while cooking.
   (b) When crawfish is tender, drain, add to white sauce and add parsley.
4. Serve over rice, toast or shells.

   This makes a wonderful hot dip.

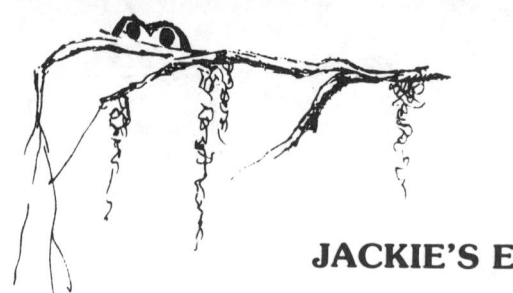

JACKIE'S ETOUFFEE

Per pound of crawfish

1 stick butter
2 large onions, chopped
½ bell pepper, chopped
3 stalks celery, chopped
Salt and pepper
Garlic to taste
1 tablespoon flour
Crawfish (1 pound per recipe) cleaned and peeled

1. Sauté first 4 ingredients to mush, then add salt and pepper, 1 clove garlic, 1 tablespoon flour per 1 pound of crawfish. Stir and let thicken.
2. Add crawfish and heat well.
3. Add hot water — about 1¾ cups — stir well and cook 15 minutes until thickened.

Serve over rice and garnish with chopped shallots.

BOILED CRAWFISH

1 sack of live crawfish, purged
1 cup cayenne pepper
1 large bell pepper, quartered
3 large onions, quartered
½ cup liquid crab boil
2 bags crab boil
½ cup Worcestershire sauce
6 lemons, quartered
2 cups salt
1 stalk celery

1. Fill a large boiling pot with water and bring to a rolling boil. Add all ingredients except crawfish and boil for 10 minutes.
2. Add crawfish and return to boil for 3-4 minutes. Turn heat off and soak crawfish in seasoned cooking water for 20-25 minutes.

NOTE: Vegetables may be added at various stages of the cooking process depending on the required cooking time.

Suggested vegetables

Small potatoes— drop in boiling water 15 minutes before adding crawfish.

Corn on the cob (fresh or frozen)— drop in boiling water when crawfish are added.

Artichokes— same as small potatoes.

Cauliflower (whole head)— drop in water after removing crawfish for 8-10 minutes.

Garlic (whole bulb)— drop in boiling water when crawfish are added. To eat squeeze soft garlic from each toe onto crackers.

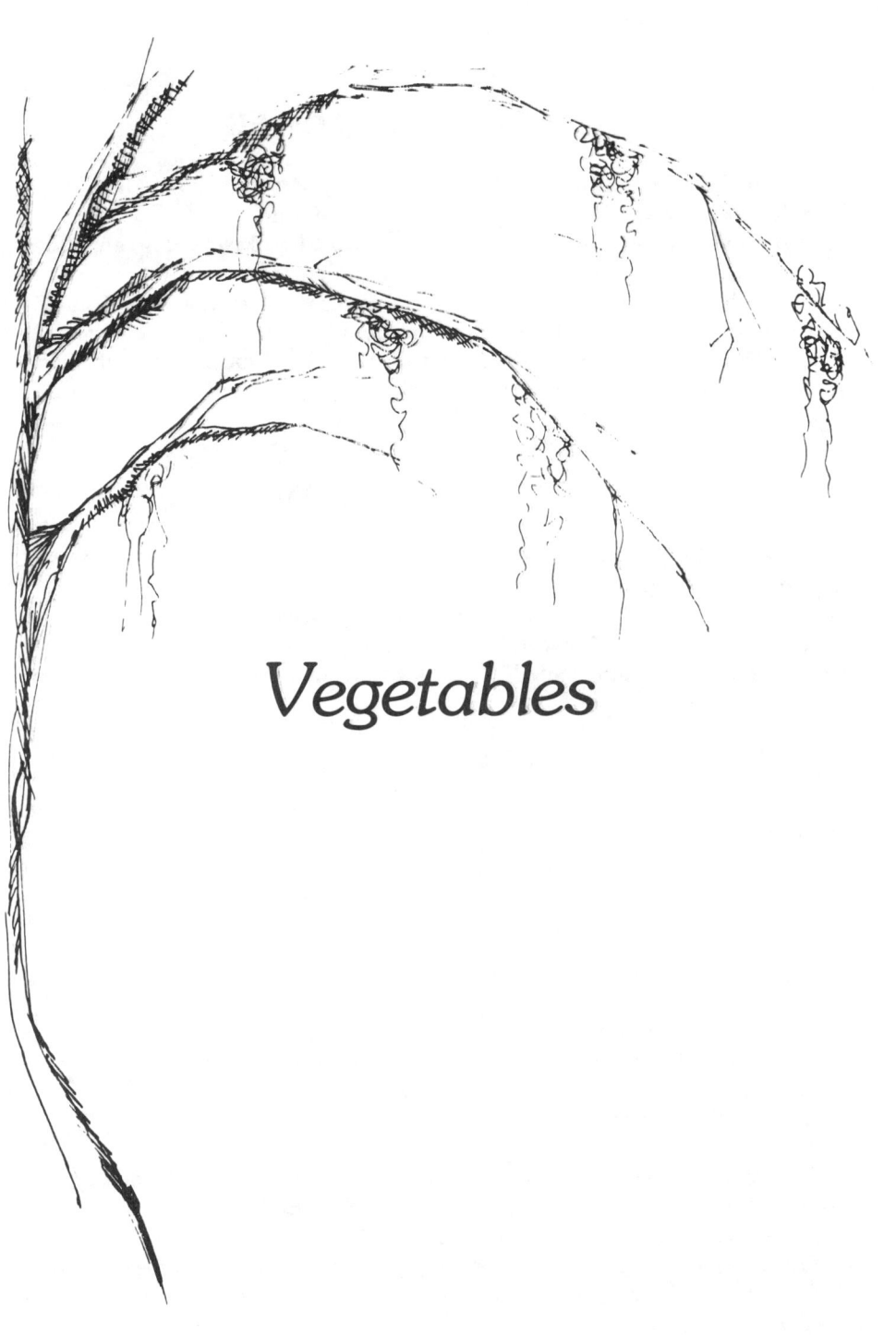

Vegetables

FROSTED CAULIFLOWER

1 medium head cauliflower
2 tablespoons water
½ cup mayonnaise

1 teaspoon mustard
Dash of salt
½ cup Cheddar cheese, shredded

1. Place cauliflower in 1½-quart dish with water in microwave.
2. Cover and cook on high for 8 to 9 minutes.
3. Combine mayonnaise, mustard, and dash of salt, spoon over cauliflower.
4. Sprinkle with cheese. Serve piping hot.

SQUASH DELIGHT

1 pound sliced yellow squash
½ cup green pepper
½ cup celery
½ cup onion (½ green, if available)
1 can water chestnuts, sliced
½ cup mayonnaise

½ cup margarine (if desired)
Salt
Red pepper
½ cup cheese
Bread crumbs

PREHEAT OVEN TO 325 DEGREES

1. Boil sliced squash just until tender. Drain. Add the rest of the ingredients.
2. Pour into a casserole dish and top with bread crumbs.
3. Bake for 45 minutes at 325 degrees.

MARINATED TOMATOES

6 very large ripe tomatoes
½ cup vegetable oil
½ cup vinegar
½ cup red table wine

1 cup minced onions
½ to 1 cup Parmesan cheese
½ cup capers

1. Slice tomatoes ¾-inch thick and arrange in a 12-inch glass baking dish.
2. Mix oil, vinegar, wine and onions in a salad bottle and shake.
3. Pour mixture over tomatoes and cover baking dish.
4. Refrigerate overnight. When ready to serve, arrange tomato slices on platter.
5. Sprinkle with Parmesan cheese and garnish with sprigs of parsley. Sprinkle capers on top.

GREEN CHILI RICE

1 cup chopped onion
¼ cup butter or margarine
3 cups cooked rice
2 cups dairy sour cream
1 cup cream style cottage cheese
1 bay leaf, crushed
½ teaspoon salt
⅛ teaspoon pepper
2 (4-ounce) cans whole green chili peppers
1 cup shredded Cheddar cheese
Snipped parsley
Tabasco to taste

1. In a small saucepan cook onion in butter or margarine until tender but not brown.
2. In a large bowl combine onion, rice, sour cream, cottage cheese, bay leaf, salt and pepper. Quarter green chili peppers lengthwise, rinse and seed. Chop half of the chili peppers.
3. Stir chopped peppers into rice mixture, turn into a 12 x 8 x 2-inch greased baking dish.
4. Place quartered chili peppers diagonally atop casserole. Sprinkle with Cheddar cheese. Bake uncovered in a 375 degree oven for 30 minutes. Sprinkle with parsley.

Makes 8 to 10 servings.

SQUASH CASSEROLE

1 pound yellow squash, cooked and mashed
¼ cup chopped bell pepper
¼ cup onions
½ cup Cheddar cheese, grated
½ cup mayonnaise
1 teaspoon sugar
¾ stick margarine
1 egg, beaten
Salt and pepper to taste
1 can water chestnuts, drained
¼ stick margarine
Ritz crackers

PREHEAT OVEN TO 350 DEGREES

1. Cook 1 pound yellow squash, mash.
2. Add bell pepper and onions (chopped fine), grated cheese, mayonnaise, sugar, ¾ stick margarine, one beaten egg, salt and pepper to taste, and water chestnuts, sliced very thin.
3. Put in buttered dish and cover with crushed Ritz cracker crumbs. Dot with ¼ stick margarine. Bake at 350 degrees for 30 minutes.

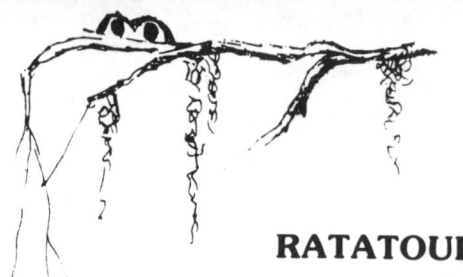

RATATOUILLE NICOISE

1 large onion
1 large green pepper
1 eggplant
2 green squash
3 tomatoes
1 clove garlic

1 bay leaf
1 teaspoon basil, oregano or thyme
Salt and pepper
½ cup olive oil
1 small glass wine

1. Clean all vegetables. Dice onion, green pepper, eggplant, and slice green squash and tomatoes.
2. Sauté onion and green pepper in olive oil for about 10 minutes.
3. Then sauté eggplant and squash. Add onion, pepper, tomatoes, garlic, salt and pepper, white wine, bay leaf, and basil, oregano or thyme.
4. Cook for about 20 minutes, or until vegetables are cooked. Better the next day. Can be served hot or cold.

TANGY MARINATED VEGETABLE KABOBS

1 large zucchini
2 medium size yellow squash
1 sweet red pepper, cut into 12 (1-inch) pieces
1 (14-ounce) can artichoke hearts, drained and halved

½ cup olive oil
¼ cup lemon juice
1 large clove garlic, crushed
¼ teaspoon salt
¼ teaspoon freshly ground pepper

1. Cut zucchini and yellow squash into 2-inch slices. Cut each slice into 4 wedges.
2. Combine wedges with sweet red pepper and artichoke hearts in a shallow dish.
3. Combine oil and remaining ingredients in a small bowl, stir well. Pour over vegetables, cover and chill 3 hours, occasionally tossing gently.
4. Soak 12 (6-inch) wooden skewers in water 30 minutes.
5. Drain vegetables, reserving marinade. Place vegetables on skewers. Grill kabobs over medium hot coals 8 to 10 minutes turning frequently. Baste with marinade.

   Yield: 6 servings.

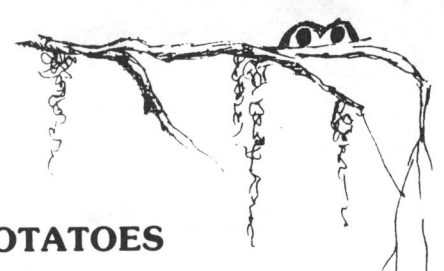

SEASONED POTATOES

3 large potatoes (2½ pounds)
3 ounces cream cheese
2 to 4 tablespoons milk
Paprika, optional

1 (8-ounce) carton onion dip
¼ cup butter
½ teaspoon garlic salt
Cheddar cheese, optional

PREHEAT OVEN TO 350 DEGREES

1. Cook peeled potatoes in boiling water until tender.
2. Drain and mash.
3. Add onion dip and mix.
4. Add cream cheese, butter, milk and garlic salt.
5. Beat and whip until smooth.
6. Spoon into greased baking dish or foil potato cups.
7. Sprinkle with grated cheese and paprika. Bake at 350 degrees for 30 minutes.

SWEET POTATO LOAF

1½ cups sugar
½ cup oil
2 eggs
⅓ cup water
1¾ cups all-purpose flour
1½ teaspoon cinnamon

1 teaspoon nutmeg
1 teaspoon soda
½ teaspoon salt
1 cup mashed sweet potatoes
½ cup chopped pecans
½ cup raisins

PREHEAT OVEN TO 350 DEGREES

1. Cream sugar and oil with electric mixer.
2. Add eggs and blend well.
3. In a separate bowl, mix all of the dry ingredients.
4. Add water to egg mixture and then add dry ingredients. Mix well.
5. Add sweet potatoes, pecans and raisins with a fork.
6. Bake in two 1 pound coffee cans or 1 large loaf pan at 350 degrees for one hour. Let cool 10 minutes. Remove from cans.

CANDIED SWEET POTATOES

4 medium potatoes, baked and peeled
3 tablespoons melted butter

½ cup brown sugar
½ teaspoon salt
2 tablespoons water

1. Cut potatoes in half lengthwise.
2. Cook butter, brown sugar, salt and water until syrup is formed.
3. Place potatoes in buttered baking dish, cover with syrup.
4. Bake at 350 degrees for 25 to 30 minutes.
   Yield: 4 servings.

ITALIAN MARINATED VEGETABLES

½ head cauliflower, broken into florets (yellow and green squash, thickly sliced, may be substituted
4 carrots, sliced
2 stalks celery, cut into 2-inch pieces
1 green pepper, cut into ¾-inch pieces
½ pound medium size fresh mushrooms or canned mushrooms
1 (3-ounce) jar pimento stuffed olives
1 cup pitted ripe olives
¾ cup white wine vinegar
¼ cup olive oil
¼ cup water
2 tablespoons sugar
¼ teaspoon white pepper
1 teaspoon salt
2 teaspoons dried whole oregano (or to taste)
2 teaspoons dried whole sweet basil (or to taste)
1 teaspoon rosemary
½ teaspoon thyme

1. Place first 7 ingredients in (13 x 9 x 2-inch) dish, set aside.
2. Combine vinegar and remaining ingredients in a small saucepan. Cook over medium heat stirring constantly until mixture boils. Remove from heat and pour over vegetables. Toss gently to coat. Cover and chill at least 8 hours, or overnight, stirring several times.
3. Drain vegetables and serve in a glass dish or on a lettuce lined platter with wooden picks.

Makes 15 to 17 appetizer servings.

Triple recipe for 50 servings.

Note: This is a tasty and eye-appealing dish which may be served as a salad or an hors d' oeuvre.

MOUNTAIN CAVIAR

2 cups blackeyed peas, cooked
½ cup thinly sliced bell pepper
3 medium onions, thinly sliced
½ cup oil
¼ cup vinegar
¼ teaspoon dried red pepper, crushed
¼ teaspoon salt
1 clove garlic, smashed

1. Drain the peas. Combine all the ingredients and refrigerate overnight. Keep covered. Remove the garlic if desired. Serve from a relish dish with a slotted spoon.

Yields: 10 to 12 servings.

CAJUN SQUASH

1 medium onion, sliced
1 clove garlic, minced
1 tablespoon olive oil
1 medium zucchini, sliced
2 medium sized yellow squash, sliced
¼ teaspoon hot sauce
2 tomatoes peeled and quartered
¼ teaspoon salt
⅛ teaspoon pepper
⅛ teaspoon dried whole oregano
⅛ teaspoon dried whole thyme

1. Sauté onion and garlic in olive oil in a skillet until crisp tender.
2. Add zucchini and yellow squash, cook vegetable mixture over medium high heat, stirring constantly, 5 minutes.
3. Add tomatoes and remaining ingredients, cook stirring constantly, 2 minutes. Serve immediately. Yield: 6 servings.

MARINATED VEGETABLE SALAD

1 (16-ounce) can whole kernel corn, drained
1 (16-ounce) can sliced carrots, drained
1 (17-ounce) can cut green beans, drained
1 medium onion, thinly sliced and separated into rings
1 green pepper, seeded and sliced
1 stalk celery, sliced diagonally
¾ cup sugar
½ cup vegetable oil
1 tablespoon celery seed or poppy seeds
1 teaspoon salt

1. Combine first 6 ingredients in a large bowl with a tight fitting lid, stir well.
2. Combine remaining ingredients, pour over vegetable mixture, stir well.
3. Cover. Chill for at least 12 hours before serving.
   This salad will keep well for several days in the refrigerator.
   Yield: 6 servings.

GOLDEN BROCCOLI

2 packages frozen broccoli
2 teaspoons salt
2 tablespoons lemon juice
Pepper to taste
1 (10-ounce) can cream of chicken soup
½ cup grated Cheddar cheese

PREHEAT OVEN TO 350 DEGREES

1. Cook broccoli in salted water as directed on package until tender. Drain.
2. Place broccoli in shallow serving dish.
3. Sprinkle with lemon juice, pepper and cover with soup.
4. Sprinkle cheese on top and place under broiler for 10 minutes or until cheese is melted and bubbly.
   Serves 8.

SPINACH MADELEINE

2 packages frozen chopped spinach
4 tablespoons butter
2 tablespoons flour
2 tablespoons chopped onion
½ cup evaporated milk
½ cup vegetable liquor
½ teaspoon black pepper
¾ teaspoon celery salt
¾ teaspoon garlic salt
Salt to taste
6 ounce roll of Jalapeño cheese
1 teaspoon Worcestershire sauce
Red pepper to taste

1. Cook spinach according to directions on package.
2. Drain and reserve liquor.
3. Melt butter in saucepan over low heat.
4. Add flour, stirring until blended and smooth, but not brown.
5. Add onion and cook until soft but not brown. Add liquor slowly, stirring constantly to avoid lumps.
6. Cook until smooth and thick; continue stirring. Add seasonings and cheese which has been cut into small pieces. Stir until melted.
7. Combine with cooked spinach. This may be served immediately or put into a casserole and topped with buttered bread crumbs. The flavor is improved if the latter is done and kept in refrigerator overnight. This may also be frozen.

   Serves 5 to 6.

   So different!

*May substitute 3-ounce roll of Garlic cheese and 3-ounces of Jalapeño cheese roll.

VEGETABLE CASSEROLE

1 onion
1 green pepper
3 cloves of garlic
1 stick butter
1 pound fresh mushrooms
4 cups fresh vegetables, cut in bite-size pieces, (carrots, cauliflower, broccoli, eggplant, or squash)
1 can cream of mushroom soup
Salt, pepper to taste
Tabasco to taste
1 cup mozzarella or Swiss cheese, shredded
Bread crumbs

1. Sauté onion, green pepper, and garlic in butter.
2. Add fresh mushrooms, 4 cups fresh vegetables, stir until crisp tender.
3. Add cream of mushroom soup, salt, pepper, Tabasco, and mozzarella or Swiss cheese. Stir well.
4. Pour in greased casserole. Top with bread crumbs. Bake at 350 degrees for 30 minutes.

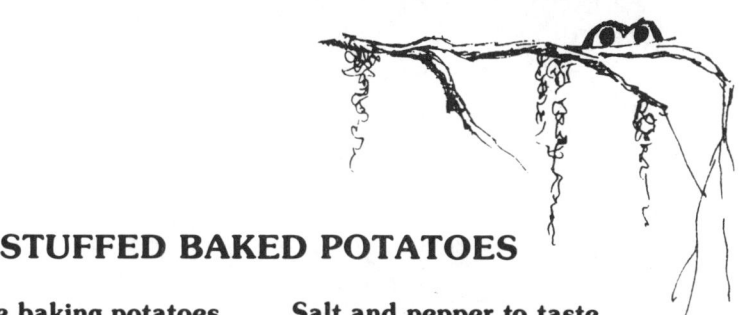

STUFFED BAKED POTATOES

8 medium white baking potatoes
1 cup milk, slightly heated
1 cup grated mild Cheddar cheese
1 stick butter
Salt and pepper to taste
2 teaspoons chopped onion tops
6 slices bacon, fried crisp and crumbled

PREHEAT OVEN TO 450 DEGREES

1. Wash potatoes, wrap in foil — punch a few holes in each potato and bake at 450 degrees until potatoes are fully cooked. About 2 hours.
2. Remove from oven, cut off slice from top of each potato and scoop out inside. Mash well to break up starch particles.
3. Add butter, salt and pepper, and milk. Mix thoroughly.
4. Add chopped onion tops and bacon and stir lightly.
5. Fill scooped out shells with potato mixture and sprinkle grated cheese on top of potato. Bake in 350 degree oven for 15 to 20 minutes or until cheese is melted and potatoes are hot. This may be prepared ahead of time and baked to serve later. Freezes well.

FRUITED YAM CUPS

6 medium sweet potatoes (or 2-pound can) drained
½ stick margarine
½ cup sugar
½ cup orange juice
¼ cup chopped pecans
1 small can crushed pineapples
1 small bottle maraschino cherries, chopped
¼ cup cherry juice
1 teaspoon vanilla
½ teaspoon almond flavoring
Orange cups
Small marshmallows

1. Cut oranges in half, juice, saving part of juice for potatoes. Remove pulp and white membrane by scraping with spoon. Scallop or flute edges with scissors.
2. Bake or boil yams, or heat canned yams. Remove skins while hot and mash.
3. Add margarine, sugar, orange and cherry juices and beat well. Do not scrape stringy fibers from beaters.
4. Fold in pineapple and juice, cherries, flavorings and pecans.
5. Fill orange cups with sweet potato mixture.
6. Top with marshmallows.
7. Put in 450 degree oven or run under broiler to brown marshmallows.

   Note: Orange shells may be prepared ahead and stored in refrigerator in plastic bag.

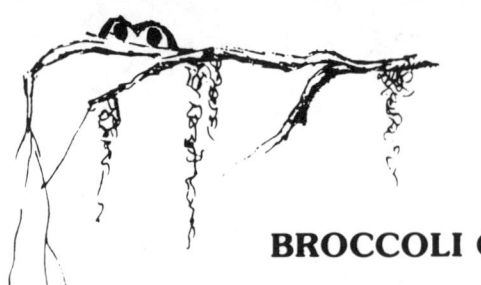

BROCCOLI CASSEROLE

2 large onions, finely chopped
1 stick margarine
2 large bags chopped broccoli
2 cans cream of mushroom soup

3 packages garlic cheese
1 large can mushrooms
1 cup bread crumbs
Salt, pepper to taste

PREHEAT OVEN TO 300 DEGREES

1. Sauté onion in margarine.
2. Add broccoli and cook until tender.
3. Add mushroom soup, cheese, mushrooms. Pour in large casserole.
4. Sprinkle bread crumbs on top. Bake in 300 degree oven until bubbly.

Serves 18 or more.

GALASHTA (CABBAGE ROLLS)

2 pounds hamburger meat
1 pound sausage
1½ cups uncooked rice
2 eggs

Salt and pepper to taste
1 or 2 large heads of cabbage
1 large can sauerkraut

PREHEAT OVEN TO 250 DEGREES

1. Par boil cabbage until leaves are pliable.
2. Mix all ingredients well except sauerkraut
3. Place a small amount of meat mixture in cabbage leaf. Roll up.
4. Line bottom of extra large pan with extra cabbage. Stack rolls on top.
5. Add sauerkraut and some water. Cook very slow in oven 2½ to 3 hours. The longer it cooks the better it is.

ARTICHOKE CASSEROLE

4 cans artichoke hearts
2 cups bread crumbs
1 cup Parmesan cheese
½ cup white wine

¼ cup olive oil
1 teaspoon onion salt
½ teaspoon garlic salt

PREHEAT OVEN TO 350 DEGREES

1. Mix artichokes, onion salt, garlic salt and Parmesan cheese. Pour in casserole dish.
2. Top with bread crumbs. Pour wine and then olive oil over bread crumbs.
3. Bake for 30 minutes at 350 degrees.

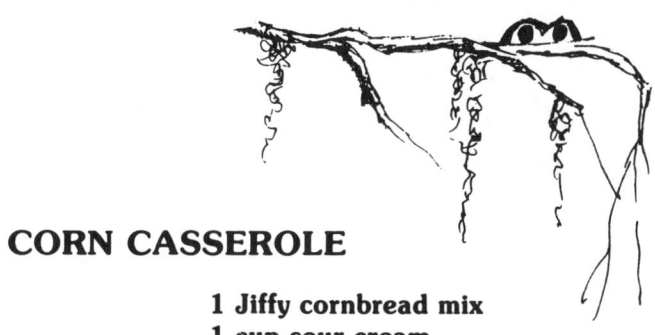

CORN CASSEROLE

1 stick butter
1 can creamed corn
1 can Niblet corn
1 Jiffy cornbread mix
1 cup sour cream

PREHEAT OVEN TO 350 DEGREES

1. Melt butter in oven while oven is preheating.
2. While butter is melting, mix all other ingredients.
3. When butter is melted, pour mixture into pan and bake for 30 minutes.

Note: Time of baking may need to be adjusted for double/triple recipe amounts.

SOUTH LOUISIANA RED BEANS

1 pound red kidney beans
Ham bone with generous amount of meat (I like to use cubes of ham)
1 pound pepperoni, sliced
1 bay leaf
Dash red pepper
Cumin powder to taste
1 large onion, chopped
1 clove garlic, chopped

1. Wash and pick over beans
2. Cover in cold water (I use 8-cups) and soak overnight.
3. Cook pepperoni, onions, and garlic until slightly browned.
4. Add beans and water in which they have soaked, then ham and more water to cover (usually 1 to 2 cups), bay leaf, red pepper and cumin powder to taste.
5. Cook slowly for several hours (this seems to take approximately 5½ hours). Cornbread goes well with red beans.

   Serves 8.

SNOWY MASHED POTATOES

4 pounds potatoes
1 (8-ounce) cream cheese, softened
1 cup sour cream
2 teaspoons salt
⅛ teaspoon pepper
1 clove garlic
¼ cup chives
½ teaspoon paprika
1 tablespoon margarine

1. Cook potatoes until tender, then mash.
2. Add cream cheese, sour cream, salt, pepper and garlic.
3. Beat in mixer until smooth and light.
4. Stir in chives.
5. Spoon into foil potato shells, dot with margarine and sprinkle with paprika.
6. Bake covered at 350 degrees for 30 minutes.

MUSHROOM CROUSTADES

Thin sliced white bread
1 tablespoon butter for pans
2 tablespoons butter
1 shallot
½ pound mushrooms
1 tablespoon flour
Grated Parmesan cheese and chopped parsley for garnish

¾ to 1 cup heavy cream
½ teaspoon salt
⅛ teaspoon cayenne
1 tablespoon chopped parsley
1½ tablespoons chopped green onion
½ teaspoon lemon juice

PREHEAT OVEN TO 400 DEGREES

1. Butter a mini-muffin tin.
2. Cut rounds from the bread with a 2-inch cookie cutter and flatten with a rolling pin.
3. Press the rounds into the muffin tin and bake in a 400 degree oven for 8 to 10 minutes or until the cups are lightly toasted.
4. Remove from the tin and cool.
5. Chop the mushrooms and shallot together.
6. Melt the 2 tablespoons of butter in a skillet.
7. Cook the mushroom mixture over moderate heat until the liquid has evaporated, about 8 to 10 minutes.
8. Sprinkle flour over the mixture and cook a minute or so.
9. Add the cream and cook until it thickens and remove from the heat.
10. Add the remaining ingredients (except the garnish) and taste for seasoning.
11. Fill the bread cups with the filling and bake at 350 degrees for 10 minutes or until they are bubbling.
12. Sprinkle with the Parmesan cheese and parsley.

GERMAN FRIED POTATOES

¼ cup bacon drippings
4 potatoes peeled and sliced
1 medium onion, sliced

½ cup water
Salt and pepper to taste

1. Heat drippings in iron skillet. Add sliced potatoes, turning until light brown.
2. Add sliced onions, cook for about 5 minutes longer. Add salt and pepper.
3. Pour water over potatoes and cover immediately with tight fitting lid. Reduce heat to low, let steam, turning potatoes occasionally. When tender remove from skillet.

   Serves 4.

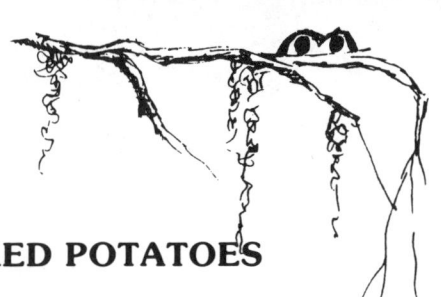

SPECIAL TWICE BAKED POTATOES

4 white Idaho potatoes
1 chopped onion
1 stick butter
⅛ teaspoon red pepper

1 teaspoon salt OR to taste
¼ teaspoon black pepper
1 cup shredded Sharp cheese
Milk

PREHEAT OVEN TO 450 DEGREES

1. Scrub potatoes, dry and pierce. Bake at 450 degrees for about 1 hour on rack without foil.
2. Melt butter and saute' onion until clear and tender.
3. Halve potatoes lengthwise. Scoop out the pulp leaving shells in tact. Mash potatoes, add red pepper, salt, black pepper, butter, onion, and cheese. Beat in enough milk for fluffy consistency. Fill 6 to 8 of the shells. Pile high and score tops with a fork. Bake in hot oven until tops are lightly brown.

    Serves 6 to 8.

BASIC VEGETABLE MIXTURE

1 onion
½ green bell pepper

2 sticks celery
1 clove garlic

1. Run vegetables through meat grinder or blender. (Makes 1 cup). You can double this recipe to suit your needs.

A cajun would die if you took his garlic and onions away.

SPINACH CASSEROLE

2 packages frozen spinach
1 package frozen artichoke hearts
  or 1 large can packed in water
1 can mushrooms (optional)

½ cup Parmesan cheese
8 ounces sour cream
Salt and pepper

1. Cook and drain spinach and artichokes as directed on package.
2. Mix all ingredients and pour in buttered casserole dish.
3. Top with more Parmesan cheese and bake at 350 degrees for 30 minutes.

STEAMED RICE

1 cup long grain rice
1½ cups cold water*

½ teaspoon shortening
1 teaspoon salt

1. Wash rice thoroughly (unless instructed otherwise on package), add water, shortening and salt. (Shortening will help prevent boiling over).
2. Cook rice in 1½ quart saucepan with a tight fitting cover on a regular 6-inch surface unit. Turn switch to high until steaming freely (leaving cover off utensil), then immediately cover and turn to lowest heat position and cook 30 minutes.
3. Do not remove cover during cooking. Rice will be dry and fluffy.

  * When using the speed unit and with some makes of ranges, use 2 cups of water.

Tasty Rice: Substitute chicken or any meat broth for water. Do not add salt. When done toss lightly with chopped parsley. Excellent served with broiled chicken or other meat.

NUTTY WILD RICE CASSEROLE

1 (6-ounce) package long grain and wild rice mix
1 cup sliced celery
½ cup pitted ripe olives, sliced
¾ teaspoon ground sage
8 ounces bulk pork sausage

1 cup chopped onions
1 (16-ounce) package frozen spinach, drained
½ cup Miracle Whip Salad Dressing
½ cup chopped pecans

PREHEAT OVEN TO 350 DEGREES

1. Prepare rice mix according to package directions, omitting the butter.
2. Cook sausage, onion, and celery until light brown. Drain.
3. Stir sausage mixture and remaining ingredients except pecans into rice.
4. Spoon into 1½-quart casserole dish.
5. Sprinkle with pecans.
6. Bake in preheated 350 degree oven for 30 minutes.

   Serves 4 to 6.

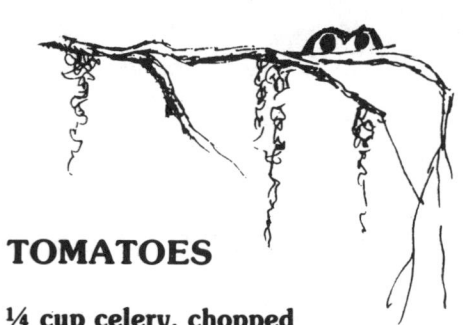

HOT STUFFED TOMATOES

8 medium size tomatoes, firm but ripe
6 green onions, chopped fine
3 tablespoons butter
3 tablespoons parsley, chopped
¼ cup celery, chopped
1½ cups bread crumbs
1 tablespoon Worcestershire sauce
A pinch of thyme
Salt and pepper to taste

PREHEAT OVEN TO 400 DEGREES

1. Hollow center of each tomato leaving the stem end for the bottom.
2. Save pulp. Lightly salt inside of each tomato.
3. Sauté onions in butter, add chopped parsley, cut up tomato pulp, and celery. Add bread crumbs and seasonings to mixture. If too dry, add a little tomato juice.
4. Stuff mixture in tomatoes. Sprinkle more bread crumbs on top of each one and add a dot of butter on top of each.
5. Place in baking dish and add just a little water to keep tomatoes from sticking. Bake at 400 degrees for 25 to 30 minutes or until crumbs are slightly brown and the tomato looks tender.

Serves 8.

CAJUN TATORS

6 to 8 large baking potatoes
1 pint sour cream
4 strips bacon
1 bunch green onions, chopped
1 (8-ounce) block mild Cheddar, cheese, grated
1½ sticks butter
1 can shrimp, drained and rinsed
1 cup white crabmeat
1 teaspoon cayenne pepper or to taste
Pet evaporated milk, if needed

1. While potatoes are baking, cook bacon until crisp. Drain and crumble.
2. In same fat, cook onions until tender. Drain.
3. In large mixing bowl combine onions, bacon, butter, sour cream, skinned potatoes, Cheddar cheese minus ½ cup. Mix until smooth. If mixture is too thick add pet milk.
4. Fold in shrimp and crabmeat. Pour into lightly greased casserole dish and add remaining cheese on top.
5. Bake at 350 degrees for 20 minutes or until cheese is melted.

Note: This is best if made two to three days ahead of time. Our family thinks these taste 100 percent better than plain old mashed potatoes.

POTATOES STUFFED WITH CRABMEAT

10 medium baking potatoes
2 sticks butter
1 cup half-and-half cream
1½ teaspoons salt
1½ teaspoons white pepper
¾ cups chopped finely green onions and tops
2 (6½-ounce) cans crabmeat
1 cup mild cheese, grated

PREHEAT OVEN TO 450 DEGREES

1. Scrub potatoes well and bake in a 450 degree oven until thoroughly done.
2. Cut the potatoes lengthwise, scoop out the pulp and mash with butter, cream, salt, and pepper. Mix thoroughly.
3. Add onions and crabmeat. Fill the reserved shells with the mixture and top with grated cheese.
4. Bake at 350 degrees for 15 to 20 minutes or until the cheese is melted. This may be made ahead of time and baked later. These also freeze beautifully.

   Serves 10.

POTATO CASSEROLE

6 red potatoes, peeled and sliced thin
1 can cream of mushroom soup
½ cup milk
1 large onion, sliced
1 tablespoon Worcestershire sauce
⅛ teaspoon Tabasco sauce
4 slices bacon

PREHEAT OVEN TO 375 DEGREES

1. Butter casserole and layer half of sliced potatoes and onion rings. Salt and pepper.
2. Combine soup, milk, Tabasco, Worcestershire and pour ½ mixture over potatoes.
3. Repeat layers. Top with bacon slices. Bake at 375 degrees for 1 hour.

SWEET POTATO CASSEROLE

3 cups cooked mashed sweet potatoes or 2 small cans, drained
1 cup sugar
½ teaspoon salt
2 eggs, beaten
½ stick margarine
¼ cup milk
½ teaspoon vanilla

PREHEAT OVEN TO 350 DEGREES

1. Combine ingredients and pour into casserole dish.
2. Top with topping and bake at 350 degrees for 35 minutes.

    8 servings.

Topping:

1 cup brown sugar, packed
⅓ cup flour
1 cup pecans, chopped
⅓ stick margarine, melted

1. Combine ingredients and sprinkle over sweet potatoes.

STUFFED ARTICHOKES

1 artichoke
½ cup bread crumbs
½ cup grated Romano or Parmesan cheese
¼ cup lemon juice
4 cloves garlic, finely chopped
¼ cup olive oil
Tony Chachere's to taste
Parsley to taste

1. Mix together bread crumbs, cheese, garlic, parsley, and Tony's.
2. Cut top and bottom from artichoke and pull leaves apart gently. Dip cut edges in lemon juice.
3. Fill each leaf with stuffing.
4. Pour olive oil over stuffed artichokes and steam in a covered pot in a small amount of water for 45-60 minutes. Done when leaf pulls out easily. Allow 1 per person.

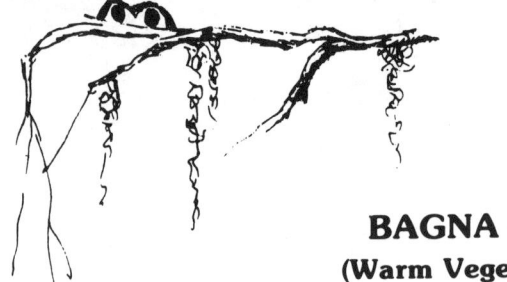

BAGNA COTTI
(Warm Vegetable Dip)

5-6 cloves garlic
5-6 anchovies, mashed

2 tablespoons + ½ cup olive oil
½ cup butter

1. Sauté garlic and anchovies in 2 tablespoons olive oil until very soft. Set aside.
2. Melt butter then add ½ cup olive oil and cooked garlic mixture. Mix well and heat throughly.
3. Serve warm as a vegetable dip.

JO'S POTATO CASSEROLE

6 white potatoes
1 teaspoon salt
¼ teaspoon black pepper
Red pepper to taste
1 stick butter or margarine, melted
½ cup milk or more if needed

½ cup chopped green onions
¼ cup chopped pimento, drained
1 cup grated Cheddar cheese
½ pint whipping cream, whipped
1 tablespoon butter or margarine, melted
½ cup corn flakes, slightly crushed

1. Boil potatoes in their jackets until just tender. Drain and let cool. This can even be done the day before.
2. Peel and grate potatoes on the large side of a grater. Combine with salt, black pepper and red pepper to taste. Add the stick of melted butter, ½ cup milk, green onions, pimento and cheese.
3. Whip cream and gently fold it into the potato mixture. Taste for seasoning.
4. Place in 9 x 13-inch baking dish.
5. Pour 1 tablespoon of the melted butter or margarine over the crushed corn flakes and ring the edge of the dish with the chips.
6. Bake in 350 degree oven for about 30 minutes or until bubbly.

Serves 6 to 8.

JO SALTER'S PRIMEVERA SALAD

Mix and Refrigerate...

1 cup mayonnaise (½-mayonnaise, ½-yogurt)
¼ cup thinly sliced green onions
¼ cup chopped parsley
½ teaspoon dried basil (to taste)
½ teaspoon salt
⅛ teaspoon pepper
3 cups chilled cooked chicken strips (any meat)

1 cup broccoli (cooked or raw)
1½ cups frozen peas (thawed), drained
1 cup matchsticks carrots
2 small matchstick zucchini
½ cup chopped red bell pepper
1 cup water chestnuts
1 cup matchstick celery

Sweets

Cakes
Desserts
Pies
Candy
Cookies

SCAVONA'S KING CAKE

Sweet Dough

3 eggs (room temperature)
½ cup sugar
1 stick butter
1 cup milk

5 cups all-purpose flour
½ teaspoon salt
2 packages dry yeast
¼ cup water (warm 105 degrees)

PREHEAT OVEN TO 350 DEGREES

1. Sprinkle yeast in warm water. Mix. Let soften. Stir, then let sit about 5 minutes, until light and bubbly.
2. Scald milk. Remove from stove. Melt butter in warm milk.
3. In large bowl beat eggs.
4. Add sugar, salt and dissolved yeast to eggs.
5. Add milk mixture. Beat well.
6. Stir in flour. Beat well. Dough will be soft.
7. Place dough into large butter bowl. Cover with a towel, put in a draft-free place and let rise until double in bulk, about 1½ hours.
8. Turn dough out on floured board and knead 10-12 times.
9. Roll dough out 24 x 10-inches.
10. Brush with melted butter.
11. Top with filling.
12. Roll dough with filling like a jelly roll. (The roll should be 24-inches long).
13. Seal edges with egg wash.*
14. Place on a large cookie sheet that has been sprayed with Pam.
15. Push baby into King's Cake.
16. Pressing ends together to seal.
17. Brush King's Cake with egg wash.
18. Cover with towel, put in warm place to rise until double in size - 45 minutes.
19. Bake in middle of preheated oven for 30 minutes at 350 degrees.
20. Remove from oven and cool.
21. Top with frosting.
22. Sprinkle colored sugar over top of cake.

Egg Wash:*

Beat together 1 egg and 1 tablespoon water.

FILLINGS FOR KING'S CAKE

Cream Cheese Filling

2 (8-ounce) packages cream cheese, softened
¾ cup sugar

1 egg, beaten
2 teaspoons vanilla

1. Combine all ingredients using electric mixer until well blended.

Cinnamon and Sugar Filling:

1½ cups sugar

1 tablespoon + 1 teaspoon cinnamon

1. Combine all ingredients.

Pineapple Raisin Filling:

1 can (1-pound 4-ounce) crushed pineapple, well drained
¾ cup sugar

1 tablespoon cornstarch
½ cup raisins

1. Combine sugar and cornstarch. Add pineapple and raisins and mix well.

★ You may buy filling at cake decoration stores or you may use Peach or Apple pie filling.

FROSTING FOR KING'S CAKE

1 box confectioners sugar, sifted
1 stick butter

3 to 4 tablespoons milk or water
1 teaspoon vanilla

1. In a large mixing bowl, combine all ingredients. Blend until smooth. Add more milk, a few drops at a time, until of spreading consistency or drizzling consistency.

TIP: Fruit juices may be substituted for milk.

DEVIL'S FOOD PEANUT LAYER CAKE

1 package (18.25-ounce) devil's food cake mix
1 package (4-serving size) vanilla pudding and pie filling
1½ cups milk
6 ounce chocolate-covered peanut-butter cups, 10 large or 21 small, chopped coarse (1½-cups)
6 ounce dark mildly sweet chocolate candy bar, *chopped fine*
¼ cup whipping cream

PREHEAT OVEN TO 350 DEGREES. Grease and flour two 9-inch round layer cake pans.

1. Prepare and bake cake mix according to package directions. Cool in pan on rack 15 minutes. Remove from pan. Cool completely on rack. *Meanwhile make filling.*
2. Stir pudding and milk in a medium size saucepan until smooth. Bring to a full boil over medium heat, stirring constantly. Pour into bowl, cover with plastic wrap and refrigerate about 15 minutes to cool slightly. Remove wrap.
3. Stir in chopped peanut-butter cups until they melt slightly into pudding. Cover surface again and return to refrigerator to cool completely.
4. Just before assembling, make icing. Put chocolate in a small bowl. Heat cream in a small saucepan over low heat until small bubbles form around edges.
5. Add to chocolate in a slow steady stream, beating constantly with electric mixer about 4 minutes until chocolate melts and mixture thickens to spreading consistency.
6. To assemble, put 1 cake layer top side down on serving plate. Spread filling to edges. Cover with remaining cake layer top side up; press gently. Spread icing on top; smooth with spatula. When icing sets, cover cake and refrigerate.

Makes 12 servings.

APPLESAUCE CAKE

¼ cup sugar
2 teaspoons cinnamon
1 yellow cake mix
3 eggs
1⅔ cups applesauce (15½-ounce jar)

PREHEAT OVEN TO 350 DEGREES

1. Mix sugar and cinnamon in small mixing bowl and set aside. Combine cake mix, eggs and applesauce. Beat two minutes at highest speed of mixer.
2. Pour ½ of batter in bundt pan.
3. Sprinkle sugar mixture, then pour rest of batter. Bake at 350 degrees for 35 to 45 minutes. Let cool 25 minutes, remove from pan. Dust with powdered sugar or drizzle with favorite icing.

ITALIAN CREAM CAKE

Cake:

1 stick margarine
½ cup Wesson oil
2 cups sugar
5 egg yolks, slightly beaten
1 cup buttermilk
1 teaspoon baking soda

2 cups flour
1 teaspoon vanilla
1 cup pecans, chopped
1 small can coconut
5 egg whites, stiffly beaten

Frosting:

1 stick margarine
1 (8-ounce) package cream cheese
1 teaspoon vanilla

1 box powdered sugar
½ cup nuts, chopped fine

PREHEAT OVEN TO 325 DEGREES

Cake:

1. Cream margarine, oil and sugar. Add egg yolks one at a time, beating after each addition.
2. Stir baking soda into buttermilk.
3. Add sifted flour into batter, alternating with buttermilk mixture.
4. Add vanilla, coconut and chopped nuts.
5. Beat egg whites and fold into mixture.
6. Pour into three greased and floured 9-inch cake pans. Bake at 325 degrees for 45 minutes. Cool and frost.

Frosting:

1. Cream together all ingredients. Frost cooled cake layers, top and sides.

4 LAYER COCONUT CAKE

1 box Duncan Hines golden vanilla cake mix

1. Mix according to directions, but *bake in 4 cake pans.*

Frosting:

1 cup sour cream
2 cups confectioners sugar

2 cups coconut
1 (10-ounce) Cool Whip

1. Mix all ingredients and spread between layers and top.
2. Sprinkle a little coconut on top. Must be kept in refrigerator.

HARVEY WALLBANGER CAKE

1 package (2-layer) size orange cake mix
1 (3¾-ounce) package instant vanilla pudding mix
4 eggs
½ cup cooking oil
½ cup orange juice
½ cup Galliano
2 tablespoons vodka

Glaze:

1 cup sifted powdered sugar
1 tablespoon orange juice
1 tablespoon Galliano
1 teaspoon vodka

PREHEAT OVEN TO 350 DEGREES

1. In large mixer bowl, combine cake mix and pudding mix.
2. Add the eggs, oil, the ½-cup orange juice, the ½ cup Galliano, and the 2 tablespoons vodka.
3. Beat on low speed of electric mixer for 1 minute; beat on medium speed for 5 minutes, scraping bowl frequently.
4. Pour into greased and floured 10-inch fluted tube pan; bake in 350 degree oven for 45 minutes. Cool in pan 10 minutes; remove to rack and pour on glaze while cake is still warm.

To make Glaze:

Combine the powdered sugar, the 1 tablespoon orange juice, the 1 tablespoon Galliano, and the vodka. Beat together well.

VANILLA POUND CAKE

1 box Duncan Hines yellow cake mix
1 box pudding mix (vanilla)
¾ cup Wesson oil
¾ cup water
4 eggs

PREHEAT OVEN TO 325 DEGREES

1. Combine cake mix, pudding mix, oil, water (½-cup). Mix well adding 1 egg at a time. If batter is too thick add rest of water.
2. Grease and flour bundt pan. Bake at 325 degrees for 1 hour and 15 minutes. Cook in top half of oven.

Icing:

2 cups powdered sugar, sifted
½ teaspoon vanilla
2 tablespoons milk (or more for a thick pouring consistency)

RUM CAKE

Cake:

1 cup margarine
2 cups sugar
4 eggs
1 teaspoon rum extract

1 cup buttermilk
3 cups cake flour
½ teaspoon baking soda
½ teaspoon baking powder

Glaze:

1 cup sugar
½ cup water

1 teaspoon rum extract

PREHEAT OVEN TO 375 DEGREES

1. Blend margarine and sugar.
2. Add eggs and rum extract and beat until well mixed. Add buttermilk, mix well.
3. Combine flour, baking soda and baking powder; add to egg mixture and blend well.
4. Bake in well-greased tube pan at 375 degrees for 45 minutes.

Glaze:

In saucepan combine all ingredients and bring to full boil. Pour over warm cake.

BETTER THAN SEX CAKE

1 box yellow cake mix
1 #2 can crushed pineapple
2 cups sugar
1 large package vanilla instant pudding
1 (8-ounce) package cream cheese

4 large bananas, sliced lengthwise
1 large container Cool Whip
1 medium jar of cherries, cut in ¼'s
1 cup pecans, chopped
1 cup coconut, shredded

1. Bake yellow cake according to directions on box in a 11 x 14-inch pan, using milk instead of water.
2. Punch cake full of holes after baking.
3. Mix pineapple and sugar together in saucepan and bring to a boil. Pour over cake.
4. Make vanilla pudding according to directions. After pudding is prepared, mix with cream cheese. Pour over cake and spread.
5. Place bananas, sliced lengthwise, over top of cake.
6. Spread Cool Whip on cake over bananas and pudding.
7. Place cherries cut into ¼ pieces on top.
8. Sprinkle pecans and coconut evenly over cake.
9. Place in refrigerator and let set.

$25,000 MARDI GRAS CAKE

⅔ cup butterscotch morsels (16-ounce) package
¼ cup water
2¼ cups all-purpose flour
1 teaspoon salt
1 teaspoon soda
1 cup buttermilk
½ teaspoon baking powder
1¼ cups sugar
½ cup shortening (use part butter or margarine)
3 eggs

PREHEAT OVEN TO 375 DEGREES

1. In a small saucepan melt butterscotch morsels and water. Cool.
2. Sift together flour, salt, soda and baking powder. Set aside.
3. In a large mixing bowl, cream well the shortening and sugar.
4. Blend in unbeaten eggs, one at a time, beating well after each addition.
5. Blend in melted butterscotch morsels and mix well.
6. Add the dry ingredients alternately with the milk, beginning and ending with the dry ingredients. Blend thoroughly after each addition. *If using an electric mixer, use a low speed.*
7. Turn into 2 (9-inch) round layer cake pans, well greased and lightly floured on the bottoms. Bake in 375 degree oven for 25-30 minutes until cake springs back when touched lightly in center. Cool in pans for 10 minutes, then remove. While cake is baking prepare the filling.

Filling:

½ cup sugar
1 tablespoon cornstarch
½ cup evaporated milk
⅓ cup water
⅓ cup butterscotch morsels
1 egg yolk
2 tablespoons butter
1 cup chopped coconut
1 cup chopped pecans or walnuts

1. In a 2-quart saucepan combine sugar and cornstarch.
2. Stir in milk, water, morsels and beaten egg yolk.
3. Cook over medium heat, stirring constantly until thick.
4. Remove from heat. Add butter, coconut and nuts. Cool.

Sea Foam Icing:

⅓ cup granulated sugar
⅓ cup brown sugar
⅓ cup water
1 tablespoon corn syrup
1 egg white
¼ teaspoon cream of tartar

(continued on page 165)

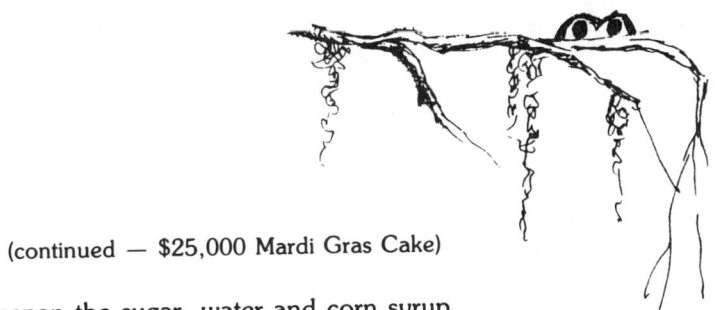

(continued — $25,000 Mardi Gras Cake)

1. Combine in saucepan the sugar, water and corn syrup.
2. Cook until a little syrup dropped in cold water forms a soft ball or if using a candy thermometer, cook to 236 degrees.
3. Meanwhile, beat the egg white with the cream of tartar until stiff peaks form.
4. Add the cooked syrup mixture to the egg white in a slow, steady stream beating constantly until thick enough to spread.

To Assemble: On the cooled cake, spread filling between layers and on top to within ½-inch of the edges. Ice sides and top edge with the Sea Foam Icing (or you can use whipped cream).

FRESH APPLE CAKE

1 cup shortening
2 cups sugar
4 eggs
2½ cups flour
1 teaspoon baking soda
1 teaspoon cinnamon

1 teaspoon allspice
½ cup water
1 teaspoon vanilla
3 medium apples, chopped
1 cup chopped pecans

PREHEAT OVEN TO 350 DEGREES

1. Cream shortening with sugar and add eggs, until light.
2. Add sifted dry ingredients alternately with water.
3. Fold in vanilla, apples and pecans.
4. Pour into prepared layer pans. Bake at 350 degrees for 30 minutes.

Frosting:

½ cup margarine
1 cup brown sugar, packed
½ cup heavy cream

½ teaspoon vanilla
1 box powdered sugar

1. Combine margarine, sugar and cream. Mix well.
2. Stir in powdered sugar and vanilla; stirring until spreading consistency.
3. Spread over cake.

HERSHEY'S PRIZE CHOCOLATE CAKE

½ cup margarine or butter
2 cups sugar
1 teaspoon vanilla

2 eggs
1¾ cups milk

Dry Ingredients

¾ teaspoon baking soda
¾ cup cocoa
1¾ cups unsifted flour

¾ teaspoon baking powder
⅛ teaspoon salt

PREHEAT OVEN TO 350 DEGREES.
Generously grease and flour two 9-inch round cake pans.

1. Cream butter, sugar and vanilla until light and fluffy, blend in eggs.
2. Combine all dry ingredients in separate bowl; add alternately with milk to the batter. Blend well. Pour into prepared pans. Bake 30-35 minutes. Recipe can be halved. Makes cupcakes and freezes well. Great with buttercream frosting.

My daughter, Debbie, uses this recipe for making a sheet cake to decorate for birthday parties. Delicious.

MISSISSIPPI MUD CAKE

2 sticks margarine or butter
2 cups sugar
1½ cups all-purpose flour
Dash salt

½ cup cocoa
4 beaten eggs
1 cup chopped pecans
1 teaspoon vanilla

1. Melt margarine and cocoa together.
2. Add all other ingredients and pour into 13 x 9 x 2-inch greased pan.
3. Bake in 350 degree oven for 30 to 35 minutes.

Icing:

1 box powdered sugar
⅓ stick margarine or butter, soft
1 teaspoon vanilla
½ to 1 cup milk, depending on consistency

⅓ cup cocoa
Dash salt
1 bag miniature marshmallows

1. As soon as cake comes from oven, cover top with marshmallows.
2. Mix margarine and cocoa. Add all other ingredients and mix until very smooth. Pour icing over marshmallowed cake while still very warm.

PATSY'S MILKY WAY CAKE

8 Milky Way bars
2 cups sugar
2½ cups flour
½ teaspoon soda
1 cup chopped nuts

1 cup butter
4 eggs
½ teaspoon salt
1¼ cups buttermilk
1 teaspoon vanilla

PREHEAT OVEN TO 350 DEGREES

1. Chop candy bars and combine with ½ cup butter in top of double boiler. Heat until melted; then set aside.
2. In large mixing bowl, combine sugar and remaining ½ cup butter. Add eggs and beat until light and fluffy.
3. Combine flour and salt.
4. Stir soda into buttermilk; add alternately with flour, beating until smooth after each addition.
5. Stir in nuts. Add vanilla and melted candy bars.
6. Pour in greased 13 x 9-inch pan. Bake 50-60 minutes at 350 degrees.

Frosting:

2½ cups sugar
½ cup butter
1 package (6-ounce) chocolate bits

1 small can evaporated milk (⅔-cup)
1 cup marshmallow cream

1. Combine sugar and milk in saucepan. Cook to soft ball stage (234-240 degrees).
2. Add chocolate bits, marshmallow cream and butter. Stir until melted and thoroughly blended. Cool and spread on cake.

TUNNEL OF FUDGE CAKE

1½ cups butter (at room temperature)
6 eggs
1½ cups sugar

2 cups flour
1 package Pillsbury Fudge Frosting Mix
2 cups chopped walnuts

PREHEAT OVEN TO 350 DEGREES

1. Cream butter, add one egg at a time, then sugar.
2. Cream at high speed until fluffy.
3. Stir in flour, add mix and nuts.
4. Grease and flour bundt pan. Bake for 60 minutes at 350 degrees. Cool 2 hours.

ORANGE SLICE CAKE

2 sticks margarine
2 cups sugar
3 eggs
1 teaspoon soda
1 cup buttermilk
3½ cups flour

½ pound chopped dates
2 cups chopped pecans
2 cups grated coconut
1 tablespoon grated orange rind
1 pound candied orange slices, chopped

1. Cream the margarine and sugar until light and fluffy. Add the eggs one at a time, beating well after each.
2. Dissolve the soda in buttermilk. Add 2½ cups flour alternately with the buttermilk to the creamed mixture.
3. Coat the dates and pecans with the remaining flour. Fold in the dates, pecans, coconut, orange rind and orange slices into the batter.
4. Bake in greased and floured tube or Bundt pan for 1½ hours at 300 degrees. Cool cake for about 10 minutes in pan then remove from pan and slowly pour glaze over cake.

Glaze:

¼ cup orange juice

2 cups powdered sugar

1. Heat juice and sugar together until mixture boils. Pour hot mixture over cake.

HEAVENLY HASH CAKE

2 sticks butter
2 cups sugar
4 eggs
1 teaspoon vanilla
4 tablespoons cocoa

1½ cups sifted flour
2 teaspoons baking powder
2 cups chopped pecans
16 marshmallows

1. Cream together butter and sugar.
2. Add other ingredients in order given.
3. Bake in 9 x 13-inch pan at 350 degrees for 30 minutes.
4. Remove from oven and cover top with marshmallows.
5. Return to oven until puffed up. Cool and spread with topping.

Topping:

½ stick margarine
3 tablespoons cocoa

6 to 8 tablespoons hot milk
1 box confectioners sugar

1. Combine all ingredients and spread on. Serve with whipped cream.

PINEAPPLE CRUSH CAKE

1 package pineapple cake mix
1 (8-ounce) package cream cheese, softened
1 package (4-serving) vanilla instant pudding and pie filling mix
2 cups cold milk
1 (8-ounce) can crushed pineapple, drained
2 cups whipped topping

Cake:

PREHEAT OVEN TO 350 DEGREES
GREASE AND FLOUR 2 (13 x 9 x 2-inch pans.

1. Prepare cake as directed on package. Divide evenly in pans.
2. Bake at 350 degrees for 20 to 25 minutes; follow package directions for doneness test and cooling.

Filling:

1. For filling, beat cream cheese, instant pudding mix, and cold milk in small mixer bowl. Beat for 2 minutes at medium speed.
2. Spread on one cooled cake layer. Spoon drained crushed pineapple over top.
3. Add second layer. Spread whipped topping on sides and top of cake.
4. Store in refrigerator until next day before serving.

    Yield: 16 servings.

VANILLA WAFER CAKE

1 cup softened butter or margarine
2 cups sugar
6 eggs
12 ounce box vanilla wafers, crushed*
½ cup milk
7 ounce package coconut
1 cup chopped nuts

1. Cream butter or margarine until fluffy. Add sugar gradually, creaming well.
2. Add the eggs one at a time, beating well after each addition.
3. Add crushed wafers alternately with milk. (You may continue using the electric mixer for this.) Fold in coconut and nuts.
4. Pour into greased and floured bundt pan. Bake at 275-300 degrees for about an hour and 15 minutes to an hour and a half. Test for doneness with toothpick.

    * Wafers must be crushed into fine crumbs. (A rolling pin or food processor works well.)

CARROT CAKE

1¼ cups salad oil
2 cups sugar
2 cups flour
2 teaspoons baking powder
1 teaspoon baking soda

2 teaspoons cinnamon
1 teaspoon salt
4 eggs
3 cups grated carrots (raw)
1 cup chopped pecans

PREHEAT OVEN TO 325 DEGREES

1. Combine oil and sugar; mix well.
2. Sift together remaining dry ingredients.
3. Sift half into sugar mixture and blend. Sift remaining ingredients; alternating with eggs, one at a time. Mix well.
4. Add carrots. Add pecans.
5. Pour into 10-inch tube pan.*
6. Bake at 325 degrees for about 1 hour, 10 minutes. Cool in pan upright.

   * If using 9-inch round cake pans, cook for approximately 25 minutes.

Frosting:

1 (8-ounce) cream cheese
1 box confectioners powdered sugar

1 teaspoon vanilla
½ stick butter
1 cup pecans (optional)

1. Using the electric mixer, mix all of the above ingredients except pecans.
2. Add pecans using a fork
3. Spread on cake.

MARTHA'S CREAM CHEESE POUND CAKE

3 cups sugar
3 cups sifted cake flour
1 (8-ounce) cream cheese
2 sticks butter

1 stick margarine
6 eggs
3 teaspoons flavoring (1 teaspoon each-vanilla, lemon, butter)

1. Bring all ingredients to room temperature.
2. Cream butter, margarine, cream cheese together using electric mixer. Add sugar and mix thoroughly.
3. Using low speed on mixer, add flour alternately with eggs and flavorings.
4. Pour batter into a well-greased, floured tube or bundt pan.
5. Start with cold oven. Bake at 275-300 degrees for 1 hour 15 minutes. Do not open door during baking.

MOM'S STRAWBERRY PECAN CAKE

1 box white cake mix
1 (3-ounce) box strawberry jello, dry
1 cup cooking oil
½ cup milk
4 eggs
1 cup frozen sliced strawberries, undrained
1 cup coconut
1 cup pecans, chopped

PREHEAT OVEN TO 350 DEGREES

1. Combine cake mix and jello, dry.
2. Add eggs, one at a time and then add remainder of ingredients.
3. Bake in 3 layers at 350 degrees for 30 minutes.

Filling:

1 stick margarine
1 box powdered sugar
½ cup drained strawberries
½ cup pecans
½ cup coconut

1. Cream sugar and margarine, adding other ingredients. Spread on cake.

CRUMP'S FIG CAKE

2 cups flour
1 teaspoon salt
1 teaspoon soda
1½ cups sugar
1 cup margarine
3 eggs
1 cup buttermilk
1 cup chopped nuts
1 cup cut fig preserves (with juice)
1 teaspoon vanilla

1. Sift flour, sugar, salt, soda; add margarine and beat well. Add eggs, one at a time and beat well.
2. Add milk gradually. Then add cut figs and nuts. Add vanilla. Bake at 325 degrees for 45 minutes if a sheet cake, or 1 hour if a tube pan (I use a tube pan.)

Sauce:

1 cup sugar
1 stick margarine
1 tablespoon corn syrup (Karo)
1 tablespoon vanilla
½ cup buttermilk
½ teaspoon soda

1. Mix these ingredients and boil for 3 minutes. Pour over hot cake after piercing cake *many times* with ice pick.
2. Let cake stand for 1 hour. Remove from pan before completely cool.

CHOCOLATE RUM CHIFFON CAKE

½ cup hot water
⅓ cup unsweetened cocoa
¼ cup dark rum
1¾ cups sifted cake flour
1⅓ cups sugar
1½ teaspoons baking soda

½ teaspoon salt
½ cup pure vegetable oil
7 eggs, separated
1 teaspoon vanilla
½ teaspoon cream of tartar
⅓ cup sugar

PREHEAT OVEN TO 325 DEGREES

1. Blend hot water and cocoa; set aside to cool; stir in rum.
2. Sift together flour, 1⅓ cup sugar, baking soda, and salt into bowl.
3. Make a well in center; add in order oil, egg yolks, vanilla and cooled rum mixture. Beat until smooth.
4. Beat egg whites and cream of tartar in large bowl with electric mixer until foamy.
5. Add ⅓ cup sugar gradually, beating well after each addition. Continue beating until meringue forms stiff, glossy peaks.
6. Pour chocolate mixture over meringue; gently fold in.
7. Pour into ungreased 10 x 4-inch tube pan. Bake 55 minutes at 325 degrees. Increase heat to 350 degrees; bake 10 to 15 minutes or until cake tests done. Invert pan; cool. Remove from pan. Frost with Seven-Minute Frosting; drizzle with Chocolate Glaze.

SEVEN-MINUTE FROSTING

3 egg whites
1 cup sugar
⅓ cup light corn syrup

3 tablespoons water
¼ teaspoon cream of tartar
1 teaspoon vanilla

1. Blend egg whites, sugar, corn syrup, water and cream of tartar in top of double boiler.
2. Beat rapidly with rotary beater over boiling water until mixture stands in stiff peaks.
3. Remove from heat; beat in vanilla.

CHOCOLATE GLAZE

1 square unsweetened or semi-sweet chocolate
1 tablespoon butter or margarine

1. Melt chocolate square with the butter in a cup over hot water; stir until smooth.
2. Drizzle over top of cake, letting mixture drip down side.

SOCK IT TO ME CAKE

1 box Duncan Hines Golden Butter Cake Mix
¾ cup Crisco oil
½ cup sugar
1 (8-ounce) sour cream
1 teaspoon vanilla
4 eggs

PREHEAT OVEN TO 350 DEGREES

1. Mix cake mix, sugar, oil and sour cream. Beat well.
2. Add eggs one at a time. Add vanilla. Beat thoroughly.
3. Pour half of batter into greased and floured tube pan. Sprinkle with:
    3 teaspoons cinnamon
    4 tablespoons brown sugar
    1 cup pecans, chopped
4. Pour in remaining batter. Bake 1 hour at 350 degrees. Cool 5 minutes, remove from pan and glaze.

Glaze:

2 tablespoons melted margarine
2 tablespoons milk
1 teaspoon vanilla
1 cup sifted powdered sugar

1. Mix all the above ingredients. Drizzle cake with the glaze.

SOUR CREAM POUND CAKE

½ pound butter
3 cups sugar
3 cups flour (not sifted)
6 eggs
Pinch of salt
¼ teaspoon soda
1 cup sour cream
1 teaspoon vanilla
½ teaspoon lemon extract
¼ teaspoon almond extract

PREHEAT OVEN TO 350 DEGREES

1. Cream butter and sugar. Add eggs one at a time, beat well after each.
2. Stir in sour cream, vanilla, lemon extract, and almond extract.
3. Sift flour, soda, and salt together. Add alternately with sour cream to mixture. Mix well.
4. Bake in a tube pan (greased and floured) at 350 degrees for 1 hour and 10 minutes or until done. Cool in pan 10 minutes.

MARBLE CHEESECAKE

Graham Crust (recipe below)
3 (8-ounce) packages cream cheese, softened
¾ cup sugar
½ cup sour cream
2 teaspoons vanilla

3 tablespoons flour
3 eggs
¼ cup Hershey's Cocoa
¼ cup sugar
1 tablespoon oil
½ teaspoon vanilla

PREHEAT OVEN TO 450 DEGREES

1. Prepare Graham Crust; cool.
2. Combine cream cheese, sugar, sour cream and 2 teaspoons vanilla in large mixer bowl; beat on medium speed until smooth.
3. Add flour, a tablespoon at a time, blending well.
4. Add eggs, one at a time, beating well after each addition.
5. Reserve 1½ cups batter; set aside.
6. Combine cocoa and sugar in small bowl. Add oil, ½ teaspoon vanilla and reserved 1½ cups batter; mix until well blended.
7. Spoon plain and chocolate batters alternately over crust, ending with dollops of chocolate on top; gently swirl with spatula or knife for marbled effect.
8. Bake at 450 degrees for 10 minutes; without opening oven, reduce heat to 250 degrees and continue baking 30 minutes. Turn off oven; cool cheesecake 30 minutes without opening door.
9. Loosen cake from rim of pan; cool completely before removing rim. Chill thoroughly.

    12 servings.

Graham Crust:

1 cup graham cracker crumbs (about 7 crackers)

2 tablespoons sugar
¼ cup butter or margarine, melted

1. Combine crumbs, sugar and butter; press mixture into bottom and ½-inch up side of a 9-inch springform pan. Bake at 350 degrees for 10 minutes.

When making peanut butter cookies, use a meat tenderizer mallet instead of a fork to quickly make the criss-cross design on the cookie dough.

MARY'S CHEESECAKE FOR A CROWD

6 (8-ounce) packages cream cheese
2 cups sugar
6 large eggs
Vanilla wafers or graham crackers

1 tablespoon vanilla
½ teaspoon salt
1 cup sour cream

PREHEAT OVEN TO 350 DEGREES

1. Have eggs and cream cheese at room temperature. Beat cream cheese first until smooth and creamy with electric mixer.
2. Add alternately other ingredients and add sour cream last.
3. Line pan with vanilla wafer crumbs or graham cracker crumbs.
4. Bake one hour at 350 degrees.

Topping #1:

1 cup sour cream
½ teaspoon vanilla

3 tablespoons sugar

1. Mix together sour cream, vanilla and sugar.
2. Place on top of hot cheesecake and bake an additional five minutes.
3. Refrigerate for 5-6 hours before serving.

Topping #2:

1 can of blueberry or cherry pie filling

1. Store cheesecake (without a topping) in freezer.
2. When ready to serve, thaw and top with can of blueberry or cherry pie filling

DEATH BY CHOCOLATE

1 box chocolate cake mix
1 cup Kahlua
4 boxes chocolate mousse
 (jello brand)

2 (12-ounce) tubs whipped topping
6 Skor candy bars

1. Bake cake according to package directions for a (9 x 13-inch) cake.
2. Prick top of baked cake with fork then poor Kahlua over the cake. Let this soak in, it can be left this way overnight.
3. Make the chocolate mousse according to package directions.
4. To assemble cake:
    Crumble up half of the cake and place it on bottom of large glass bowl. Layer half of the mousse, then half of the whipped topping and half of the Skor candy bars, which have been broken into small pieces. Repeat layers.
    Serves 18

BANANA SPLIT CAKE

Crust:

½ cup butter or margarine, melted

1 (13½-ounce) package graham cracker crumbs

1. Mix melted butter and graham cracker crumbs.
2. Press into a 13 x 9 x 2-inch baking dish.

Filling:

1 cup butter or margarine
2 eggs

1 (1-pound) box powdered sugar

1. Mix ingredients at high speed in electric mixer until smooth and creamy. Spread over crust.

Topping:

4 bananas
1 (1-pound 4-ounce) can crushed pineapple, drained

1 (9-ounce) carton frozen whipped topping
¾ cup chopped pecans
Cherries

1. Slice bananas over filling.
2. Spread with crushed pineapple and cover with whipped topping.
3. Sprinkle with pecans and garnish with cherries. Refrigerate overnight.

NO GREASE STAINS

To keep your cookbook or magazine free of spills and spatters, slip it into a gallon-size clear plastic bag before you start cooking.

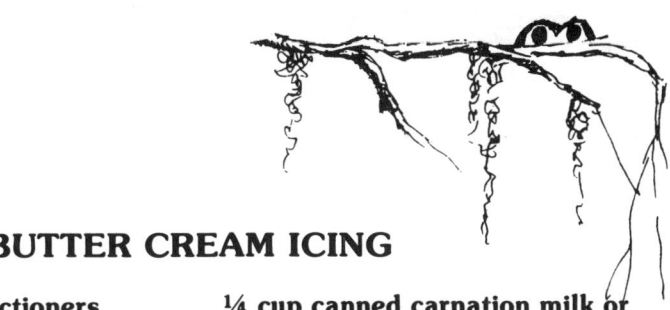

BUTTER CREAM ICING

1 pound sifted confectioners powdered sugar
1 stick butter
¼ cup canned carnation milk or half-and-half
1 teaspoon vanilla

1. Combine all ingredients and mix well.

SNOW WHITE ICING

1 pound sifted confectioners powdered sugar
¼ cup Crisco
3 ounces cream cheese
¼ cup canned carnation milk or half-and-half
1 teaspoon vanilla

1. Cream Crisco and cream cheese.
2. Add milk and confectioners sugar using an electric mixer.
3. Add vanilla flavoring.

   This is an excellent icing for birthday cakes.

SEVEN MINUTE ICING

2 egg whites
¼ teaspoon cream of tartar
⅛ teaspoon salt
6 tablespoons cold water
1½ cups sugar
1 teaspoon vanilla

1. Put all ingredients, except vanilla, in top of double boiler over boiling water.
2. Beat with rotary beater for 7 minutes, or an electric beater for 4 minutes, or until icing is stiff enough to stand in peaks.
3. Remove from heat and add vanilla. If any graininess appears add a few drops of lemon juice and beat until smooth. Spread on cake immediately.

CUSTARD CREAM FILLING

⅔ cup sugar
3 tablespoons flour
3 tablespoons cornstarch
¼ teaspoon salt
2 eggs, beaten
2 cups milk
1 teaspoon vanilla

1. Mix sugar, flour, cornstarch and salt in medium saucepan.
2. Add beaten eggs and milk. Beat with eggbeater until smooth.
3. Cook over medium heat, stirring constantly until mixture boils and thickens. Remove from heat. Cover with plastic wrap to keep skim from forming. When cool, add vanilla and beat in thoroughly.

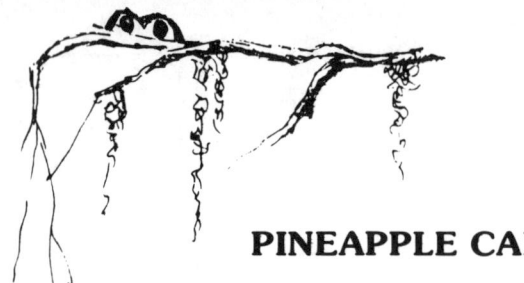

PINEAPPLE CAKE FILLING

3 tablespoons cornstarch
½ cup sugar

1 no. 2 can crushed pineapple
1 tablespoon butter

1. Mix cornstarch and sugar together in saucepan. Add pineapple, blend.
2. Cook over medium heat, stirring constantly until syrup thickens and becomes transparent.
3. Remove from heat. Stir in butter. Cool completely before spreading on cake.

LEMON CAKE FILLING

¾ cup sugar
2 tablespoons cornstarch
⅛ teaspoon salt
2 egg yolks, beaten

¾ cup orange juice and water
   (about 6 tablespoons of each)
3 tablespoons lemon juice
1 tablespoon grated lemon rind
1 tablespoon butter

1. In top of double boiler, mix sugar, cornstarch and salt.
2. Stir in egg yolks. Add juices and water. Cook over boiling water, stirring constantly until mixture is very thick.
3. Remove from heat, stir in lemon rind and butter. Cool before spreading on cake.

STRAWBERRY CAKE FILLING

2 cups (10-ounce) package
   unsweetened frozen
   strawberries
2 tablespoons cornstarch

½ cup sugar
1 tablespoon lemon juice
1 tablespoon butter

1. Combine cornstarch and sugar in saucepan. Add berries and lemon juice. Blend thoroughly.
2. Cook over low heat, stirring constantly, about 10 minutes or until mixture boils and thickens.
3. Remove from heat and add butter. Cool completely before spreading on cake.

You can use fresh strawberries. For raspberry filling, use 10-ounce sweetened raspberry and omit sugar.

HASTY COBBLER

½ cup sugar
½ cup flour
1 teaspoon baking powder
½ cup milk
½ cup juice from fruit or water

½ stick butter or margarine
2 tablespoons sugar
2 cups drained fruit (canned or cooked apples, sliced peaches, apricots, berries)

PREHEAT OVEN TO 375 DEGREES

1. Grease 9-inch shallow baking dish (for cakes) with a tablespoon of margarine.
2. In a small mixing bowl, combine ½ cup sugar, flour and baking powder.
3. Add milk to make batter — do not over mix.
4. Pour batter into a greased dish.
5. Add fruit and juice, then dot with butter. Sprinkle with 2 tablespoons sugar. Bake uncovered at 375 degrees for 30 minutes. Serve warm or cold, plain or with cream.

PEACH COBBLER

6 fresh peaches, peeled and sliced
1 cup sugar
2 tablespoons flour

½ stick margarine
Dash cinnamon

1. Mix flour, sugar, margarine and peaches in small saucepan. Cook on low heat until thickened.
2. Pour into buttered 9 x 9-inch dish.

Pastry:

1 cup flour
⅓ cup shortening

½ teaspoon salt
4 tablespoons milk

1. Blend flour, salt and shortening. Gradually add milk. Mix well. Chill 30 minutes for easier rolling.
2. Roll out on floured board to approximately a 9-inch square. Cut in 1-inch wide strips.
3. Place on top of peach mixture (lattice form).
4. Melt ½ stick margarine and pour over top. Bake at 350 degrees for 30-45 minutes.

BEST DESSERT EVER

1 stick butter
¼ cup light brown sugar, packed
1 cup flour, sifted
½ cup chopped pecans
½ gallon vanilla ice cream

PREHEAT OVEN TO 400 DEGREES

1. Cream butter and sugar with fork or pastry cutter.
2. Add flour and blend with fork.
3. Stir in pecans.
4. Spread very flat in 13 x 9-inch pan. Bake for 10 minutes or until golden brown.
5. Remove from oven and stir.
6. Reserve ¾ cup of mixture for topping.
7. Press remainder on bottom of 13 x 9-inch pan and let cool.
8. Fill with ½ gallon vanilla ice cream.
9. Sprinkle ¾ cup mixture on top of ice cream.
10. Cover air tight and freeze.

Fudge Sauce:

½ cup cocoa
½ stick butter
1½ cups sugar
1 cup cream
⅛ teaspoon salt
1 teaspoon vanilla

1. Combine cocoa, sugar, butter and cream in saucepan.
2. Stir and bring to boil. Let boil 5 minutes, while stirring.
3. Remove from heat, add vanilla and salt.
4. Keep fudge sauce in refrigerator until ready to serve. Cut dessert into 2 x 2-inch square, top with 1 teaspoon fudge sauce and serve.

This is truly the best dessert ever.

MAW HELEN'S BANANA PUDDING

1 (5¼-ounce) instant vanilla pudding
1 can condensed milk
1 medium (12-ounce) Cool Whip
3 cups milk
1 large box vanilla wafers
4 or 5 bananas

1. Mix instant pudding according to box directions. Then mix in condensed milk and Cool Whip.
2. Alternate layers of vanilla wafers, bananas and pudding in a large bowl. Garnish by standing vanilla wafers around edge of bowl then sprinkling wafer crumbs on top.

MISSISSIPPI MUD PIE

Crust:

1 stick margarine
1 cup flour
¾ cup chopped pecans

PREHEAT OVEN TO 350 DEGREES

1. Cream margarine and flour with pastry cutter or two knives.
2. Add pecans and mix with fork.
3. Spread very flat in 13 x 9-inch pan and bake at 350 degrees for 15 minutes or until golden brown.
4. Remove from oven and stir. Let cool; press mixture on bottom of pan.

Filling:

1 cup powdered sugar
1 (8-ounce) package cream cheese
½ large Cool Whip

1. Using the electric mixer, blend sugar and cream cheese.
2. Fold Cool Whip into cream cheese mixture.
3. Spread on top of crust.

Chocolate Filling:

2 small packages instant chocolate pudding
3 cups milk
1½ teaspoon vanilla

1. Mix pudding, milk and vanilla and beat until thick.
2. Place on top of cream cheese filling.

Top with ½ large container of Cool Whip, ¼ cup chopped pecans and cherries.

TEASIE'S BANANA PUDDING

1 large box instant vanilla pudding
3 cups milk
1 (8-ounce) package cream cheese
1 (12-ounce) Cool Whip
1 can sweetened condensed milk
1½ pounds vanilla wafers
9 large bananas, sliced

1. Gradually add and mix sweetened condensed milk to cream cheese.
2. Prepare instant pudding according to the directions and add to mixture.
3. Fold in Cool Whip to mixture.
4. Alternate vanilla wafers, bananas and pudding mix in layers in a very large dish.

BITS 'N' BERRIES
— Just For Kenny —

1 (14-ounce) can sweetened condensed milk
1½ cups cold water
1 (3½-ounce) package instant vanilla pudding
2 cups heavy cream, whipped
36 vanilla wafers
1 quart strawberries, halved
¼ cup Nestle little bits semi-sweet chocolate

1. In large mixing bowl, combine sweetened condensed milk and water. Add instant pudding mix; beat until well blended. Chill 5 minutes.
2. Fold in whipped cream.
3. Spoon 2 cups pudding into 3-quart round glass serving bowl; top with half of each of the vanilla wafers, strawberries and ¼ cup Nestles little bits semi-sweet chocolate and 2 cups pudding. Repeat layering, ending with pudding.
4. Garnish with additional strawberries and ¼ cup little bits. Chill thoroughly. Refrigerate leftovers.

Makes 8 to 10 servings.

Note: 2 cups blueberries, sliced peaches, sliced nectarines, plum halves or grapes may be substituted for strawberries.

CLEMENTINE'S TOO EASY PEACH COBBLER

5 to 6 peaches, peeled, pitted, sliced
1½ cups sugar
2 tablespoons flour
1 egg
1 stick butter, melted
5 slices white bread

PREHEAT OVEN TO 350 DEGREES

1. Place peaches in buttered 8 x 8-inch pan.
2. Cut crusts off bread and slice each slice into 5 fingers and place over peaches.
3. In a bowl, mix sugar, flour, egg and butter and pour over bread. Bake for 35 to 45 minutes in 350 degree oven until golden brown.

Never fold whipped cream into a warm mixture as the warmth will deflate the cream. To hasten cooling of the warm mixture, place bowl with mixture in a large bowl or pan of ice water and stir until chilled.

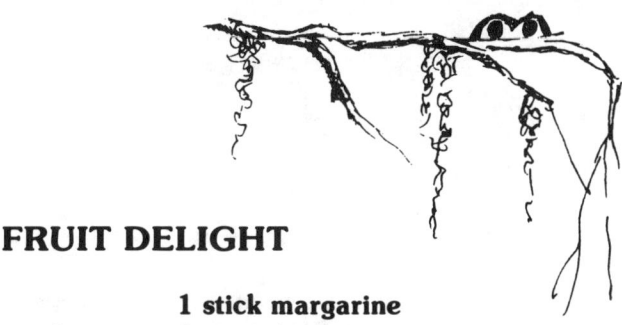

FRUIT DELIGHT

1 can cherry pie filling
1 large can crushed pineapple
1 box yellow cake mix
1 stick margarine
1 cup pecans

PREHEAT OVEN TO 350 DEGREES

1. Butter a 13 x 9-inch pan.
2. Cover bottom with cherries — topped with undrained pineapple.
3. Spread dry cake mix over pineapple.
4. Drizzle melted margarine over dry cake mix.
5. Sprinkle with pecans. Bake at 350 degrees for 1½ hours.

FRUIT PIZZA

1 package sugar cookie dough
1 cup powdered sugar
8 ounce cream cheese
5 ounce Cool Whip
½ cup water
1 tablespoon cornstarch
¾ cup orange juice (I substitute any fruit juice or juice drained from pineapple)

Lemon juice for bananas
3 bananas, sliced
1 can pineapple chunks, drained
1 jar cherries, drained-cut in halves
2 kiwi, sliced

PREHEAT OVEN TO 350 DEGREES

1. Spread cookie dough on 15 x 12 x 1-inch cookie sheet.
2. Cook 13 minutes at 350 degrees.
3. Mix cream cheese and sugar, using an electric mixer. Fold in cool whip using a spoon.
4. Spread on cooled cookie dough.
5. Mix water, cornstarch, fruit juice. Boil 1 minute. Cool completely.
6. Sprinkle bananas with small amount of lemon juice. Arrange bananas, cherries, pineapple and kiwi on top of cookie and cream cheese mixture.
7. Pour mixture of water, cornstarch and fruit juice over fruit for glaze.

   Serves 15 to 20.

BREAD PUDDING

1 (10-ounce) loaf stale French bread, broken (or 8-cups any type bread)
4 cups milk (or ½ milk, ½ heavy cream)
2 cups sugar
4 tablespoons butter, melted

3 eggs
2 tablespoons vanilla
1 cup raisins
1 cup shredded coconut
1 cup chopped pecans
1 teaspoon cinnamon
1 teaspoon nutmeg

1. Combine all ingredients; mixture should be very moist but not soupy.
2. Pour into buttered 9 x 9-inch baking dish. Place on middle rack of non-preheated oven.
3. Bake at 350 degrees for approximately 1 hour 15 minutes, until top is golden brown.
4. Serve warm with Amaretto sauce. (See next recipe).

   Makes 20 to 24 servings.

Amaretto Sauce:

½ cup butter (1 stick)
1½ cups powdered sugar
1 egg, yolk or whole

½ cup Amaretto, rum or bourbon, (to taste)

1. Cream butter and sugar over medium heat until all butter is absorbed.
2. Remove from heat and blend in egg yolk.
3. Pour in Amaretto gradually to your own taste, stirring constantly. Sauce will thicken as it cools.
4. Serve warm over warm bread pudding.

   Makes enough sauce for above bread pudding recipe.

DRUNKEN GRAPES

3 pounds seedless grapes, washed and stemmed
⅓ cup confectioners sugar
Juice of half a lemon

½ cup Cointreau, orange-flavored liqueur
1 cup heavy cream, whipped

1. Clean and prepare grapes. Sprinkle confectioners sugar over grapes until they are coated.
2. Mix lemon juice and Cointreau. Stir the liquid mixture into the grapes. Pour cream mixture over grapes and stir from bottom every 30 minutes for 4 hours while the grapes are refrigerated. Serve at party or meeting, on a luncheon plate, as a side dish at brunch or as a dessert.

APPLE DUMPLINGS

Pastry:

1½ cups sifted flour
½ cup shortening
½ teaspoon salt
4½ tablespoons water
6 apples

1 tablespoon sugar
1 tablespoon butter
¼ teaspoon cinnamon
½ teaspoon vanilla extract

1. Combine salt and flour.
2. Cut shortening into flour using pastry blender or two knives.
3. Add water and mix with a fork. (Do not over stir.)
4. Divide pastry into 6 sections.
5. Roll out on slightly floured pastry board.
6. Place an apple which has been peeled and cored in the center of pastry.
7. In center of apple place 1 tablespoon sugar, 1 tablespoon butter, ¼ teaspoon cinnamon and ½ teaspoon vanilla extract.
8. Fold corners of dough over apples and place in baking dish.

Syrup:

½ cup water
½ stick butter

½ cup sugar

1. Heat all the above ingredients in a saucepan.
2. Pour over apples.
3. Bake 35-40 minutes at 425 degrees. Serve piping hot topped with ice cream or cream.

OREO COOKIE CAKE

3 roll package Oreo cookies
1 stick margarine
½ gallon vanilla ice cream, softened

1 small can Hershey's chocolate syrup
1 medium Cool Whip, thawed
½ cup toasted pecans, chopped

1. Crush cookies between sheets of wax paper or in food processor. Save ½ of crumbs.
2. Mix crumbs with 1 stick melted margarine. Press into bottom of 13 x 9-inch pan and chill.
3. Spread ice cream over crumbs, then cover with chocolate syrup.
4. Top with Cool Whip, then garnish with crumbs and pecans.
5. Freeze before serving.
6. Serve frozen — allow to soften a few minutes for easier cutting.

DESSERTS FROM THE ICE CREAM FREEZER

Proportions of ice to salt. For ice cream and sherberts, allow 1 part of salt to 8 parts of ice. The ice and salt may be arranged in layers in the freezer until a layer of ice reaches above the top of the can. Ice cream is improved by standing for at least one hour.

UNCOOKED HOMEMADE ICE CREAM

4 eggs
2 cups sugar
1 can evaporated milk
3 cartons half-and-half (one pint each)
2 teaspoons vanilla

1. Mix eggs and add sugar. Combine well and add other ingredients.
2. Fill freezer container with mixture and add homogenized milk to desired level of freezer. Freeze until firm.

OLD-FASHIONED COOKED CUSTARD ICE CREAM

8 eggs
1⅓ cups sugar
1 quart plus 1 cup whole milk
½ pint whipping cream
2 tablespoons flour
Pinch of salt
2 teaspoons vanilla

1. Beat eggs until light and fluffy. Beat in sugar.
2. Add milk and cream, reserving some of the liquid to mix with flour. Mix flour with reserved milk forming a smooth paste. Add to the custard mixture along with the salt.
3. Cook over low fire stirring constantly. Continue to cook until it begins to thicken and coats spoon. Remove from fire and add vanilla.
4. Allow to cool, then pour into an electric ice cream freezer.

   Makes 1 gallon.

Waterproof Boxes

To waterproof storage boxes, spray the cardboard, inside and out, with common shellac and let it sit outside to dry for a few hours. All but floodwaters will be repelled by the sealant, including unwanted bugs.

MADELANE'S PINK LEMONADE PIE

1 (9-inch) baked pie crust
1 (8-ounce) package cream cheese
1 (14-ounce) can Eagle Brand sweetened condensed milk
1 (6-ounce) frozen lemonade thawed
1 small Cool Whip

1. In large bowl beat cream cheese until light and fluffy. Stir in sweetened condensed milk and lemonade concentrate.
2. Fold in whipped cream. Pour into pie crust.
3. Chill two hours.

   Hint: If it isn't pink enough add a few drops of red food color. Cut small pieces as it is so rich.

EASY CHOCOLATE PIE

1 (6-ounce) box Jello chocolate pudding and pie filling
2 teaspoons vanilla flavor
1 baked Pillsbury all ready pie crust

1. Cook chocolate pie filling according to directions on back of box.
2. Remove from heat, add vanilla. Cool. Place plastic wrap on surface of pudding while cooling.
3. Pour into baked pie shell. Cover with plastic wrap and put in refrigerator.
4. Top pie with Cool Whip. Garnish with chocolate leaves. Serve.

Variations

Banana Pie — Use vanilla pudding, and vanilla flavor. Slice 3 bananas into baked pie shell. Pour cooked pie filling over bananas. Follow the above directions.

Coconut Pie — Add 1½ cups coconut instead of bananas. Garnish with coconut.

STRAWBERRY PIE

1 package frozen strawberries
1 package cool whipped cream
Graham cracker crust
4 tablespoons cornstarch
1 cup sugar
3 tablespoons strawberry Jello (½ package)
1½ cups water
1 Cool Whip (for topping)

1. Mix cornstarch, sugar and jello, add water. Heat and stir until thick. Let cool.
2. Add strawberries to jello mixture, then pour into crust.
3. Chill at least 2 hours, top with Cool Whip.

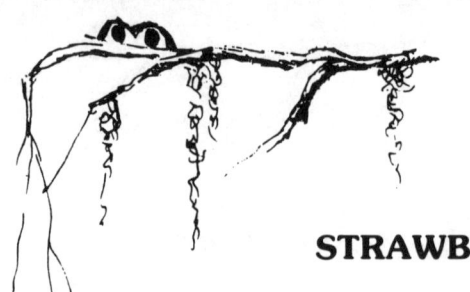

STRAWBERRY PIE II

1 (12-ounce) box vanilla wafers
1 stick margarine
½ cup chopped pecans
2 envelopes Dream Whip

1 can condensed Eagle Brand milk
2 lemons (juice)
1 pint strawberries, sliced

1. Crush wafers and add melted margarine and pecans.
2. For the bottom crust of the pie, place 1 cup of the vanilla wafer mixture into a 9 x 13 inch dish, put the remainder in another pan. Bake both at 350 degrees for 5 minutes.
3. Prepare Dream Whip according to directions on package. Using one recipe of Dream Whip, add condensed milk, lemon juice and strawberries to form strawberry filling.
4. Place all of the strawberry filling on top of the first vanilla wafer mixture in the 9 x 13 inch baking dish.
5. Using a fork, crumble the remaining vanilla wafer mixture and sprinkle over pie. Top with the second Dream Whip. Cool at least 3 hours before serving. Garnish with fresh whole strawberries with leaves.

FRESH STRAWBERRY PIE

Makes 1 pie:

1 pint fresh strawberries
1 cup sugar
2 tablespoons cornstarch
1 cup water

4 tablespoons strawberry Jello (dry)
1 pie crust

1. Bake pie crust. Cool.
2. Mix sugar, cornstarch, and water. Cook until thick and clear.
3. Remove from stove.
4. Add Jello and stir, cool.
5. Place fresh, sliced berries in pie shell.
6. Pour mixture over berries and cover, and refrigerate overnight.
7. Top with Cool Whip and serve.

Tape a small magnet to one end of your vacuum cleaner head to use for picking up small metal items (such as screws, nails, safety pins) before they can damage your vacuum cleaner.

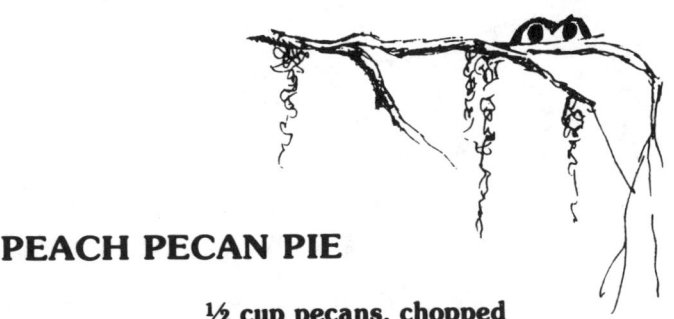

PEACH PECAN PIE

3 egg whites
1 cup sugar
12 soda crackers (saltines), rolled fine
½ teaspoon baking powder
½ cup pecans, chopped
1 teaspoon vanilla
½ pint whipping cream
1 (15-ounce) can sliced peaches, drained

1. Butter a 9-inch pie pan. Combine egg whites, sugar, crushed crackers, baking powder, pecans and vanilla. Spread mixture into pie plate.
2. Bake at 320 degrees for 30 minutes. The pie crust will rise while baking and fall when cooling.
3. Let pie crust cool. Fold drained peaches and whipped cream together, sweeten to taste and spread over pie crust. Refrigerate until ready to serve.

Note: This is easy to make and is one of my favorite desserts.

GRASSHOPPER PIE

1 (6-ounce) package Nestle semi-sweet real chocolate morsels
1 tablespoon shortening
1½ cups finely chopped nuts
½ pound marshmallows (about 35 large)
⅓ cup milk
¼ teaspoon salt
3 tablespoons green creme de menthe
3 tablespoons white creme de cacao
1½ cups heavy cream, whipped

1. Line a 9-inch pie pan with aluminum foil.
2. Combine over hot (not boiling) water, Nestle semi-sweet real chocolate morsels and shortening, stir until morsels are melted and smooth.
3. Add chopped nuts, mix well. Spread evenly on bottom and up sides (not rim) of foil-lined pie pan, chill in refrigerator until firm (about 1 hour). Lift chocolate shell out of pan, peel off foil and place shell on serving plate, chill in refrigerator until ready to use.
4. Combine over hot (not boiling) water, marshmallows, milk and salt, heat until marshmallows melt. Remove from heat.
5. Add liquers, stir until blended.
6. Chill in refrigerator until slightly thickened (about 1 hour). Gently fold in whipped cream. Pour filling into shell and chill in refrigerator until firm (about 1 hour).

    Makes 1 (9-inch) pie.

FRENCH APPLE PIE

1 unbaked pie crust
½ cup sugar
3 tablespoons flour
1 teaspoon ground cinnamon
⅛ teaspoon salt
5 medium size apples, pared and sliced

PREHEAT OVEN TO 425 DEGREES

1. Combine sugar, flour, cinnamon and salt.
2. Stir in apples.
3. Prepare topping. (See recipe below).
4. Place apple filling in pie crust. Place topping on top. Topping should be crumbly.
5. Cover with foil and bake 40 minutes at 425 degrees, remove foil and bake another 10 minutes. (Place pie in center of oven to bake).

Serve with ice cream or Cool Whip.

Topping

1 cup flour
½ cup margarine
½ cup brown sugar

1. Using a pastry blender cut margarine into flour and sugar.

MARGARITA PIE

1¼ cups finely crushed pretzels
½ cup plus 2 tablespoons margarine or butter, melted
¼ cup sugar
1 (14-ounce) can sweetened condensed milk (NOT evaporated milk)
⅓ cup lime juice from concentrate
3 to 4 tablespoons tequila
2 tablespoons triple sec or other orange flavored liqueur
1 cup (½ pint) whipping cream, whipped (2 cups Cool Whip)

Additional whipped cream and pretzels for garnish, optional.

1. Combine crumbs, margarine and sugar, press firmly on bottom and up side of lightly buttered (9-inch) pie plate.
2. In large mixing bowl, combine sweetened condensed milk, lime juice, tequila and triple sec, mix well. Fold in whipped cream. Add 1 drop green food color for good color.
3. Pour into prepared crust. Freeze 4 hours or chill 2 hours. Garnish with additional whipped cream and pretzels if desired. Return leftovers to freezer or refrigerator.

Makes 1 (9-inch) pie.

FRANKIE'S BEST-EVER LEMON PIE

1 baked pie shell
1¼ cups sugar
6 tablespoons cornstarch
2 cups water
⅓ cup lemon juice

3 eggs, separated
3 tablespoons butter
1½ teaspoons lemon extract
2 teaspoons vinegar

1. Mix sugar and cornstarch together in top of double boiler.
2. Add the two cups of water.
3. Combine egg yolks with juice and beat.
4. Add to rest of mixture. Cook until thick over boiling water for 25 minutes. This does away with starchy taste.
5. Now add lemon extract, butter and vinegar and stir thoroughly.
6. Pour into a deep, 9-inch pie shell and let cool. Cover with meringue and brown in oven.

Never Fail Meringue:

1 tablespoon cornstarch
2 tablespoons cold water
½ cup boiling water
3 egg whites

6 tablespoons sugar
1 teaspoon vanilla
Pinch of salt

1. Blend cornstarch and cold water in a saucepan.
2. Add boiling water and cook, stirring until clear and thickened. Let stand until COMPLETELY cold.
3. With electric beater at high speed, beat egg whites until foamy.
4. Gradually add sugar and beat until STIFF, but not dry.
5. Turn mixer to low speed, add salt and vanilla.
6. Gradually beat in cold cornstarch mixture.
7. Turn mixer again to high speed and beat well.
8. Spread meringue over cooled pie filling. Bake at 350 degrees for about 10 minutes. This meringue cuts beautifully and never gets sticky. Enjoy!

Oil on your driveway or parking lot? Soak and then scrub the spot with mineral spirits, then quickly blot up the residue with newspaper. Once the pavement is dry, scrub with a mixture of Tide, bleach, and a gallon of cold water.

FRESH PEAR PIE

2 (9-inch) pie crusts
½ cup + 2 tablespoons sugar
⅓ cup all-purpose flour
1 teaspoon cinnamon

4 cups sliced pared fresh pears
  (about 7 medium pears)
2 tablespoons lemon juice
3 tablespoons margarine or butter
1 tablespoon vanilla

PREHEAT OVEN TO 425 DEGREES

1. Prepare pastry for a 2 crust pie. I use Pillsbury All Ready Pie Crust (frozen).
2. Stir together sugar, flour, cinnamon, mix with pears.
3. Turn into pastry-lined pie pan, sprinkle with lemon juice, vanilla and dot with butter.
4. Cover with top crust which has slits cut in it, seal and flute. Sprinkle with 2 tablespoons of sugar. Cover edge with 2 to 3-inch strip of aluminum foil to prevent excessive browning, remove foil last 15 minutes of baking. Bake for 50 minutes or until crust is golden brown and juice begins to bubble through slits in crust.
5. Serve hot with Cool Whip or ice cream.

To Freeze Pear Pie Filling:

1. Place sliced pears into plastic bag.
2. Add 2 tablespoons lemon juice, toss to coat pears with lemon juice.
3. Stir together sugar, flour and cinnamon. Add to plastic bag. Toss to mix all ingredients. Seal and freeze.
4. When you are ready to make a pie, remove from freezer, thaw a little, place in pie crust and add vanilla and butter. Follow recipe for completing the pie.

Glass sparkles when cleaned with half vinegar and half water, applied with common newsprint. The vinegar causes quick drying and the newsprint leaves no oils.

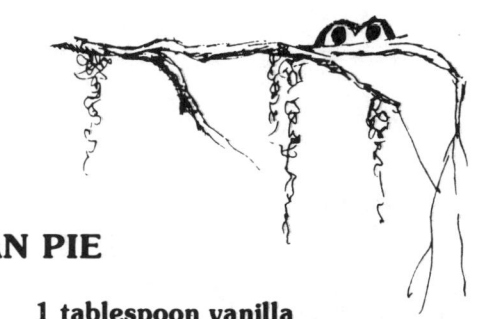

PECAN PIE

3 eggs, slightly beaten
1 cup Karo light or dark syrup
1 cup sugar
2 tablespoons margarine, melted

1 tablespoon vanilla
1½ cups pecan halves
1 unbaked (9-inch) pastry shell

PREHEAT OVEN TO 350 DEGREES

1. Stir together first 5 ingredients until blended. Add nuts. Pour into pastry shell. Bake in 350 degree oven 50 to 60 minutes or until knife inserted halfway between center and edge comes out clean. Cool.

Variations

Chocolate Pecan Pie: Decrease sugar to ⅓ cup. Add 4-ounces melted semi-sweet chocolate.

Pumpkin Pecan Pie: Pumpkin Layer — Stir together 1 egg, 1 cup canned pumpkin, ⅓ cup sugar, ½ teaspoon ground cinnamon, ¼ teaspoon ground ginger and ⅛ teaspoon ground cloves until blended. Spread evenly in bottom of unbaked pastry shell. Pecan Layer — Stir together 2 eggs, ⅔ cup corn syrup, ⅔ cup sugar, 2 tablespoons melted margarine and ½ teaspoon vanilla. Add 1 cup pecans. Carefully spoon over pumpkin layer. Bake in 350 degree oven 60 minutes or until filling is set around edges.

BROWNIES

4 eggs
2 cups sugar
1½ cups flour, sifted
¾ cup cocoa

2 sticks butter
2 teaspoons vanilla
3 cups pecans

PREHEAT OVEN TO 375 DEGREES
Grease and flour a 9 x 9 x 2-inch baking pan.

1. Melt butter and cocoa over low heat, beat eggs until light, add all other ingredients.
2. Mix well.
3. Add vanilla and pecans.
4. Bake 20 to 25 minutes.

Icing:

Just melt 1 stick butter, add 1 box sifted confectioners sugar, ⅔ cup cocoa and stir until right consistency. (Add a little extra cream if needed). Add 2 teaspoons vanilla and spread over cake while warm.

FOOLPROOF PIE DOUGH

4 cups flour
2 teaspoons salt
1 tablespoon sugar
1¾ cups shortening

½ cup water
1 tablespoon vinegar
1 beaten egg

1. Combine flour, salt and sugar. Cut shortening into flour mixture.
2. Add water, vinegar and egg. Mix with fork.
3. Cut into five parts. Roll into balls.
4. Wrap airtight. Freeze to use as needed.

Makes 5 single crusts.

KENTUCKY DERBY PIE

2 eggs, slightly beaten
1 cup sugar
½ cup all-purpose flour
½ cup butter, melted and cooled
1 cup chopped pecans
1 (6-ounce) package semi-sweet chocolate morsels

1 teaspoon vanilla extract
1 unbaked 9-inch pastry shell
1 cup whipping cream
1 tablespoon bourbon
¼ cup sifted powdered sugar

1. Combine first 4 ingredients in a medium mixing bowl, beat with an electric mixer just until blended.
2. Stir in pecans, chocolate morsels, and vanilla. Pour filling into pastry shell, and bake at 350 degrees for 45 to 50 minutes.
3. Beat whipping cream and bourbon until foamy, gradually add powdered sugar, beating until soft peaks form. Serve pie warm with the whipped cream.

CHOCOLATE PIE

1 (9-inch) graham cracker crumb pie crust (bake in oven for 10 minutes)
12 marshmallows, large

½ cup milk
6 (1-ounce) milk chocolate candy bars with almonds
1 cup chilled whipping cream

1. Heat together milk, marshmallows and candy.
2. Stirring until melted. Cool.
3. Whip whipping cream until it stands in peaks.
4. Fold whipped cream into marshmallow mixture.
5. Turn into pie shell and cool for 3 to 4 hours. Freezes well.

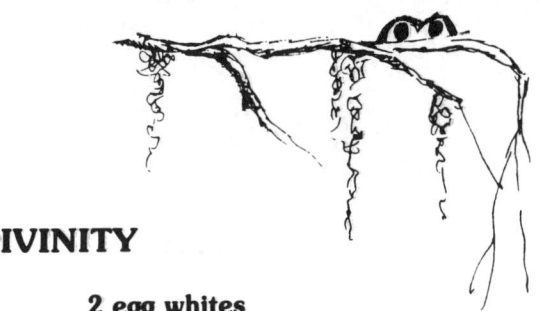

DIVINITY

2½ cups sugar
½ cup white Karo
½ cup water
Raisins or nuts

2 egg whites
Pinch salt
2 teaspoons vanilla

1. Place sugar, Karo and water in boiler. Boil to hard boil stage.
2. While syrup is cooking, beat egg whites until stiff but not dry.
3. Add syrup to egg whites, beating it in a little at a time (use electric mixer).
4. Beat in vanilla, salt, and nuts. As soon as mixture loses its gloss, drop by teaspoon on waxed paper.

CREAMY PRALINES

1½ cups sugar
¾ cup light brown sugar, packed
½ cup milk

¾ stick butter
1½ cups pecans
1 teaspoon vanilla

1. Combine all ingredients except vanilla in a heavy pot.
2. Bring to boil, stirring frequently. Cook to soft ball stage 238-240 degrees, on candy thermometer.
3. Remove from heat, add vanilla and beat with a spoon until shine has gone and it is cool. Drop on wax paper. Place a few sheets of newspaper beneath the waxed paper.

GRAHAM CRACKER PRALINES

1 box graham crackers
1½ cups pecans, chopped

1 cup brown sugar
2 sticks margarine

PREHEAT OVEN TO 350 DEGREES

1. Spray a 15 x 12 x 1-inch pan with Pam then line with whole graham crackers.
2. Sprinkle with pecans.
3. Boil margarine and brown sugar for 3 minutes, then pour over graham crackers.
4. Bake for 10 minutes at 350 degrees. Cut while warm into 3 x 1-inch bars. Cool and store in air tight container.

CYNTHIA'S HARD CANDY

¾ cup water
2¾ cups sugar
1½ cups Karo
3 or 4 drops red or green food coloring

2 teaspoons oil of cinnamon or spearmint or peppermint

1. Cover 3 large cookie sheets or cake pans with at least ¼-inch powdered sugar.
2. Combine first 3 ingredients in saucepan, bring to a boil using a candy thermometer.
3. Cook until thermometer reads 300 degrees. Take off stove and stir in coloring and flavoring.
4. Make rows in sugar and pour candy in.
5. Let candy set, then break into small pieces.

   Be sure to have pans ready before you start.

PEANUT BUTTER BALLS

1 pound box powdered sugar
1½ cups crunchy peanut butter
2 sticks margarine

½ teaspoon vanilla
12 ounce semi-sweet chocolate
⅛ block paraffin wax

1. Using electric mixer, blend peanut butter, vanilla and margarine. Add powdered sugar gradually.
2. Chill, roll into balls, the size of a large marble.
3. Melt 12-ounces semi-sweet chocolate and ⅛ block paraffin wax in microwave or double boiler.
4. Dip peanut butter balls into chocolate with tooth pick. Place on wax paper to cool.

   Makes 60.

BLIND DATES

1 packet dried dates
Salted peanuts

Granulated sugar

1. Cut a slit in each date and remove the stone. Fill the dates with the salted peanuts and roll in granulated sugar.
2. Pack in layers of waxed or greaseproof paper, foil or paper cases in tins or boxes.

ARDETH'S BARS

12 double graham crackers
1 cup brown sugar (light)
1 cup butter (the real thing)

1 (11¾-ounce) package milk
  chocolate chips
1 cup finely chopped pecans

PREHEAT OVEN TO 400 DEGREES

1. Line a jelly roll pan with sides with foil. Then line the bottom with whole graham crackers. Mine takes 12 double graham crackers, but if the size varies you can cut crackers to fill the gap.
2. Combine brown sugar with butter, bring to a boil, boil 3 minutes, stirring constantly. Pour this mixture evenly over the graham crackers and bake for 5 minutes in a preheated 400 degree oven. Watch it carefully so it won't burn. Crackers will sort of "lift up".
3. Remove from oven and immediately pour the milk chocolate chips over the crackers and spread evenly. Cover chocolate with pecans. Allow to cool before cutting. This will freeze, but should be used approximately within 3 weeks.

CHOCOLATE FUDGE

2 cups granulated sugar
3 to 4 tablespoons cocoa or 1
  square chocolate
½ cup cream
½ cup milk

Few grains of salt
2 tablespoons corn syrup
1 tablespoon butter
1 teaspoon vanilla
½ to 1 cup nut meats (if desired)

1. Combine sugar, cocoa or chocolate, cream, milk, syrup and salt in a deep pan and heat.
2. Stir until sugar is completely dissolved and the mixture boils.
3. Boil until the test for soft ball stage is given when a little of the mixture is tested in cold water.
4. Remove from the fire and add butter and vanilla.
5. Cool until only warm, beat until thick and creamy. Add nuts, if used, and pour into a buttered pan. Mark in squares.

ROCKY ROAD HALLOWEEN SQUARES

1 (12-ounce) package semi-sweet chocolate morsels
1 (14-ounce) can Eagle Brand sweetened condensed milk
2 tablespoons butter or margarine
2 cups dry roasted peanuts
1 (10½-ounce) package miniature white marshmallows

1. In top of double boiler, over boiling water, melt morsels with sweetened condensed milk and butter, remove from heat.
2. In large bowl, combine nuts and marshmallows, fold in chocolate mixture.
3. Spread in wax paper lined 13 x 9-inch pan. Chill 2 hours or until firm. Remove from pan, peel off wax paper, cut into squares. Cover and store at room temperature.

TUNNEL OF FUDGE

18 ounce semi-sweet chocolate chips
1 large can evaporated milk
1 (7-ounce) bottle of Kraft marshmallow cream
1 stick margarine
4½ cups of sugar
Pinch of salt
4 cups of chopped pecans

1. Mix sugar, milk, margarine, and salt in heavy pan. Stir well. Bring to a boil. Reduce heat, cook 8 minutes on low heat stirring constantly. Remove from heat and add remaining ingredients. Pour into bundt pan which has been sprayed heavily with shortening. Chill.
2. To remove fudge from pan, turn upside down on serving tray and cover with hot dish towels until it falls from pan. Made the day before, it comes out more easily. Made that morning, it is very difficult to remove that night.
3. A small toothpick holder or small glass jar fits in the center of the mold and filled with tiny flowers makes an appealing sweet. Also, causes lots of conversation!

KATHLEEN'S CHOCOLATE DELIGHT

½ pound white chocolate, melted
1 box Ritz crackers
1 cup pecans, finely chopped

1. Dip Ritz crackers in chocolate.
2. Roll in pecans.
3. Place on wax paper and freeze for a few minutes.

This is a special treat to add to a Christmas box of goodies.

PEANUT BRITTLE

1 cup sugar
½ cup white Karo
¼ cup water

1 cup raw shelled peanuts
1 teaspoon soda

1. Combine sugar, Karo and water. Cook until mixture spins a thread.
2. Add peanuts. Cook until peanuts begin to pop, cut off fire.
3. Add soda and stir until candy becomes yellow. Pour into buttered platter. Simply delicious!

CHINESE CHEWS

1 (6-ounce) package semi-sweet chocolate pieces
1 (6-ounce) package butterscotch pieces

1 (3-ounce) can chow mein noodles
1 (6½-ounce) can cocktail peanuts (optional)

1. Melt chocolate and butterscotch pieces in a 2 quart glass dish in microwave oven for 2 minutes. Stir until smooth.
2. Add noodles and nuts.
3. Stir until well coated. Drop by teaspoonful onto waxed paper. Harden in refrigerator until firm.

   Makes 4 dozen.

WHITE CHOCOLATE FUDGE

1 (8-ounce) package cream cheese, softened
4 cups sifted powdered sugar
1½ teaspoons vanilla extract

12 ounces vanilla flavored candy coating, melted
¾ cup chopped pecans

1. Beat cream cheese at medium speed with an electric mixer until smooth. Gradually add sugar and vanilla, beating well.
2. Stir in candy coating and pecans.
3. Spread into a butter 8-inch square pan. Refrigerate until firm. Cut into small squares.

   Yield: 2 pounds.

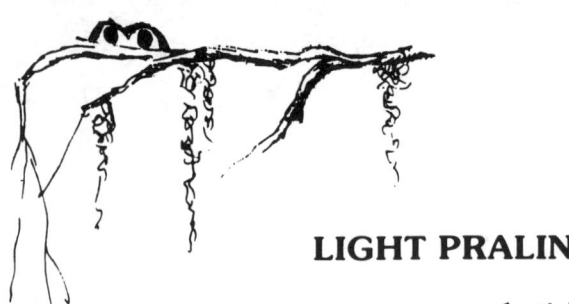

LIGHT PRALINES

4 cups sugar
1 large can evaporated milk
1 can condensed milk

1 stick butter
2 teaspoons vanilla
1 quart pecans

1. Dissolve sugar in evaporated and condensed milk. Add butter and bring to a boil over low heat, stirring constantly, until candy thermometer registers 228 degrees. Continue cooking, without stirring, until the thermometer registers 236 degrees or mixture forms soft ball in water.
2. Remove from heat, add vanilla and pecans. Beat with wooden spoon until thickened but still glossy.
3. Drop by spoonfuls on waxed paper. If mixture begins to harden while turning out, place over hot water.

CREAMY PRALINES

1½ cups light brown sugar
1½ cups granulated sugar
1 cup evaporated milk
½ teaspoon cream of tartar

⅛ teaspoon salt
½ cup (1 stick) margarine
2 teaspoons vanilla
2 cups pecan halves

1. Put 2 sheets of waxed paper over newspaper on counter or use foil. Have ready one cup of water with a large ice cube to test soft ball stage, or use a candy thermometer.
2. Cook together sugars, milk, salt and cream of tartar, stirring constantly until firm soft ball stage, or until thermometer registers 240 degrees.
3. Remove from heat and add butter and vanilla. Stir until mixture begins to thicken.
4. Beat about a minute, add pecans and continue to beat until mixture begins to thicken.
5. Drop quickly onto waxed paper by small spoonfuls. Let cool until firm.

Makes about 50 (2-inch) pralines.

After a soup has been refrigerated or frozen, taste for seasoning. Foods lose flavor when they are chilled or frozen.

NELL'S NUT GOODIE BARS

Step 1 — First Layer:

1 (12-ounce) package milk chocolate chips

1 (12-ounce) package butterscotch chips
2 cups peanut butter (chunky)

1. Melt in double boiler. Pat or spread half of mixture in 10 x 15-inch jelly roll pan. Freeze.

Step 2 — Second Layer:

2 pounds powdered sugar
1 cup margarine
½ cup evaporated milk

¼ cup vanilla pudding mix (not instant)
½ teaspoon maple or vanilla flavoring

1. In a large mixing bowl place 2 pounds powdered sugar. In a separate bowl, mix margarine, evaporated milk and pudding mix, pour over powdered sugar. Add ½ teaspoon maple or vanilla flavoring and beat until smooth.
2. Spread over hardened chocolate mixture. Freeze.

Step 3 — Third Layer

2 cups coarsely chopped salted peanuts

1. Reheat remaining chocolate mixture. Add 2 cups coarsely chopped salted peanuts. Spread over 2nd layer and return to freezer until hard. Cut into small pieces. Keep in freezer or refrigerator.

Gum in your pocket? Ice it down...it will get brittle and break off easily. Or the messy approach is applying peanut butter, whose oils help break down the gum.

MARTHA WASHINGTON BALLS

1 can flaked coconut
1 cup pecans, chopped
1 can sweetened condensed milk

¼ pound soft margarine
2 boxes powdered sugar

1. Blend all ingredients and roll by hand into small balls about ¾-inch in diameter.
2. Chill in refrigerator, (about 1 hour or longer).
3. Insert toothpick into each ball and dip into chocolate paraffin mixture to coat thoroughly.
4. Place on waxed paper to harden. Remove toothpicks.

   Chocolate-Paraffin Mixture: Melt 1 teaspoon paraffin and one large (12-ounce) package chocolate bits in a small sauce pan on the lowest heat position (10-15 minutes). Use for dipping, as directed above.

HEAVENLY HASH

36 ounces Hershey's plain milk chocolate (3 giant bars of 9¾-ounces and 1½ bars of 4¾-ounces)

5 (1-ounce) bars cocoa butter
1 pound large marshmallows, cut in halves
1 quart pecans, chopped large

1. Melt chocolate and cocoa butter in double boiler.
2. Oil wax paper in a large box or cake pan. Spread less than half of chocolate mixture over bottom.
3. Space marshmallows (cut marshmallows in half and you will not use the whole bag).
4. Mix pecans in the remainder of chocolate and pour over marshmallows.
5. Put in refrigerator. Cut into desired size when hard.

   Yields about 4 pounds.

To peel tomatoes, remove stem with the tip of a knife. Immerse tomatoes in boiling water for 10 to 20 seconds; green tomatoes may take longer. Place in cold water to cool. Peel should slip off easily.

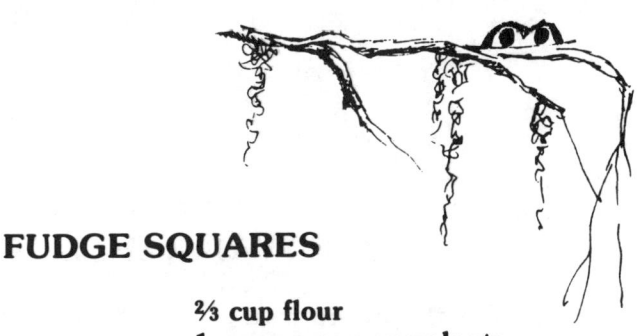

FUDGE SQUARES

1 stick butter
2 cups sugar
4 squares chocolate, melted
4 eggs, beaten
⅔ cup flour
1 cup pecans or walnuts
2 teaspoons vanilla

1. Cream butter and sugar, add chocolate. Stir in rest of ingredients.
2. Spread in greased 8-inch square pan. Bake at 350 degrees for 35 minutes.

Icing:

1 can condensed milk
1 (12-ounce) package chocolate morsels
1 teaspoon vanilla

1. Mix and melt over a double boiler until chocolate morsels are well blended.
2. Spread on cake while still warm, and cut into squares. Let cool in pan. Freezes well.

FANTASY FUDGE

3 cups sugar
¾ cups butter
⅔ cups evaporated milk
1 (12-ounce) package semi-sweet chocolate pieces (2 cups)
1 pint jar marshmallow creme
1 cup chopped nuts
1 teaspoon vanilla

Grease 13 x 9-inch pan

1. Combine sugar, butter, and milk. Bring to a rolling boil. *Boil for 5 minutes, stirring constantly* (scorches easily).
2. Remove from heat, stir in chocolate pieces till melted.
3. Add marshmallow creme, vanilla, and nuts, beat until well blended.
4. Pour into *greased* 13 x 9-inch pan. Cool.

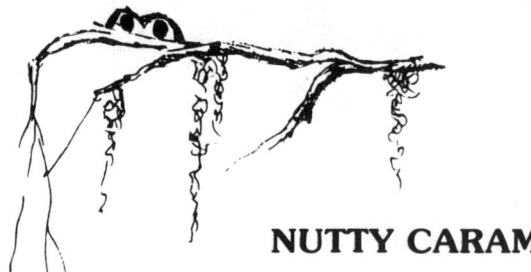

NUTTY CARAMEL CORN

6 quarts freshly popped corn (about 1 cup unpopped corn)
1 cup pecan halves
1 cup cashews
1 cup butter or margarine

2 cups firmly packed brown sugar
½ cup light corn syrup
1 teaspoon salt
½ teaspoon baking soda
1 teaspoon vanilla extract

1. Combine first 3 ingredients in a large roasting pan, set aside.
2. Melt butter in a large saucepan, stir in brown sugar, corn syrup and salt.
3. Bring to a boil over medium heat, stirring constantly. Boil 5 minutes, without stirring (temperature will register about 250 degrees).
4. Remove from heat, stir in soda and vanilla. Pour over popped corn and nuts, stir well.
5. Bake at 225 degrees for 1 hour, stirring every 15 minutes. Cool and break into pieces, if desired. Store in an airtight container.

Yield: 5 quarts.

PRALINE POPCORN CRUNCH

10 cups popped corn
1½ cups whole pecans
½ cup slivered almonds
1⅓ cups sugar
1 cup butter

¼ cup praline liqueur
¼ cup light corn syrup
1 tablespoon praline liqueur
¼ teaspoon salt

PREHEAT OVEN TO 325 DEGREES

1. Butter baking sheet and large bowl.
2. Toast pecans and almonds till light brown. About 12 to 15 minutes at 350 degrees.
3. Mix popped corn and nuts in large bowl.
4. Combine sugar, butter, ¼ cup praline liqueur and corn syrup in heavy 2 quart saucepan. Cook over medium heat, stirring occasionally to 275 degrees.
5. Remove from heat, quickly stir in 1 tablespoon liqueur and salt.
6. Pour over popped corn and nuts, mixing until evenly coated.
7. Immediately spread mixture on buttered baking sheet. Let stand 1 hour. Break into bite size pieces.

Makes about 14 cups.

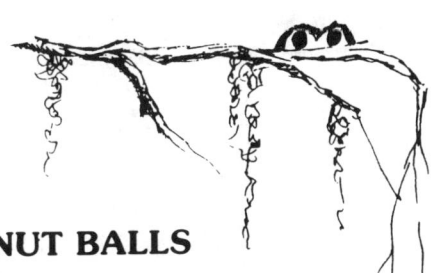

ORANGE COCONUT BALLS

1 small can frozen orange juice, undiluted
1 box powdered sugar
1 stick butter
1 large package vanilla wafers
1 large can Angel Flake coconut
1 tablespoon vanilla

1. Leave orange juice in refrigerator overnight to thaw.
2. Cream sugar and butter.
3. Crush vanilla wafers fine, add to sugar mixture.
4. Blend in orange juice and vanilla, mixing well.
5. Form into small balls and roll in coconut. Refrigerate.

Makes about 100 balls.

HOLIDAY ROCKY ROAD

2 bars of milk or special dark chocolate (8-ounces each)
1 cup coarsely chopped nuts
½ cup golden raisins or snipped dried apricots
1½ cups miniature marshmallows
Red candied cherry halves

1. Melt chocolate bars, broken into pieces, in top of double boiler over hot, not boiling, water. Stir until smooth.
2. Remove from heat, stir in nuts, raisins or apricots, and marshmallows just until coated.
3. Drop heaping spoonfuls into paper-lined miniature muffin pans or turn into buttered (8-inch) square pan. Place cherry halves on top, chill completely. Cut into squares.

About 4 dozen cups or 25 pieces.

"TRASH" CANDY

1 bag pretzel sticks
1 big box Honey Comb cereal
1 small jar dry roasted peanuts
2 small packages almonds (or English walnuts)
1 (14-ounce) box raisins
2 packages almond bark

1. Mix pretzels, cereal, peanuts, raisins, and almonds or walnuts in a large dish pan or mixing bowl.
2. Melt almond bark in microwave.
3. Pour over mixture and mix well. Pour onto waxpaper till cool, then break into pieces.

Note: Half recipe and melt 1 package almond bark, then do the other.

DEBBIE'S CHEWY CHOCOLATE COOKIES

1¼ cups butter
2 cups sugar
2 eggs
2 teaspoons vanilla extract
2 cups all-purpose flour, sifted
¾ cup Hershey's Cocoa
1 teaspoon baking soda

½ teaspoon salt
2 cups (12-ounce package) Reese's peanut butter chips or 2 cups (12-ounce) Hershey's semi-sweet chocolate chips or 1½ cups chopped (coarse) pecans

PREHEAT OVEN TO 350 DEGREES

1. In large mixer bowl cream butter and sugar until light and fluffy. (Using electric mixer.)
2. Add eggs and vanilla, beat well.
3. Combine flour, cocoa, baking soda and salt in another bowl.
4. Gradually add flour mixture into creamed mixture and beat.
5. Remove electric mixer. Stir in chips or pecans.
6. Drop by teaspoonfuls on to ungreased cookie sheet.
7. Bake 7 to 8 minutes. (Do not overbake, cookies will be soft. They will puff while baking and flatten while cooling). Cool slightly, remove from cookie sheet on to wire rack. Cool completely.

   Makes about 4½ dozen cookies.

NEIMAN'S $250 COOKIE RECIPE

2 cups butter
2 cups sugar
2 cups brown sugar, packed
4 eggs
2 teaspoons vanilla
4 cups flour
5 cups blended oatmeal

1 teaspoon salt
2 teaspoons baking powder
2 teaspoons baking soda
24-ounces chocolate chips
1 (8-ounce) grated Hershey bar
3 cups chopped nuts

PREHEAT OVEN TO 375 DEGREES

1. Blend oatmeal. Measure and blend in a blender to a fine powder.
2. Cream butter and both sugars. Add eggs and vanilla.
3. Mix together with flour, oatmeal, salt, baking powder and baking soda.
4. Add chips, candy and nuts.
5. Roll into balls and place 2-inches apart on cookie sheet.
6. Bake for 6 minutes at 375 degrees. Makes 112 cookies, but recipe can be halved.

SCOTCH SHORTBREAD

1¼ cups all-purpose flour
3 tablespoons cornstarch
¼ cup sugar

½ cup (¼ pound) butter, cut into chunks (do not substitute margarine)
1 tablespoon sugar

PREHEAT OVEN TO 325 DEGREES

1. In a large bowl, combine flour, cornstarch, and the ¼ cup sugar, with your fingers, work in butter until mixture is crumbly and no large particles remain. Shape into a firm lump.
2. Place dough (it will still be crumbly) in an 8 or 9-inch springform pan, press firmly and evenly over bottom of pan. Impress edge of dough with tines of a fork (as you would a pie crust), prick surface evenly.
3. Bake in a 325 degree oven for about 40 minutes or until a pale golden brown. Using a sharp knife, cut into 8 to 12 wedges while still warm, sprinkle with the 1 tablespoon sugar. Let cool, then remove pan rim and lift out cookies.
4. Wrap airtight and store at room temperature for up to a week. Freeze for longer storage.

   Makes 8 to 12 cookies.

Note: I used a 9-inch square pan, reduced baking time to 25 to 30 minutes.

Scotland's traditional cooky-cake has the charm of utter simplicity — there's practically nothing to it but flour, sugar, and butter. Still the flavor keeps you coming back for more.

FRUIT CAKE COOKIE

1 cup butter
16 ounces brown sugar
2 eggs
½ cup buttermilk
3½ cups flour
1 teaspoon salt

½ teaspoon soda
2 cups dates
2 cups mixed candy fruit
1 cup pecans
1 tablespoon + 1 teaspoon bourbon

PREHEAT OVEN TO 400 DEGREES

1. Cream butter and sugar until light and fluffy.
2. Add eggs and beat well.
3. Stir in buttermilk.
4. Combine flour, salt and soda. Add to cream mixture.
5. Stir in remainder of ingredients.
6. Chill overnight. Drop by teaspoonful on cookiesheet. Bake at 400 degrees for 8 to 10 minutes. Cool on wire rack.

   Makes 4 dozen.

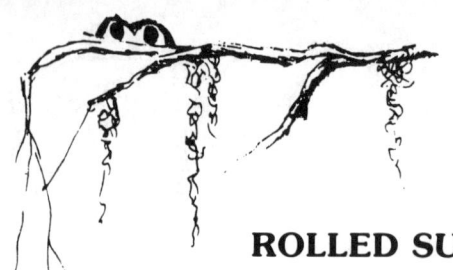

ROLLED SUGAR COOKIES

1½ cups powdered sugar (sifted)
1 cup margarine (soft)
1 large egg

1 teaspoon vanilla
½ teaspoon almond extract

Mix the above ingredients then add:

2½ cups flour (sifted)
1 teaspoon baking soda

1 teaspoon cream of tarter

PREHEAT OVEN TO 375 DEGREES

1. After the flour mixture has been added, divide in half and cover and refrigerate for 2 hours.
2. Roll each half in 3/16-inch thick on lightly dusted surface. Cut into shapes and sprinkle with granulated sugar.
3. Bake on lightly greased baking sheet for 7 to 8 minutes at 375 degrees in a preheated oven.

   Makes about 5 dozen cookies.

KATHY'S FANTASTIC BROWNIES

1 (14-ounce) package caramels
1 (14-ounce) can sweetened condensed milk
1 (18½-ounce) package german chocolate cake mix

¾ cup butter, melted
1 cup chopped pecans
1 (6-ounce) package semi-sweet chocolate chips

PREHEAT OVEN TO 350 DEGREES

Grease and flour 13 x 9 x 2-inch baking pan.

1. In top of double boiler, melt caramels and ⅓ cup of the sweetened condensed milk. Keep warm and set aside.
2. In large mixing bowl, combine cake mix, butter, remaining sweetened condensed milk and pecans.
3. Beat at high speed in mixer until very well combined.
4. Press half of dough into bottom of a greased and floured 13 x 9 x 2-inch baking pan.
5. Bake at 350 degrees for 6 minutes.
6. Sprinkle chocolate chips over partially baked dough.
7. Spread warm caramel mixture over chocolate chips.
8. Crumble remaining dough on top. Continue baking for 15 minutes or until sides pull away from pan. Do not overcook.

   Yield: 3 to 4 dozen.

PECAN PIE BARS

Crust:

3 cups flour
½ cup sugar
1 cup margarine
½ teaspoon salt

Filling:

4 eggs, slightly beaten
1½ cups Karo light or dark corn syrup
1½ cups sugar
3 tablespoons margarine, melted
1½ teaspoon vanilla
2½ cups chopped pecans

PREHEAT OVEN TO 350 DEGREES

Grease bottom and sides of 15 x 10 x 1-inch baking pan.

1. Prepare crust: In large bowl with mixer at medium speed beat flour, sugar, margarine and salt until mixture resembles coarse crumbs, press firmly and evenly into pan. Bake in 350 degree oven for 20 minutes. While crust is baking prepare filling.
2. In large bowl stir eggs, corn syrup, sugar, margarine and vanilla until blended, stir in pecans. Spread evenly over hot crust. Bake in 350 degree oven for 25 minutes or until set. Cool on wire rack.

   Makes 48 bars.

CHRISTMAS TREE COOKIES

1 cup shortening
¾ cup sugar
1 egg
2¼ cups sifted flour
⅛ teaspoon salt
¼ teaspoon baking powder
1 teaspoon almond extract
Green vegetable coloring

1. Cream shortening and add sugar gradually. Mix well. Add unbeaten egg, mix.
2. Add sifted dry ingredients, flavoring and a few drops of vegetable coloring into mixture *slowly*. Mix well.
3. Fill cookie press using tree plate. Press out dough onto cookie sheet. Decorate with tiny candies. Bake at 375 degrees for 10-12 minutes.

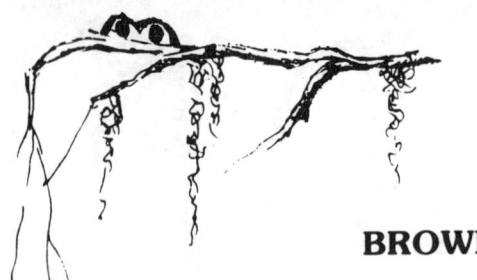

BROWNIES II

2 squares semi-sweet chocolate
8 tablespoons (1 stick) butter
2 eggs
1 cup sugar

1 teaspoon vanilla
½ cup sifted all-purpose flour
⅛ teaspoon salt
¾ cup chopped walnuts

1. Melt chocolate and butter in a small saucepan over low heat, cool.
2. Beat eggs in a small bowl with electric mixer, gradually beat in sugar until mixture is fluffy and thick.
3. Stir in chocolate mixture and vanilla. Fold in flour and salt until well blended, stir in walnuts.
4. Spread evenly in an 8 x 8 x 2-inch greased baking pan. Bake in moderate oven, 350 degrees, for 30 minutes, or until shiny and firm on top. Cool in pan on wire rack.
   Makes 16 brownies.

CHOCOLATE CHIP COOKIES

1 box yellow cake mix
2 tablespoons water
1 (6-ounce) package semi-sweet chocolate chips

½ cup chopped pecans (optional)
½ cup cooking oil
2 eggs

PREHEAT OVEN TO 350 DEGREES

1. Blend cake mix with cooking oil, water and eggs until thoroughly mixed and smooth using electric mixer.
2. Remove from electric mixer, stir in chocolate chips and pecans.
3. Drop by teaspoonful onto ungreased cookie sheet.
4. Bake at 350 degrees for 10 to 12 minutes. Top of cookies will look pale. Cool on cookie sheet for about 1 minute, then remove to rack to finish cooling.

CACOONS

2 sticks margarine
½ cup sugar
2 tablespoons vanilla
2½ cups flour

Powdered sugar
½ teaspoon salt
2 cups finely chopped pecans

PREHEAT OVEN TO 375 DEGREES

1. Cream shortening, sugar, and vanilla.
2. Add sifted flour and salt. Blend thoroughly. Add pecans.
3. Shape into 1-inch ovals. Bake at 375 degrees for 20 minutes or until light brown.
4. Roll in powdered sugar immediately or sugar will not stick. Cool.

CHRISTMAS JEWELS OR THUMB PRINT

1 cup butter
½ cup sugar
3 hard cooked egg yolks

1 teaspoon vanilla
2 cups sifted flour
Red Currant jelly (or your choice)

PREHEAT OVEN TO 375 DEGREES

1. Cream together butter and sugar until light and fluffy.
2. Break up egg yolks and beat into creamed mixture, blend well.
3. Add vanilla. Gradually stir in flour. Chill 1 hour.
4. Shape dough into 1 inch balls and place 1 inch apart on ungreased baking sheet.
5. Make a small dent in top of each cookie with thumb or finger.
6. Bake at 375 degrees for 10 minutes. Remove from oven and fill dents with jelly. Return to oven and bake for 1 or 2 more minutes to set jelly.

   Makes about 5 dozen.

MAGIC COOKIE BARS

1½ cups Kellogg's corn flake crumbs
½ cup melted margarine
1⅓ cups (3½-ounces) flaked coconut

1 cup coarsely chopped walnuts
3 tablespoons sugar
1 cup (6-ounces) semi-sweet chocolate morsels
1 can sweetened condensed milk

PREHEAT OVEN TO 350 DEGREES

1. Using the food processor with cutting blade, crumb the cornflakes. Measure corn flake crumbs, sugar and margarine into 13 x 9 x 2 inch baking pan, mix thoroughly. With back of tablespoon press mixture evenly and firmly in bottom of pan to form crust.
2. Scatter chocolate morsels over crust.
3. Spread coconut evenly over chocolate morsels.
4. Sprinkle walnuts over coconut.
5. Pour sweetened condensed milk evenly over walnuts.
6. Bake in oven at 350 degrees for 25 minutes. Cool and cut into 2 x 1-inch bars.

   Yields: 54

NELL'S CREME DE MENTHE SQUARES

1¼ cups butter or margarine
½ cup unsweetened cocoa powder
3½ cups sifted powdered sugar
1 beaten egg
1 teaspoon vanilla

2 cups graham cracker crumbs
¼ cup green creme de menthe
1½ cups semi-sweet chocolate pieces

For bottom layer:

In saucepan combine ½ cup of the butter or margarine and the cocoa powder. Heat and stir until well blended. Remove from heat, add ½ cup of the powdered sugar, the egg, and vanilla. Stir in graham cracker crumbs. Mix well. Press into the bottom of an ungreased 13 x 9 x 2-inch baking pan.

For middle layer:

Melt another ½ cup of the butter. In small mixer bowl combine melted butter and creme de menthe. At low speed of electric mixer beat in the remaining 3 cups powdered sugar until smooth. Spread over the chocolate layer. Chill 1 hour.

For top layer:

In small saucepan combine the remaining ¼ cup butter and chocolate pieces. Cook and stir over low heat until melted. Spread over mint layer. Chill 1 to 2 hours. Cut in small squares. Store in refrigerator. Seal each piece in clear plastic wrap for gifts.

Makes about 96 squares.

THE CAKE

Bottom Layer:

1 box yellow cake mix
1 stick soft butter

1 tablespoon water
1 egg

1. Mix the above well.
2. Batter will be very stiff.
3. Pat in bottom of 9 x 13-inch cake pan which has been slightly greased.

Second Layer:

8 ounces cream cheese, softened
3 eggs

1 teaspoon vanilla
1 box powdered sugar

1. Mix the soft cream cheese with one egg at a time.
2. Beat well after each egg.
3. Add the powdered sugar and vanilla.
4. Pour this over the cake batter and bake at 350 degrees for 45 minutes or until top is lightly browned.
5. Cool and slice in small squares.

NUT ROLL

2 cups milk, lukewarm
1 cup sugar
2 teaspoons salt

1. Mix together the above ingredients.
2. Crumble into mixture 2 cakes of yeast. Stir until yeast is dissolved.
3. Stir in:
    4 eggs
    1 cup shortening or margarine (or ½ cup of each)
    8 cups flour (not all at once), mix in small amount with spoon, then hands. Use enough flour to make dough easy to handle.
4. Knead dough until smooth and elastic.
5. Place dough in greased bowl, turning once to bring greased side up. Cover with damp cloth and let rise in warm place until double in size. (1½-2 hours).
6. Punch down, turn dough over. Let rise until almost double (30-45 minutes).
7. Divide dough into 6 portions. Let it rest covered for 10 minutes.
8. Roll each portion into rectangle — rather thin. Spread dough with butter, spread with nut mixture (little less than a cup).
9. Roll up tightly. Seal well by pinching edges of roll together. Cover and let rise 20 minutes.
10. Bake at 375 degrees for 30 minutes. Cover and let cool.

Nut Roll — Filling:

3 pounds ground walnuts
3 teaspoons vanilla
1¼ cups sugar
4 egg whites, stiffly beaten
3 tablespoons sweetened condensed milk

Mix well.

Spritz Tip

Keep a spray bottle filled with water and a little lemon juice in the refrigerator. Whenever you set out a tray of cut-up fresh fruits, spray the fruit with the lemon water to prevent discoloring.

SUPER CHOCOLATE CHIP COOKIE

½ cup (1 stick) butter or
  margarine, softened
⅓ cup firmly packed brown sugar
¼ cup white sugar
1 egg
1 teaspoon vanilla
½ cup chopped nuts (optional)
1⅓ cups unsifted, all-purpose flour
½ teaspoon baking soda
¼ teaspoon salt
1 package (6-ounce) semi-sweet
  chocolate morsels

PREHEAT OVEN TO 350 DEGREES

1. Grease a 13-inch round pizza style pan. In large bowl, measure butter and sugars. With a mixer at high speed, cream butter mixture until light and fluffy, occasionally scraping bowl with spatula.
2. Beat in egg until well blended. Beat in vanilla. Reduce speed to low and gradually beat in flour, baking soda, and salt until well mixed. With wooden spoon, fold in chocolate morsels and nuts.
3. With rubber spatula, spread dough to edge of pan. Be sure to uniformly distribute dough throughout pan, otherwise, some parts will be too chewy (undercooked), and others too dry and brittle (overcooked).
4. Bake 15 to 20 minutes or until golden brown. The cookie is done when it feels set and dry to the touch. Remove from oven and let cool in pan. After it is completely cooled, decorate using a decorating tube with a prepared chocolate icing. Edge cookie with a shell or zig-zag border. This makes a wonderful gift for birthdays or special occasions.

FAMOUS OATMEAL COOKIES

¾ cup shortening
1 cup firmly packed brown sugar
½ cup granulated sugar
¼ cup water
1 egg
1 teaspoon vanilla
3 cups oats, uncooked
1 cup all-purpose flour
1 teaspoon salt (optional)
½ teaspoon baking soda

PREHEAT OVEN TO 350 DEGREES

1. Beat together margarine, sugars, egg, water and vanilla until creamy.
2. Add combined remaining ingredients, mix well.
3. Drop by rounded teaspoonfuls onto greased cookie sheet.
4. Bake at 350 degrees from 12 to 15 minutes. For variety, add chopped nuts, raisins, chocolate chips or coconut.

   Makes about 5 dozen cookies.

You may substitute an egg white for the whole egg and reduce the cholesterol in this recipe to 0 mg. Cholesterol is only found in the egg yolk.

CHOCOLATE VALENTINE COOKIES

Cookie:

1 cup sugar
1 cup margarine or butter, softened
¼ cup milk
1 teaspoon vanilla
1 egg

2¾ cups Pillsbury's Best All-Purpose or Unbleached Flour
½ cup unsweetened cocoa
¾ teaspoon baking powder
¼ teaspoon baking soda

PREHEAT OVEN TO 350 DEGREES

1. In large bowl, beat sugar and 1 cup margarine until light and fluffy.
2. Add milk, vanilla and egg; blend well.
3. Lightly spoon flour into measuring cup; level off.
4. Stir in flour, cocoa, baking powder and soda. Chill dough 1 hour for easier handling.

1. Heat oven to 350 degrees. On floured surface, roll out dough, ⅓ at a time, to ⅛-inch thickness.
2. Cut with floured 2½-inch heart-shaped cookie cutter.
3. Place half of the cutout hearts 1-inch apart on ungreased cookie sheets.
4. Cut a 1-inch heart-shape from the centers of remaining hearts. Place cutout hearts on cookie sheets. Chill excess dough and reroll. Bake at 350 degrees for 9 to 11 minutes or until set. Immediately remove from cookie sheets; cool.

Frosting:

2 cups powdered sugar
½ cup margarine or butter, softened

2 to 3 tablespoons maraschino cherry juice or milk
Red food color
Powdered sugar, if desired

1. In small bowl, beat frosting ingredients adding 1 tablespoon cherry juice at a time for desired spreading consistency. Tint with red food color. Frost bottom side of whole cookie. Top with cutout cookie. Dust with powdered sugar. Makes 4 dozen sandwich cookies.

PEANUT BLOSSOMS

½ cup shortening
¾ cup peanut butter
⅓ cup sugar
⅓ cup packed brown sugar
1 egg
2 tablespoons milk
1 teaspoon vanilla

1½ cups unsifted all-purpose flour
1 teaspoon baking soda
½ teaspoon salt
Granulated sugar
9-ounce package Hershey's kisses (48)

PREHEAT OVEN TO 375 DEGREES

1. Cream shortening and peanut butter; add sugar and brown sugar.
2. Add egg, milk, and vanilla; beat well.
3. Combine flour, baking soda and salt in another bowl.
4. Gradually add flour mixture to creamed mixture, blending thoroughly.
5. Shape dough into 1-inch balls; roll in granulated sugar.
6. Place on ungreased cookie sheet. Bake at 375 degrees for 10 to 12 minutes.
7. Remove from oven; immediately place unwrapped kiss on top of each cookie, pressing down so that cookie cracks around the edge. Remove from cookie sheet; cool.

  Makes about 4 dozen cookies.

HEATH BARS

2 cups light brown sugar
2 cups all-purpose flour
½ cup margarine, melted
1 egg
1 teaspoon salt
1 teaspoon soda

1 teaspoon vanilla
1 cup milk
6 Heath candy bars (1.4-ounces each or smaller if desired), crushed
½ cup chopped pecans

1. Mix the sugar, flour and melted margarine together. Remove 1 cup of the sugar and flour mixture, set aside to reserve for the topping.
2. In separate bowl beat egg, add the salt, soda, vanilla and milk.
3. Add the brown sugar mixture and mix well.
4. Pour batter into a lightly greased 9 x 13-inch pan.
5. Crush candy bars and mix them with the remaining 1 cup of sugar and flour mixture. Add the chopped nuts. Sprinkle over the batter.
6. Bake in 350-degree oven for 30 to 35 minutes.

Preserves and Relishes

PEACH DAIQUIRI JAM

3 pounds fully ripe peaches, peeled and finely chopped
1 package Sure Jell
5 cups sugar
¼ cup light rum

1. Combine peaches and Sure Jell in very large saucepan. Place over high heat and bring to full rolling boil for one minute, stirring constantly.
2. Add sugar and stir. Bring to rolling boil again and boil two minutes, stirring constantly.
3. Remove from heat, add rum. Skim off film with metal spoon for 5 minutes to keep fruit from floating.
4. Pour into hot, scalded jars. Seal.

Yields: 6½ pints.

PEPPER JELLY

¾ cups ground or blended bell peppers (finely ground)
¼ cup ground or blended hot peppers
6½ cups sugar
1½ cups apple cider vinegar
1 bottle of certo
Parafin

1. Combine blended peppers, sugar and vinegar in large boiler.
2. Bring to a full rolling boil, stirring often. Let stand 10 minutes.
3. Stir in a bottle of certo. Let stand another 10 minutes.
4. Pour into sterile jars. Cover with melted parafin. Seal.

Makes 7 or 8 jelly glasses.

JEZEBEL SAUCE

(Good over pork, beef, cream cheese)

1 (10-ounce) jar pineapple preserves
1 (10-ounce) jar apple jelly
1 (6-ounce) size prepared horseradish
½ of a (1.12-ounce) box of dry mustard
1 teaspoon black pepper

1. Melt jelly and preserves over low heat.
2. Add other ingredients and refrigerate.

DILLYBEANS

2 pounds tender "stringless" beans
2 cups water
2 cups white distilled vinegar
1½ teaspoons pickling salt, or to taste
⅓ cup sugar
2 bay leaves
2 small onions, peeled and thinly sliced
8 hot red peppers
8 cloves garlic, peeled
8 sprigs fresh dill

1. Wash beans and snip off ends. Discard any that are wilted or discolored.
2. In a saucepan combine water, vinegar, pickling salt, sugar, bay leaves, and onions. Bring liquid to a boil and simmer for 10 minutes.
3. Drop beans into boiling water and cook for just 5 minutes. They must still be crisp. Drain immediately and rinse in cold water.
4. Pack beans upright in 8-ounce jars with a couple of slices of onion. Add 1 hot pepper, 1 clove garlic, and a sprig of dill to each jar and pour the hot vinegar mixture over the beans to overflowing. Seal immediately.

Makes 8 (8-ounce) jars or 4 pints.

Note: Thinly cut carrots and other firm vegetables may be used in place of or in addition to the beans.

AUNT EDNA'S PICKLED SQUASH

8 cups cubed squash
2 cups thin slices of squash
2 cups thin slices of green pepper rings
1 large onion (cut in rings)
1 jar pimento red pepper
Hot pepper to taste

For syrup:

3 cups sugar
2 cups vinegar
2 tablespoons mustard seed
2 tablespoons celery seed

1. Soak squash in 3 quarts of water with ⅔ cup of salt for 1 hour; drain.
2. Mix sugar, vinegar, mustard seeds and celery seeds in a large pot making syrup mixture.
3. Boil syrup and add vegetables. Let come to a good boil.
4. Fill jars and seal.

BREAD AND BUTTER PICKLES

7# cucumbers, thin sliced — Soak in 2 gallons of water with 1 cup of pickling lime in crockery or enamel ware for 24 hours. Rinse in cold water 3 times. Drain well. Pack in ice and water for 3 hours.

Drain — Use a mixture of 2 quarts of vinegar, 4 pounds sugar (9 cups), 1 tablespoon salt. Soak overnight in mixture; add 2 teaspoons of pickling spices to taste and boil 35 minutes. Pack in jars and seal.

Makes 12 pints.

SQUASH PICKLES

8 cups sliced squash (about 2¼-pounds)
2 large onions, sliced (about 1¼-pounds)
4 cups chopped green pepper
2 cups sliced cauliflower
1¼ cups sliced carrots
1½ cups sliced celery
1 (2-ounce) jar sliced pimento, drained
½ cup salt
4½ cups sugar
3 cups white vinegar (5% acidity)
3 tablespoons pickling salt
1 tablespoon celery seeds
1 tablespoon mustard seeds
1½ teaspoons ground turmeric

1. Combine first 7 ingredients in a large glass bowl, sprinkle with ½ cup salt. Cover and let stand about 2 hours.
2. Drain and rinse in cold water. Drain well.
3. Pack vegetables in hot pint jars, leaving ½-inch headspace.
4. Combine sugar and remaining ingredients in a saucepan, stirring well.
5. Bring mixture to a boil, and cook 1 minute.
6. Pour hot vinegar mixture over vegetables, leaving ½-inch headspace. Wipe jar rims.
7. Cover at once with metal lids, and screw on bands.
8. Process in boiling water bath 15 minutes.

Yield: 5 pints.

DILL PICKLES

Wash cucumbers and pack in jar.
To each quart add:

1 tablespoon celery seed
1 tablespoon mustard seed
1 tablespoon dill
1 pod red pepper
1 clove garlic

In a large pot, add 5 cups water, 2 cups vinegar, and ½ cup salt. Bring to a rolling boil, pour over cucumbers and add pinch of alum. Seal and turn bottom side up over night.

FIG STRAWBERRY JAM

6 cups peeled and crushed figs
2 packages (6-ounces each) strawberry jello

6 cups sugar

1. Combine figs and sugar in a large saucepan. Bring to a full boil. Add two 6-ounce packages strawberry jello.
2. Bring to a boil. Cook on medium heat for 24 minutes, stirring constantly. Remove from heat.
3. Skim off any foam.
4. Fill sterile jar quickly to ⅛-inch of top.
5. Wipe jar rim. Cover quickly with flat lid. Screw band on tightly.

Makes 4½ pints.

PICKLED OKRA

2 pounds tender okra
5 pods hot red or green pepper
5 cloves garlic, peeled
1 quart white vinegar

½ cup water
8 tablespoons salt
1 tablespoon celery seed or mustard seed (optional)

1. Wash okra and pack in 5 pints hot, sterilized jars, with 1 pepper pod and 1 garlic clove per jar. Pack okra alternately, top to bottom.
2. Bring remaining ingredients to a boil. Pour over okra and seal. Let stand several weeks before using.
3. Chill for crispness.

HENNIGAN'S TOMATO SAUCE

18 average tomatoes, peeled and chopped
4 bell peppers, chopped
2 hot peppers, chopped
6 large onions, chopped

3 tablespoons salt
2 cups vinegar
1 teaspoon celery seed
10 tablespoons dark Karo Syrup
1 cup sugar

1. Combine all of the ingredients.
2. Cook 3-4 hours or until thick.
3. Seal in sterile jars.

Makes 6 pints.

PINEAPPLE FIG CONSERVE

2 pounds ripe figs
1 cup crushed pineapple
2 medium lemons, cut in small pieces
½ teaspoon salt
1 cup chopped pecans
Sugar

1. Wash figs and cut in pieces. Mix with pineapple and lemons and put into a boiler with an equal amount of sugar and the ½ teaspoon salt.
2. Bring slowly to boiling point and simmer gently until thickened, but still a little runny. Stir in nuts; put in hot jars.

CRANBERRY RELISH

3 peeled oranges
3 cups sugar
1 pound fresh cranberries
1 small can of crushed pineapple with juice

1. Grind all the above ingredients together using food processor.
2. Place in refrigerator.

DOUBLE BATCH PEACH JAM

8 cups prepared fruit (about 6 pounds fully ripe peaches)
¼ cup fresh lemon juice
2 teaspoons Ever-Fresh Fruit Protector (optional)
11 cups sugar
2 boxes Sure • Jell Fruit Pectin
1 teaspoon margarine or butter

1. Peel, pit and finely chop peaches. Measure 8 cups into 8-quart saucepot. Stir in lemon juice and fruit protector.
2. Measure sugar into separate bowl. (Scrape excess sugar from cup with spatula to level for exact measure.) Stir fruit pectin into fruit in saucepot. Add margarine. Bring to full rolling boil on high heat, stirring constantly. Quickly stir in all sugar. Return to full rolling boil and boil exactly 1 minute, stirring constantly. Remove from heat. Skim off any foam with metal spoon.
3. Ladle quickly into hot sterilized jars, filling to within ⅛-inch of tops. Wipe jar rims and threads. Cover with two-piece lids. Screw bands tightly. *Invert jars 5 minutes, then turn upright. After jars are cool, check seals.

   Makes about 14 cups or about 14 (1-cup) jars or 7 (1-pint) jars.

   Serving Ideas: This makes a summery gift for friends and relatives. Try as a sunny topping for pancakes or waffles.

Children's Corner

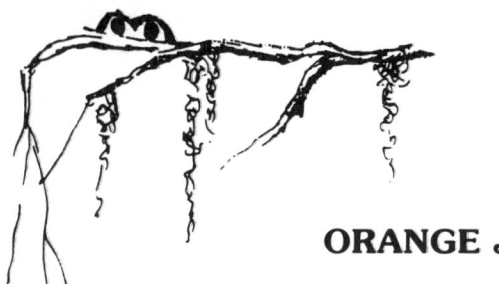

ORANGE JULIUS

½ can (6-ounce) frozen orange juice
½ cup milk
½ teaspoon vanilla
½ cup water
¼ cup sugar

1. Mix all of the above ingredients in blender.
2. Add 8-10 ice cubes. Blend.
3. Serve.

STRAWBERRY-ORANGE FROST

1 cup fresh or frozen strawberries
1 cup orange juice
2 tablespoons sugar
1 cup cracked ice

1. Blend all ingredients in an electric blender for 1 to 1½ minutes or until smooth.

   Serves 3 to 4.

   Especially for Jennifer and Allyson.

TOAD IN HOLE

1 egg
1 slice bread
3 tablespoons butter

1. Cut a circle out of center of bread slice. Fry bread in butter until brown and crisp on one side. Turn over and break egg into circle. Fry over low heat for 5 minutes.

EGGS FILLET

4 to 6 strips bacon
4 to 6 eggs
Salt
Pepper

1. Broil bacon slightly (3 minutes on each side) remove.
2. Line cups in a muffin tin with bacon strips.
3. Break eggs separately into cups and pour into center of bacon strips.
4. Sprinkle each "fillet" with salt and pepper.
5. Bake at 375 degrees for 12-15 minutes. Serve hot.

   Featherweight Coffee Cake and Eggs Fillet makes a delightful oven meal for a slumber party.

FEATHERWEIGHT COFFEE CAKE

¼ cup shortening or butter
1 egg, slightly beaten
½ cup milk
1 cup all-purpose flour, sifted

½ teaspoon salt
¼ cup sugar
3 teaspoons baking powder

Topping:

3 tablespoons sugar

1 teaspoon cinnamon

PREHEAT OVEN TO 375 DEGREES

1. Melt shortening on low heat, cool sightly.
2. Mix with egg and milk.
3. Sift dry ingredients together into a bowl.
4. Pour the liquid mixture into dry ingredients and stir only long enough to smooth out the lumps.
5. Pour batter into greased 8-inch square cake pan.
6. Combine 3 tablespoons sugar and cinnamon. Sprinkle this mixture over the unbaked cake. Bake at 375 degrees for 12-15 minutes.

Featherweight Coffee Cake and Eggs Fillet makes a delightful oven meal for a slumber party.

TUNA BURGERS

½ cup corn flake crumbs (1½ cups flakes)
1 (7-ounce) can flaked tuna
1 tablespoon finely chopped onion (optional)
1 tablespoon chopped dill pickles

2 tablespoons finely chopped celery
¼ teaspoon salt
4 or 5 buns, split and buttered
4 or 5 slices processed American cheese
½ cup mayonnaise

1. Combine cornflakes crumbs and tuna. (Rinse tuna in cold water to remove fishy taste.)
2. Add mayonnaise, onion, pickle, celery, salt and pepper. Mix lightly.
3. Shape into 4 or 5 patties, size of the buns.
4. Place each patty on bottom half of a bun and place on broiler rack. Place pan in oven so patties are 4 to 5-inches from broiler rack.
5. Broil until golden brown, about 5 minutes.
6. Top each patty with a slice of cheese.
7. Place top half of bun on broiler pan, broil until cheese melts and buns brown. (1 or 2 minutes). Remove from broiler. Serve hot.

CARAMEL APPLES

4 large red delicious apples, washed and dry
1 pound caramel candies
1 pound chopped pecans
1 pound chocolate candy wafers
4 sucker sticks
1 teaspoon water
1 tablespoon Paramount Crystals

1. Wash and dry apples, insert sucker sticks into stem end of each apple.
2. Combine Caramels and water and melt in double boiler over hot water. Place apple over caramel and spoon caramel on to apple until coated.
3. Roast pecans in over at 325 degrees for 15 minutes. Roll each apple in pecans, pressing down on apple.
4. Melt chocolate in double boiler. Add 1 tablespoon of Crystal and stir.
5. Place each apple in the bowl of chocolate and use spoon to cover entire apple. Cool and wrap.

FINGER PAINTS

NOT FOR EATING

Prepare inexpensive finger paints for children. To make "paint", mix ½ cup cornstarch with ¾ cup cold water in a medium-sized saucepan. In the meantime, soak 1 envelope of unflavored gelatin in ¼ cup cold water. Stir 2 cups of hot water into the starch mixture and cook over medium heat until it comes to a boil and is smooth. Remove from heat and blend in softened gelatin. Add ½ cup detergent (powder) or soap flakes and stir until dissolved. This makes about 3 cups. Divide into portions — in jars or bowls.

A powdered dye or food coloring may be used for color. Add 1 teaspoon of dye for each cup of mixture or a few drops of food coloring for the desired shade. For white, add white tempra paint powder.

PLAYDOUGH

NOT FOR EATING

2 cups flour
2 cups boiling water
1 cup salt
4 teaspoons cream of tartar
2 tablespoons Wesson oil.

1. Oil sides and bottom of a saucepan.
2. Mix dry ingredients.
3. Add oil and water.
4. Cook 3 minutes or until mixture an be worked into a ball. Work with hands. Food coloring or powdered dye may be used for coloring.
5. Place in Zip-loc bag.

NUTTY PUTTY

NOT FOR EATING

1 tablespoon liquid starch
2 tablespoons white glue
3 drops food coloring (optional)

Plastic egg or a screw top jar
Bowl

1. Put starch in bowl.
2. Add glue and let set 5 minutes.
3. If desired, add coloring.
4. Mix until starch is absorbed and color is spread smoothly. (HINT: The longer you mix, the better it gets.)
5. Store in plastic egg or small jar overnight before using to pick up pictures from comics.
6. Use to bounce, pick up pictures from comics or newspaper, and mold into shapes.

Hints:
1. If left in open air, it will melt, then turn hard.
2. Add 1 teaspoon more starch for a tougher, more rubbery, putty.
3. Last several days if stored airtight.
4. If putty dries out or gets tough, just dip into warm water and knead.

CARAMEL MORSEL BARS

49 (14-ounce) bag Kraft caramels
3 tablespoons water
5 cups crisp rice cereal or toasted oat cereal
1 cup peanuts

1 (6-ounce) package (1 cup) Nestle Semi-Sweet Real Chocolate Morsels
1 (6-ounce) package (1 cup) Nestle Butterscotch Flavored Morsels

1. Melt caramels with water in saucepan over low heat. Stir frequently until sauce is smooth. Pour over cereal and nuts; toss until well coated.
2. With greased fingers, press mixture into greased 13 x 9-inch baking pan.
3. Sprinkle morsels on top; place in 200 degree oven for 5 minutes, or until morsels soften. Spread softened morsels until blended to form a frosting. Cool; cut into bars.

JACK-O-'LANTERN TREATS

¼ cup margarine or butter
1 package (10-ounce about 40) regular marshmallows or 4 cups of miniature marshmallows
5 cups Kellogg's Marshmallow Krispies cereal

1. Melt margarine in large saucepan over low heat. Add marshmallows and stir until completely melted. Cook over low heat 3 minutes longer, stirring constantly.
   Remove from heat.
2. Add Marshmallow Krispies cereal. Stir until well coated.
3. To make five Jack-O'-Lanterns, divide cereal mixture into five equal parts. Form pumkin-shaped balls and stems. Decorate with frosting and Halloween candies.

   Yield: 5 Jack-O'-Lantern Treats.

Note: Best results are obtained when using fresh marshmallows.

BUNNY CAKE

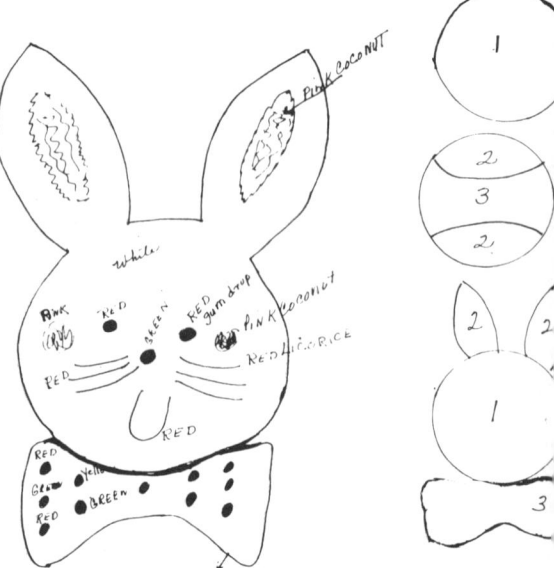

INSTRUCTIONS

1. Start with 2 (9-inch) layers.
2. Cut according to diagram.
3. Arrange bunny on a tray.
4. Top with white frosting.
5. Sprinkle lavishly with coconut.
6. Tint a small amount of coconut pink for his ears by adding a few drops of red food coloring diluted in water.
7. Decorate with gumdrops and licorice for mouth and whiskers.

HEARTTHROB COOKIE DOUGH
(Valentine Cookie)

2 cups all-purpose flour
½ teaspoon baking powder
⅛ teaspoon salt
1 cup sugar

1 cup shortening
1 egg
1 teaspoon vanilla
¼ teaspoon peppermint extract

1. Stir together flour, baking powder, and salt; set aside.
2. Beat sugar and shortening with an electric mixer till fluffy.
3. Add remaining ingredients; beat well. Add flour mixture; beat well.
4. Tint and shape as directed for each cookie variation.

Baking Directions:

Place cookies on ungreased cookie sheet. Bake in a 375 degree oven 8 to 10 minutes or till golden.

Remove: Cool on a wire rack.

Inside-Out Cookies

Divide 1 dough recipe in half. To ½, mix in 10 drops red food coloring. On a lightly floured surface, roll dough, one color at a time, ¼-inch thick. Cut with different-size heart-shape cookie cutters. Using a smaller cookie cutter, cut hearts from the center of each cookie. Remove smaller hearts and interchange them so that the cookies have a contrasting colored heart in the center. Reroll dough scraps and repeat. Bake as directed. Makes about 30 (2 to 3-inch) cookies. Reserve scraps for Bleeding Heart Cookies.

   Makes 30.

Bleeding Heart Cookies:

So simple — just use the dough scraps.

Mix dough scraps lightly with your hands so dough looks marbled. On a lightly floured surface, roll dough ¼-inch thick. Cut with 2-inch heart-shaped cutter. Bake as directed.

Makes 12.

BIG BIG CINNAMON ROLLS

3 (1-pound each) loaves frozen bread dough, white or honey wheat
¼ cup melted margarine
½ cup granulated sugar
½ cup brown sugar
1 teaspoon cinnamon
½ cup walnuts (optional)
½ cup raisins (optional)
Glaze (recipe follows)

1. Let frozen bread dough thaw and rise until double.
2. Punch down dough and pat loaves together.
3. Roll out dough to a (16 x 10-inch) rectangle. The dough should be ½ to ¾-inch thick.
4. Spread top of dough with all but 2 tablespoons of melted butter.
5. Sprinkle sugars, cinnamon, nuts and raisins evenly over dough. With back of spoon, gently pat sugars into dough. With long side of dough, roll up jelly-roll fashion, pulling the dough towards you as you roll up.
6. Cut into 9 even slices. The rolls will be large.
7. Place slices into a (13 x 9-inch) greased cake pan. They should be touching on all sides.
8. Let rise until rolls are puffy and fill the entire pan (approximately 30 to 60 minutes in a warm area).
9. Bake at 375 degrees for 35 to 45 minutes. Rolls should be golden brown and make a hollow sound when gently tapped on top. Remove pan from oven.
10. Brush rolls with remaining melted butter. Let rolls cool in pan. Drizzle with glaze.

Glaze:

1 cup confectioner's (powdered) sugar
1 teaspoon vanilla
1 tablespoon milk

1. Mix together until smooth and thin enough to drizzle over rolls.

CHOCOLATE-COVERED BANANA POPS

3 ripe, large bananas
9 wooden ice cream sticks or skewers
2 cups (12-ounce package) semi-sweet chocolate chips
2 tablespoons shortening
1½ cups coarsely chopped unsalted roasted peanuts

1. Peel bananas; cut each into thirds. Insert wooden stick into each banana piece; place on wax paper-covered tray. Cover; freeze until firm.
2. In top of double boiler over hot, not boiling, water melt chocolate chips and shortening.
3. Remove bananas from freezer just before dipping. Dip each piece into warm chocolate, covering completely; allow excess to drip off. Immediately roll in peanuts.
4. Cover, return to freezer. Serve frozen.

Makes 9 pops.

Party Ideas

LUAU CENTER PIECE

Supplies:

2 cucumbers
2 bell peppers
1 pineapple
2 florist's frogs
Slices of cantaloupe
    or peach

Purple grapes
Boston fern
Long toothpicks
Flowers

Pineapple Hut:

1. Cut the top leaves off pineapple, leaving attractive lower leaves. Place longer leaves across top of pineapple and secure with T pins.
2. Cut a door in pineapple hut and pull open, leaving one side attached.
3. Slice a piece off the bottom so the pineapple will set flat.
4. Using a large tray, line with fern. Follow directions for making cucumber palm trees and arrange on tray with hut.
5. Garnish with a slice of cantaloupe for boat with two toothpicks. Cover the top of the hut with flowers.
6. Hang purple grapes from palm trees to resemble coconuts.

SOMBRERO SALAD

1 medium pineapple, cut in wedges; reserve top
½ small watermelon
1 cantaloupe
½ honeydew melon
Coconut bananas (see separate recipe)
1 to 2 pints strawberries
Mint sprigs
Green and purple grapes

1. Place sombrero on a platter. Secure the top of the pineapple into the peak of the sombrero with skewers or turkey lacers.
2. Line the brim of a sombrero with plastic wrap. Cut watermelon, cantaloupe, and honeydew melon into serving-size pieces.
3. Place fruit attractively around the sombrero's base.
4. Garnish with sprigs of mint. Using toothpicks, hang small clusters of grapes around crown of sombrero. Cover brim of sombrero with damp paper towels and plastic wrap. Refrigerate until served. Serve with fruit dressing if desired.

GUACAMOLE SPREAD

Mexico's delicious contribution to the world of salads.

2 large avocados, pitted and peeled	½ (4-ounce) can chopped green chilies (about ⅓ cup)
2 tablespoons dairy sour cream	Tabasco sauce to taste
⅛ teaspoon garlic powder	½ small onion, chopped
¼ teaspoon salt	1 small tomato, chopped
1 teaspoon lemon or lime juice	

1. In a medium bowl or food processor fitted with the metal blade, mash avocado.
2. Add sour cream, garlic powder, salt, lemon or lime juice, green chilies and Tabasco sauce.
3. Stir in onion and tomato; mix well.
4. If not serving immediately, place a piece of plastic wrap against the surface of the guacamole to prevent it from turning dark. May be refrigerated up to 2 days or frozen.

   Makes about 2 cups.

FIESTA DIP

Assemble this colorful platter just before serving.

3 recipes Guacamole spread	2 (4-ounce) cans chopped ripe olives, drained
2 cups shredded Cheddar cheese (8-ounce)	Jalapeño peppers, if desired
1½ cups shredded Monterey Jack cheese (6-ounce)	Taco chips
3 medium tomatoes, chopped	Parsley sprigs, if desired

1. As close to serving time as possible, spread Guacamole Spread on 16-inch round platter. Place Cheddar cheese, Monterey Jack cheese, tomatoes and olives in pie-shaped wedges or in 1-inch concentric circles on guacamole.
2. Garnish with parsley sprigs and jalapeño peppers, if desired. Serve with taco chips.

   Makes 16 servings.

GARNISHES

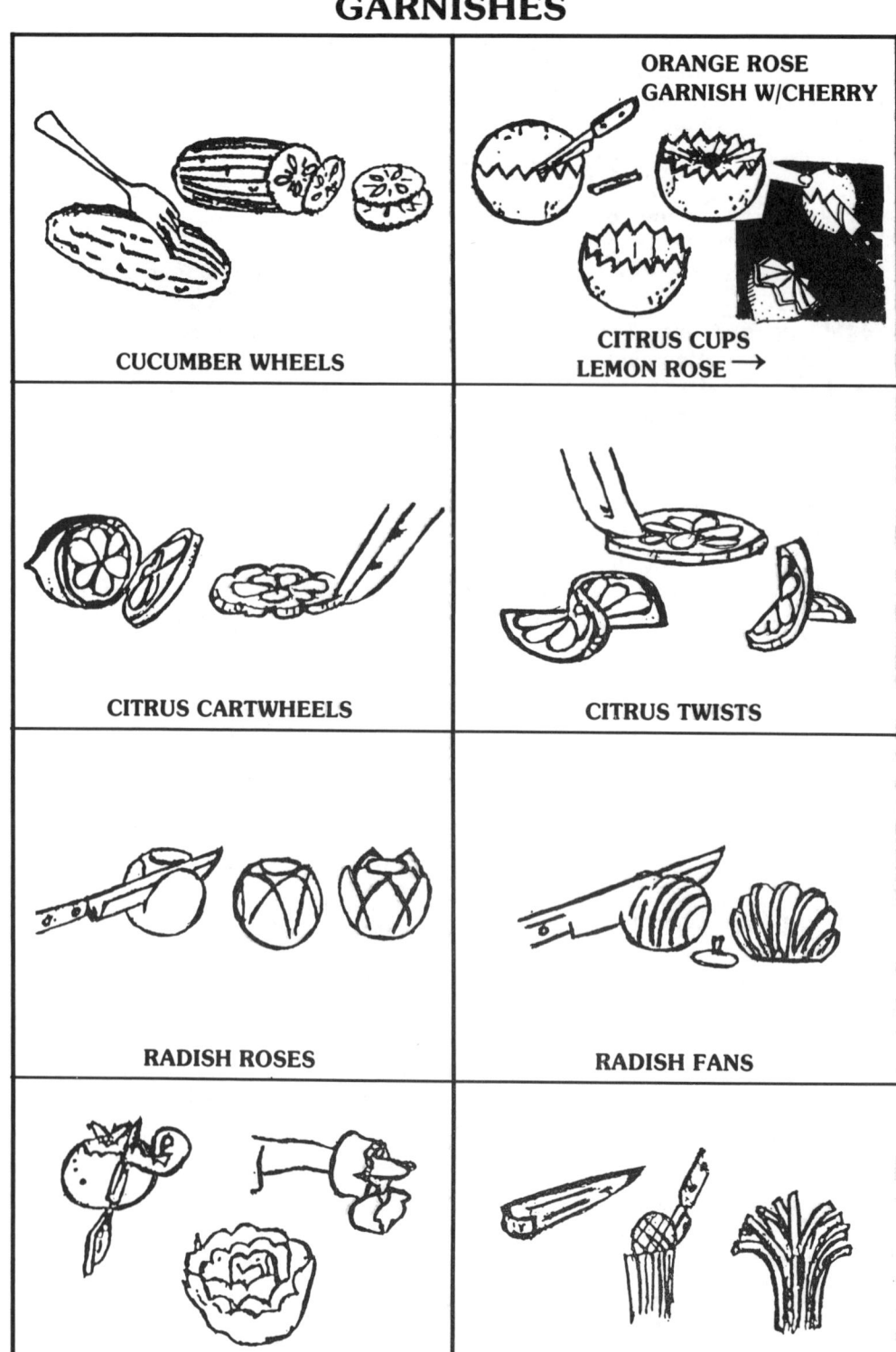

CUCUMBER PALM TREES

2 cucumbers
2 green bell peppers
2 florist's frogs
Purple grapes, if desired

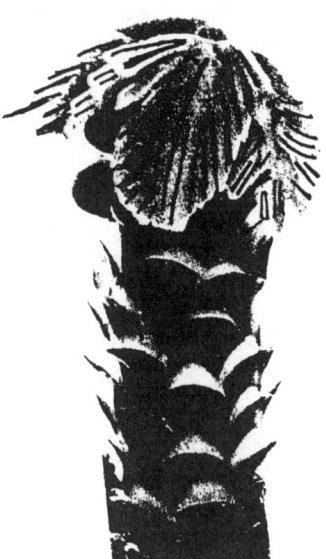

Trunk of Palm Trees:

1. Use a sharp paring knife to cut small gashes diagonally into the skin of 2 cucumbers to resemble bark.
2. Make the cuts very thin and at least ½-inch long. Cut both ends off the cucumbers to make flat surfaces.
3. Place the cucumbers in ice water in the refrigerator for two or three days to allow the cuts to open.

Leaves for the Palm Trees:

1. To begin, remove the bottoms of 2 green peppers. Remove cores and seeds by cutting up into the peppers from the bottom, leaving the tops intact.
2. Cut sections to resemble leaves, leaving them connected at the top.
3. Make diagonal cuts along each side of the leaves but do not cut through the center of the leaves.
4. Place the peppers in ice water in the refrigerator for two or three days to allow leaves to open.

Make the parts for this centerpiece two or three days ahead and store them in ice water to give the vegetables time to open. Be sure to have two florist's frogs on hand so the cucumber trees will stand steady.

CHOCOLATE DIPPED STRAWBERRIES

2 pints strawberries
6 ounce semi-sweet chocolate morsels
1 tablespoon shortening

1. Rinse berries and dry on paper towels. (Chocolate will not stick to wet berries). Set aside.
2. Place chocolate plus 1 tablespoon shortening in saucepan. Melt or microwave.
3. Hold berries by stem and dip into chocolate. Place on wax paper.

FOOTBALL PARTY DIP

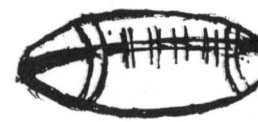

4 (8-ounce) packages cream cheese
2 packages Hidden Valley Ranch Original Ranch Party Dip
1¾ cups diced red bell pepper
2 cans (2¼-ounce) diced black olives, drained
1 (4-ounce) can diced green chilies drained, pat dried with paper towels

1. Blend 4 cream cheese packages (8-ounce each) and 2 packages of Hidden Valley Ranch Original Ranch Party Dip.
2. Stir in 1¾ cups diced red bell peppers. Drain and dry 2 cans (2¼-ounce dry wt. each) diced black olives and 1 can (4-ounce) diced green chilies. Add to mixture. Chill one hour.
3. Using a spatula, form a football shape on a platter. Chill 4 hours or overnight. Decorate football using vegetable slices and cheese strips. Serve with assorted breads, crackers and vegetables.

   * *Variation:* delete olives, bell pepper and chilies. Roll in a jar of McCormick Seasoned Pepper. Decorate football.

CHOCOLATE LEAVES

24 non-poisonous leaves such as camellia or rose leaves
4 ounces semi-sweet chocolate

1. Wash and dry the leaves. Line a baking sheet with wax paper.
2. Melt the chocolate in the top of a double boiler over hot water. Spread the melted chocolate over the underside of the leaves. Place the leaves chocolate-side up on the lined baking sheet.
3. Refrigerate them until the chocolate is firm. The chocolate-covered leaves may be frozen.
4. To remove the leaf from the chocolate, hold the leaf's stem and pull gently. The chocolate and the leaf will separate. Discard the leaves and use the chocolate leaves to garnish desserts.

WATERMELON WHALE

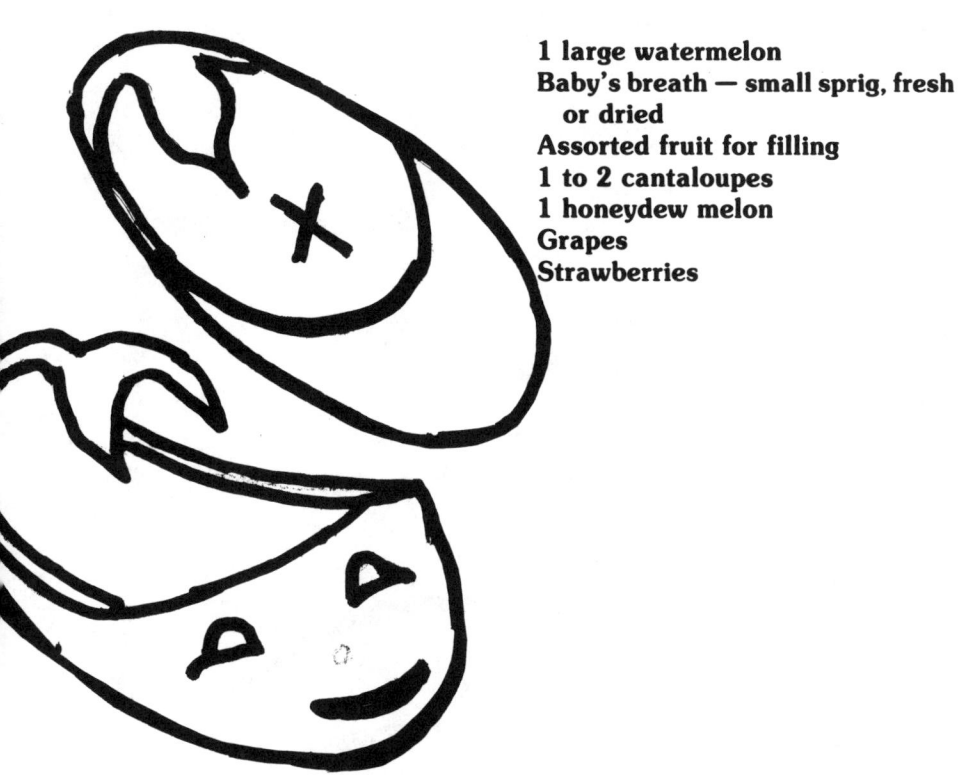

1 large watermelon
Baby's breath — small sprig, fresh or dried
Assorted fruit for filling
1 to 2 cantaloupes
1 honeydew melon
Grapes
Strawberries

1. To carve the melon use the stem end as the nose.
2. Place the tail pattern on the facing page on the melon and use a sharp pointed pencil to trace the opening of the shell. Measure the depth of each side and mark before cutting so they will be even. Using a knife with a sharp, thin blade cut an X in the top of the melon to relieve pressure then cut along the outline aiming the knife tip toward the center of the melon.
3. Cut away the unwanted shell in pieces. Scoop out watermelon fruit leaving shell about 1-inch thick. Reserve watermelon and add to other fruit to fill whale.
4. To complete whale, use eye and mouth pattern to trace for face on stem (nose) end. Cut eyes completely through shell. Cut mouth only halfway through shell so juices won't run out. Whale covered in plastic will keep for several days in the refrigerator.
5. To serve make small hole in forehead and insert flowers to resemble spouting water. Fill with assorted fruits that have been cut into bite size pieces.
6. Place on large tray and bank with leaves, flowers, mint, etc.

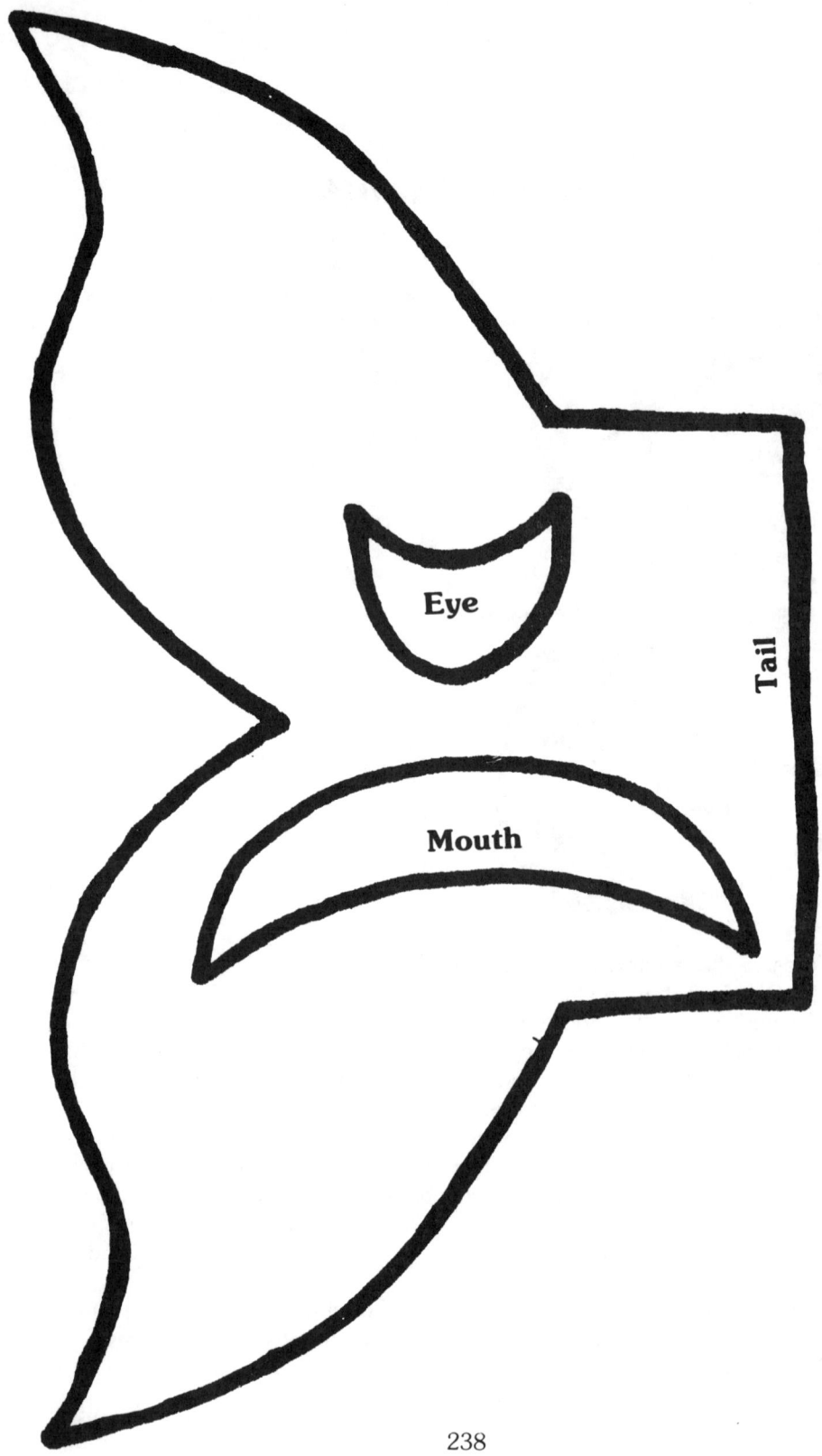

FROSTED GRAPES

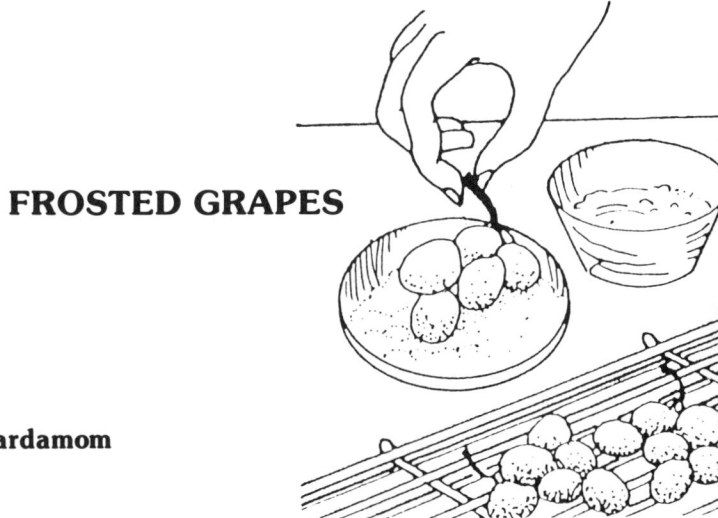

FROSTED GRAPES...

1 egg white
½ cup sugar
1 teaspoon cinnamon
½ teaspoon ground cardamom
1 pound grapes

1. In a small bowl, beat the egg white until it's frothy.
2. In another small bowl, mix the sugar, cinnamon and cardamom.
3. Cut the bunches of grapes into small clusters. Dip grapes into the egg white.
4. Shake off the excess egg white and roll the grapes in the sugar mixture until they are coated. Refrigerate them on a rack until the coating is set or overnight.

Grapes are an elegant garnish for a fruit or dessert platter.

ICE RING

6 cups water
5 or 6 large green garden leaves such as lemon leaves (not holly)
2 lemons, cut in half
1 (1-pound 1-ounce) can cling peach halves, drained
4 strawberries
2 candied cherries, halved

1. Fill a 6 cup ring mold half full of water. Freeze until solid.
2. Remove from freezer, place leaves shinyside up on top of ice. Cut a slice from bottom of lemon halves, so they sit flat. Alternate peach and lemon halves on leaves; tops of fruit should be even and slightly below top of mold. Place a strawberry on each peach half and a cherry half on each lemon half.
3. Carefully pour a small amount of water around fruit and leaves. Return to freezer until frozen.
4. Add more water to fill mold to the top, if necessary. Freeze mold overnight or for several weeks.
5. The day before serving, unmold ice ring by dipping bottom of mold in cold water; turn out on heavy foil. Wrap ring securely in foil; return to freezer. To serve, unwrap and float ice ring fruit-side up in punch bowl.

Makes 1 ice ring.

CHOCOLATE-ALMOND COFFEE SPOONS

4 ounces imported chocolate
⅛ teaspoon almond extract

Plastic or metal spoons
Plastic wrap and ribbon

1. Break chocolate into pieces and place in a 1-cup measure.
2. Microwave (medium-50 percent) 2½ to 3½ minutes or until melted, stirring twice. Stir in almond extract. Dip spoons into chocolate, tapping excess. Place on waxed paper. Set in cool place until set.
3. When chocolate is firm, place a small piece of plastic wrap over chocolate-coated spoon. Secure plastic with a ribbon. Use chocolate-coated spoons to stir hot beverages.

   Makes 32 coated spoons.

Notes: Use only imported chocolate not chocolate coatings which contain too much paraffin.

Your favorite flavoring such as rum, vanilla, amaretto, hazelnut may be substituted.

★ ★ Use only pure flavorings as imitation may cause chocolate to harden on contact.

FLORAL ICE CUBES

24 fern sprigs
24 statice sprigs
12 roses

12 small carnations
24 (3-ounce) paper cups
1 (1-quart) bottle distilled water

1. Place a fern sprig and statice sprig into each 3-ounce paper cup. Add a rose or small carnation, stem end up, to each cup.
2. Fill cups with water to within ½-inch from top. Freeze until firm.
3. Fill a punch bowl halfway with crushed ice. Place champagne or wine bottles in bowl, and arrange floral ice cubes around the bottles.

   Yield: 2 dozen floral ice cubes.

   For a true touch of unexpected elegance to champagne or wine on ice, try these Floral Ice Cubes.

Table Settings

TIPS FOR TABLE SETTING

The arrangement of dishes, flatware, glasses, and linen for one person is called a cover. The cover for each person should be approximately 24-inches wide. The tableware used will depend on the food served.

— Position the plate so that it will be directly in front of the diner. If food is served on plates from the kitchen, allow enough empty space on the cover for the plate.

— Knives are at the right of the plate, with the blades facing toward the plate.

— Spoons are to the right of the knives.

— Forks are to the left of the plate.

— Each type of flatware is placed in order of its use. For example the fork to be used first is farthest from the plate.

— Place the water glass just above the tip of the largest knife. Other glasses are placed to the right of the water glass.

— The napkin goes to the left of the forks, with the folded edge farthest from the fork.

— Silk flowers dusty? Place flowers and 2 cups of rice in a large paper bag. Shake well.

— Bows wrinkled, use curling iron to press them.

— Pine cones make a good filler in dried flower arrangements.

— Short on space — use a washing machine or wheel barrow to ice down drinks.

— Brown bag with a cup of sand and a candle make a beautiful table decoration for outdoor parties — or line the walk way with them.

— Place a coffee filter on the bottom of your dinner plate to keep it from scratching the table.

— To dry flowers, cut and hang upside down inside. Roses, bachelor's button, and cock's comb are excellent for drying.

— Antique quilts make beautiful table cloths.

— Rugs make a rugged table cloth for Mexican parties or barbecues.

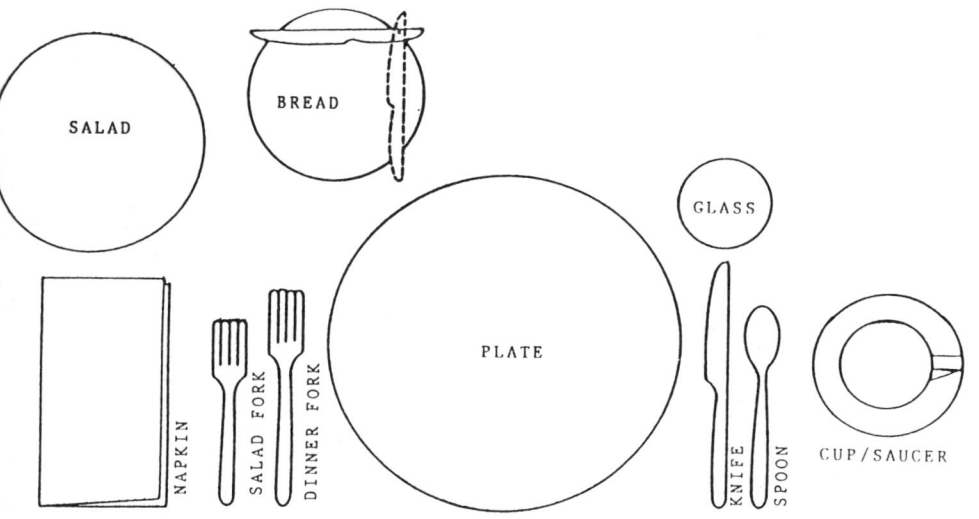

INFORMAL SETTING

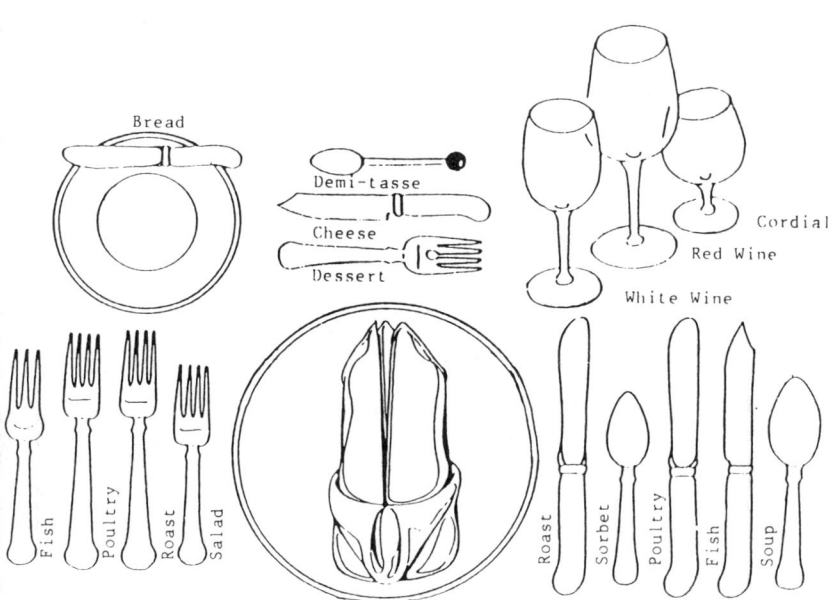

FORMAL SETTING

ORGANIZING A BUFFET

Dessert and coffee is usually served on a small side table.

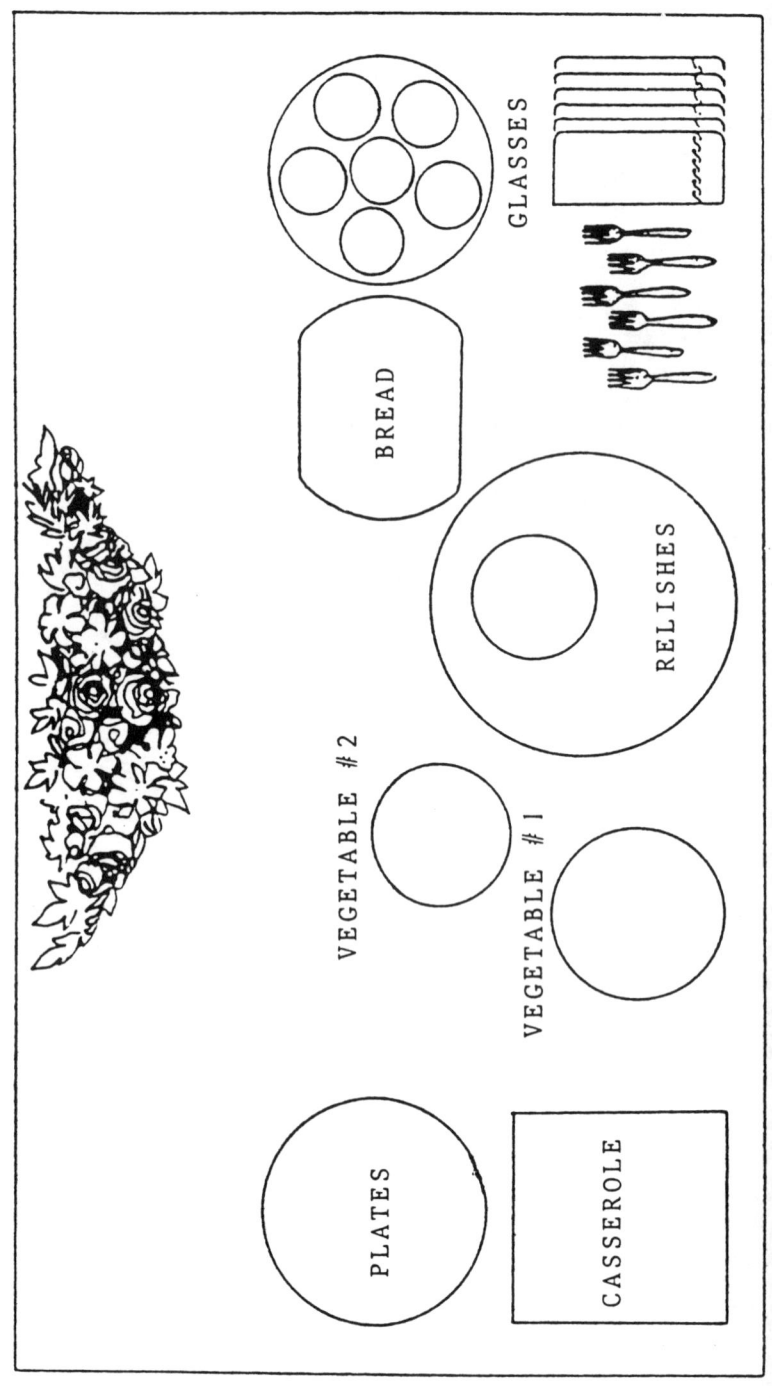

BUFFET SERVER

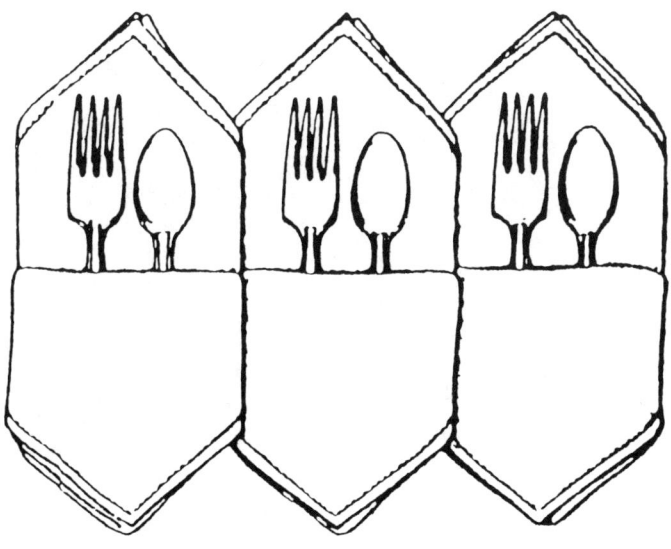

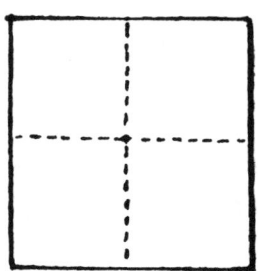

A buffet is a convenient way to serve a meal, and one way to make it uncomplicated for your guests is to have the silverware and napkins together in a convenient package.

1. Fold the napkin in quarters.

2. Place the napkin so the free points are at the upper left.

3. Fold the upper left corner of the top layer down to the lower right corner.

4. Fold under the top right and bottom left corners.

BISHOP'S HAT

1. Fold in half.

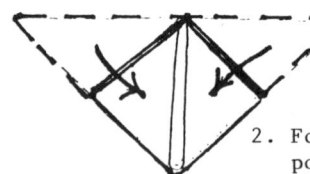

2. Fold left and right points to bottom point.

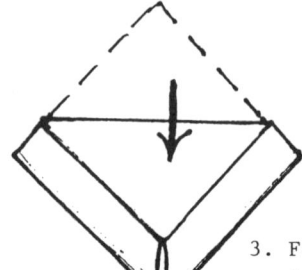

3. Fold top corner to 1" of bottom corner.

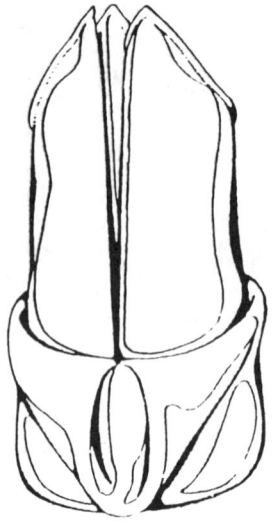

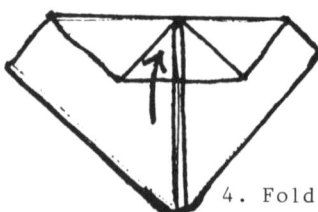

4. Fold corner back to edge.

5. Turn right side up.

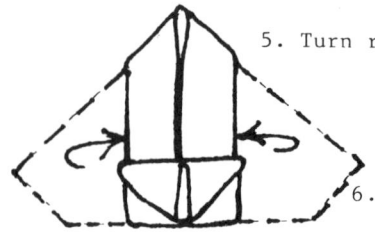

6. Fold back sides and tuck in back.

VARIATION: FLEUR DE LYS

Turn down two peaks of hat to make Fleur de Lys.

Facts From the Chef

In the Kitchen

Baking powder (2 teaspoons)	½ tsp. baking soda + 1¼ tsp. cream of tartar
Buttermilk (1 cup)	1 cup yogurt; or 1 Tbsp. vinegar or lemon juice + enough milk to make 1 cup (let mixture stand 5 minutes)
Chocolate, semisweet bits (6-ounce bag)	6 Tbsp. unsweetened cocoa powder + 7 Tbsp. granulated sugar + ¼ cup solid vegetable shortening
Chocolate, unsweetened (1 square)	3 Tbsp. unsweetened cocoa powder + 1 Tbsp. salad oil or solid vegetable shortening
Corn syrup (1 cup)	1 cup sugar boiled in ¼ cup whatever liquid the recipe calls for until syrupy
Cream, heavy (1 cup)	⅓ cup butter + ¾ cup milk
Cream, sour (1 cup)	1 cup cottage cheese + 1 Tbsp. lemon juice whirred in blender until smooth
Egg (1, in cake batter)	2 Tbsp. mayonnaise
Garlic (1 clove)	⅛ tsp. garlic powder
Honey (1 cup)	1¼ cups granulated sugar + ¼ cup whatever liquid recipe calls for
Lemon juice (1 tsp.)	½ tsp. vinegar
Milk, whole (1 cup)	½ cup evaporated milk + ½ cup water
Mustard, dried (1 tsp.)	1 Tbsp. prepared mustard
Rolling pin	Wine bottle filled with cold water
Wine for cooking, red (about ½ cup)	½ cup cranberry-juice cocktail + 1 Tbsp. lemon juice
Wine for cooking, white (about ½ cup)	½ cup white grape juice + 1 Tbsp. white vinegar

Handyman's Special

Clamp	Spring clothespin; clip-on earring; masking tape; pants hanger; partly open drawer
Drain opener	1 cup each salt and baking soda flushed with kettle of boiling water
Funnel	Plastic bag or rubber glove finger with corner clipped away
Glue for paper	Raw egg white
Ice scraper	Teflon spatula
Measuring tape	Quarter (1-inch diameter); pack of cigarettes (2-inches wide); dollar bill (6⅛-inches long)
Moving dolly	Skateboard
Packing material	Popcorn, marshmallows
Wood filler	A little instant coffee powder mixed in Spackle

Personal Effects

Antistatic spray	1 part fabric softener + 8 parts water
Blemish cream	Dab of lemon juice several times a day
Blusher	Dab of lipstick in a few drops of face cream
Cream rinse	Dab of fabric softener in glass of warm water
Earring-post back	A piece of wide rubber band or pencil eraser
Emery board	The striking strip of a matchbook
Eye cream	Caster oil applied all around eyes
Facial mask	Whipped egg white applied for 20 minutes
Facial scrub	A paste of uncooked oatmeal and water applied to face and allowed to dry (rub off with fingers using back-and-forth motion)
Ice pack	A bag of frozen vegetables (don't refreeze)
Moisturizer	A tiny dab of petroleum jelly on wet, freshly washed face Continue wetting face until jelly is evenly spread and skin is not greasy
Setting lotion	Flat beer; or 1 tsp. sugar or gelatin dissolved in 1 cup warm water
Shoehorn	A tablespoon
Toothpaste	2 parts baking soda + 1 part grated orange peel

Cleaning Up

Brass polish	Worcestershire sauce or lemon juice
Copper polisher	Little salt in a dash of vinegar or lemon juice
Furniture polish	Mixture of ⅓ cup each linseed oil, turpentine, vinegar. Apply with dry cloth and wipe off
Leather upholstery cleaner	Milk
Mirror shiner	Cold tea
Oven cleaner	Set oven at "warm" 20 minutes; turn off. Put small dish ammonia and large pan boiling water overnight on top and bottom shelf, respectively. Air out; clean with soap and water
Prewash stain remover	Liquid Lestoil or hair shampoo
Shoe polish	Furniture polish or window spray for leather; petroleum jelly for patent leather; rug shampoo for canvas (rub in with toothbrush)
Spot cleaner, clothes	2 parts water to 1 part rubbing alcohol
Spot cleaner, upholstery/carpet	Very foamy shaving cream (but test first in an inconspicuous corner)
Wood floor scratch-concealer	Brown shoe polish mixed with floor wax

WHITE SAUCES

Kind	Butter	Flour	Salt	Pepper	Milk
Thin	3 Tblsps	2 Tblsps.	1 tsp	¼ tsp.	2 cups
Medium	4 Tblsps.	4 Tblsps.	1 tsp.	¼ tsp.	2 cups
Thick	6 Tblsps.	8 Tblsps.	1 tsp.	¼ tsp.	2 cups

Steps in Making Sauces

(1) Melt the fat in a saucepan or the top of a double boiler. Stir in the flour.
(2) Remove from direct heat and pour in the liquid. Cold liquids may be added all at once. Hot liquids must be stirred in gradually.
(3) Stir slowly but steadily over direct heat until the sauce boils. Season to taste.
(4) If the sauce is not to be served immediately, set the saucepan over hot water and cover it tightly so that a crust will not form on the surface. Otherwise the crust will give the sauce a lumpy appearance when it is stirred into the liquid beneath.

First Aid to Sauces

It is no disgrace to have the first attempt at sauce-making fall short of the standard for a perfect product.

(1) **Sauce too thick?** Add more of the liquid used in the sauce or use water. Since the flavoring is diluted, taste and re-season if necessary.

(2) **Sauce too thin?** Remember that sauces thicken very quickly on cooling and that a sauce served at the table will always be thicker than when it leaves the stove. If the sauce is too thin it may be remedied in one of two ways. *(a)* An extra egg yolk may be beaten slightly, thinned with a little of the sauce, then stirred into the sauce and heated below the boiling point for not more than 1 minute. The egg yolk adds richness as well as body to the sauce. *(b)* An additional half-tablespoon of flour may be mixed to a paste with cold liquid and stirred into the thin sauce. Stirring must be continued until the sauce boils.

(3) **Sauce lumpy?** Lumps may sometimes be disposed of by vigorous beating with a spoon or egg beater. Obstinate lumps must be strained out and the sauce reheated.

HERBS AND SPICES

—add flavor without fat or calories—

1/3 to 1/2 tablespoon dried = 1 tablespoon fresh

Common Usages:

HERBS:

- Anise — cookies, cakes, breads
- Basil — tomatoes, fish, eggs, spaghetti sauce
- Bay — stock, soup, stew, stuffing, marinade
- Chervil — salad, eggs, soup, veal, chicken
- Chives — eggs, salad, potatoes, cream cheese
- Coriander — Caribbean and Mexican dishes
- Cumin — chili, enchilada, curry, beans, rice
- Dill — fish, potatoes, salad, cucumber
- Horseradish — cocktail sauce, boiled meat, fish sauces, Marjoram, sweet and wild (oregano)/Spanish and Mexican dishes, lamb, mushrooms, sausage, soup, salad
- Mint — iced tea, fruit, peas, lamb, jelly, juleps
- Mustard — sauces, salad dressing, pickles, cold meats, frankfurters
- Parsley — salad, meats, soup, stew
- Rosemary — lamb, poultry, sauces, potatoes, spinach
- Saffron — paella, bouillabaise, rice
- Sage — stuffing, pork, goose, herb bread
- Savory — poultry, salad, peas, string beans, horseradish, sauce, pork
- Sorrel — soup, sauces
- Tarragon — salad, chicken, soup, fish, vinegar, sauces
- Thyme — tomatoes, lamb, veal, pork, stock
- Fine Herbs — a combination of chopped herbs, usually parsley, basil, chives and chervil, added to omelets, sauces, cream soups
- Bouquet garni — a combination of herbs tied together in a cheesecloth bag and put in soup, stews and ragouts. Typically, 3 sprigs parsley, 2 sprigs thyme, white part of one leek, 1 celery stalk

SPICES:

- Allspice — pickles, relishes, cakes, cookies, pot roast, stew, meatloaf
- Cardamom — marinade, mulled wine, coffee, bread, cake, Swedish meatball
- Cloves — ham, mulled wine, tea, fruit, chutney, pickles, boiled meats, soup
- Curry Powder — curry, eggs, marinade, sauce
- Ginger — cookies, cakes, puddings, pot roast, fruit, sweet potatoes, squash, carrots
- Nutmeg — egg nog, spice cake, compote, applesauce, meatloaf, spinach
- Pepper — WHITE with sausage, pale-colored food and sauces;
  BLACK with dark sauces, red meats, salads;
  CAYENNE in some sauces, used sparingly

RICE COOKERY

Measurements and Yields for Various Kinds of Rice

Type of Rice	Uncooked Rice	Liquid	Salt	Butter Margarine	Approx. No. of ½ cup servings	Approx. Yield
Regular Milled White Long Grain Rice	1⅓ cups (9 ozs.)	2⅔ cups	1½ tsp.	1 Tbsp.	8	1 qt.
	5½ cups (2 lbs. 6 ozs.)	2¼ qts	2 Tbsps.	2 Tbsp.	32	1 gal.
Regular Milled White Medium Grain Rice	1½ cups (10½ ounces)	2½ cups	1½ tsps.	1 Tbsp.	8	1 qt.
	1½ qts. (2 lbs. 10 ozs.)	9½ cups	2 Tbsps.	2 Tbsps.	32	1 gal.
Brown Rice	1¼ cups (8 ozs.)	3 cups	1½ tsps.	1 Tbsp.	8	1 qt.
	1¼ qts. (2 lbs.)	3 qts.	2 Tbsps.	2 Tbsps.	32	1 gal.

Liquids other than water which can be used include: chicken stock, beef broth, bouillon, consomme, tomato or vegetable juice (1 part water, 1 part juice), fruit juices such as orange or apple (1 part water, 1 part juice), maraschino cherry juice (3 parts water, 1 part juice).

Wine and Alcohol Substitutes

- For sherry and light wines: Use equal quantities of lemon juice or chicken bouillon, or equal amounts of lemon juice combined with celery water, made by boiling leaves and coarse celery stalks.

- In Chinese and other recipes requiring small amounts of light wine such as one or two tablespoons, plain water will usually do when the recipe includes other fairly strong seasonings such as soy sauce.

- For white wines with fish: Substitute an equal amount of bottled clam juice or fish stock. Some use white grape juice for fish. Others say it is too sweet.

- For red wines: Keeping in mind the flavor combinations of the other ingredients, try substituting apple juice or grape juice for red wines.

- All the citrus juices are good in cases when a tart flavor will blend with other seasonings used. Orange juice with an added bit of grated orange rind is better in mincemeat than rum.

- Cranberry juice, diluted slightly, is good in marinating and barbecue recipes. It can also be combined with lemon juice. Cranberry juice has been recommended as excellent for pot roasts and stews, with the idea that the acid content helps tenderize the meat.

- Ginger ale is recommended for some baked and roasted meats, in recipes that call for basting a leg of lamb with champagne or white wine. Ginger ale is also good with desserts served over fruit.

- Grenadine, which is a liquid form of sugar made from pomegranate juice and is brilliant scarlet in color, is free from any trace of alcohol and is excellent as a sweetening agent and dessert topping.

A NITTY-GRITTY GUIDE TO GLUES
THE 10 KINDS OF GLUE

WHAT YOU NEED TO KNOW	Epoxy (fast)	Epoxy (slow)	Contact Cement	Rubber Cement	Polyvinyl (white)	Household Cement	Cyanoacrylate (instant glue)	Mastic	Silicone (caulk)	Casein Glue
Brand names	Miracle Fast-Set, Foxy Poxy, Devcon, Magic America Epoxy	Weldwood, Devcon Clear or Fiberglass Evercoat	Weldwood or Goodyear Contact Cement	Weldwood Rubber Cement	Elmer's Glue-All, DuPont White or Sears White Glue	LePage's Household Cement	Krazy Glue, Duro Super Glue-3, Sears Super Glue No. 3	Franklin Construction Adhesive, Ruscoe Pan-L-Bond	Dow, General Electric, Sears or Devcon Silicone Adhesive	Weldwood Casein, National Casein Co. No. 30
Setting time	5 minutes	24 hours	30 to 60 minutes	10 to 15 minutes	30 to 60 minutes	10 to 15 minutes	Instantly	3 hours	24 hours	24 hours
Requires Clamping or Holding	Yes	Yes	No	No	Yes	Yes	Yes (3 to 5 seconds)	No	Yes	Yes
Strength	Strong	Very strong	Fairly strong	Weak	Very strong	Strong	Very strong	Fairly strong	Fairly strong	Very strong
Waterproof or water-resistant	Water-resistant	Waterproof	Waterproof	Waterproof	No	No	Water-resistant	Check instructions	Very waterproof	No
Flammable	Yes	Yes	Check	Yes	No	Yes	Yes	Check	Yes	No
Toxic	Yes	Yes	Yes	Yes	No	Yes	Yes	Check	Yes	No
Solutions to thin Wet Glue	Soapy water	Soapy water	Water or paint thinner	Rubber cement thinner	Water	Acetone	Acetone	Check instructions	Alcohol	Water
Solvents to dissolve Dried Glue	None	None	Contact cement or paint thinner	Rubber cement thinner	Hot water	Acetone	Acetone	Check instructions	None	None

WHICH GLUE SHOULD I USE? A SIMPLE CROSS-REFERENCE GUIDE

If you need to attach a ceramic tile to a wood-and-tile coffee table, simply go across the top of the chart to "Wood" and down the right-hand column to "Tile (ceramic)" and you'll find out the glues that will make them stick.

WOOD	GLASS & CHINA	RUBBER	METAL (plumbing, etc.)	LEATHER	PLASTIC* (hard)	PLASTIC* (soft)	TILE* (vinyl)	TILE (ceramic)	PLASTIC-LAMINATE (Formica)	
Polyvinyl (white), casein glue, epoxy, rubber cement, contact cement, household cement, mastic.	Epoxy, contact cement, silicone, household cement.	Contact cement, rubber cement, silicone.	Contact cement, household cement, silicone.	Polyvinyl (white), contact cement, silicone, household cement, rubber cement, mastic.	Contact cement, epoxy, household cement.	Rubber cement, contact cement, household cement.	Plastic resin, contact cement, household cement.	Epoxy, silicone, mastic, household cement, contact cement.	Contact cement, casein glue, silicone, polyvinyl (white), household cement, epoxy, mastic.	WOOD
Epoxy, contact cement, silicone, household cement.	Cyanoacrylate, epoxy, household cement.	Cyanoacrylate, rubber cement, contact cement.	Cyanoacrylate, contact cement, household cement, silicone.	Cyanoacrylate, contact cement, silicone, rubber cement, household cement, mastic.	Epoxy, cyanoacrylate, household cement.	Rubber cement, contact cement, household cement.	Contact cement, plastic resin, household cement.	Epoxy, silicone, mastic, household cement, cyanoacrylate.	Contact cement, cyanoacrylate, epoxy, household cement, silicone.	GLASS & CHINA
Contact cement, rubber cement, silicone.	Cyanoacrylate, rubber cement, contact cement, silicone.	Cyanoacrylate, rubber cement, contact cement, silicone.	Silicone, cyanoacrylate.	Cyanoacrylate, contact cement, silicone, rubber cement.	Cyanoacrylate, contact cement, rubber cement.	Rubber cement, contact cement.	Rubber cement, contact cement, plastic resin, cyanoacrylate.	Contact cement, rubber cement, cyanoacrylate, silicone.	Contact cement, rubber cement, cyanoacrylate, silicone.	RUBBER
Contact cement, household cement, silicone, epoxy.	Cyanoacrylate, contact cement, household cement, silicone, epoxy.	Silicone, cyanoacrylate.	Cyanoacrylate, epoxy, silicone, contact cement, household cement.	Cyanoacrylate, silicone, contact cement, household cement.	Contact cement, epoxy, household cement, cyanoacrylate.	Contact cement, household cement, cyanoacrylate.	Contact cement, household cement, cyanoacrylate.	Contact cement, household cement, silicone, cyanoacrylate, epoxy.	Contact cement, household cement, silicone, cyanoacrylate, epoxy.	METAL (plumbing, etc.)
Polyvinyl (white), contact cement, silicone, household cement, rubber cement, mastic.	Cyanoacrylate, contact cement, silicone, rubber cement, household cement, mastic.	Cyanoacrylate, contact cement, silicone, rubber cement.	Cyanoacrylate, contact cement, silicone, household cement.	Contact cement, silicone, rubber cement, household cement.	Contact cement, rubber cement, household cement, cyanoacrylate.	Contact cement, rubber cement, household cement, cyanoacrylate.	Contact cement, rubber cement, household cement, plastic resin.	Contact cement, silicone, rubber cement, household cement, cyanoacrylate.	Contact cement, silicone, rubber cement, household cement, cyanoacrylate.	LEATHER
Contact cement, epoxy, household cement.	Epoxy, cyanoacrylate, household cement.	Cyanoacrylate, contact cement, rubber cement.	Contact cement, epoxy, cyanoacrylate.	Contact cement, rubber cement, household cement, cyanoacrylate.	Epoxy, cyanoacrylate, contact cement, household cement.	Contact cement, rubber cement, household cement, epoxy.	Contact cement, rubber cement, household cement.	Contact cement, household cement, cyanoacrylate.	Contact cement, rubber cement, household cement, epoxy, cyanoacrylate.	PLASTIC (hard)
Rubber cement, contact cement, household cement.	Rubber cement, contact cement, household cement.	Rubber cement, contact cement.	Contact cement, household cement.	Contact cement, household cement, rubber cement, cyanoacrylate.	Contact cement, rubber cement, household cement, epoxy.	Rubber cement, contact cement, household cement.	Rubber cement, contact cement, household cement.	Rubber cement, contact cement, household cement.	Rubber cement, contact cement, household cement.	PLASTIC (soft)
Plastic resin, contact cement, household cement.	Contact cement, mastic, plastic resin, household cement, cyanoacrylate.	Rubber cement, contact cement, plastic resin, cyanoacrylate.	Contact cement, household cement, cyanoacrylate.	Contact cement, rubber cement, household cement, cyanoacrylate, plastic resin.	Contact cement, rubber cement, household cement.	Rubber cement, contact cement, household cement.	Plastic resin, contact cement, rubber cement, household cement.	Plastic resin, contact cement, rubber cement, household cement, cyanoacrylate.	Plastic resin, contact cement, rubber cement, household cement, cyanoacrylate, mastic.	TILE* (vinyl)
Epoxy, silicone, mastic, household cement, contact cement.	Epoxy, silicone, mastic, household cement, cyanoacrylate.	Contact cement, rubber cement, cyanoacrylate, silicone.	Contact cement, household cement, silicone, cyanoacrylate, epoxy.	Contact cement, silicone, rubber cement, household cement.	Contact cement, rubber cement, household cement.	Rubber cement, contact cement, rubber cement, household cement.	Plastic resin, contact cement, rubber cement, household cement, cyanoacrylate.	Cyanoacrylate, silicone, contact cement, epoxy, household cement, rubber cement, mastic.	Cyanoacrylate, silicone, contact cement, epoxy, household cement, rubber cement, mastic.	TILE (ceramic)
Contact cement, casein glue, silicone, polyvinyl (white), household cement, epoxy, mastic.	Contact cement, cyanoacrylate, epoxy, household cement, silicone.	Contact cement, rubber cement, cyanoacrylate, silicone.	Contact cement, household cement, silicone, cyanoacrylate, epoxy.	Contact cement, silicone, rubber cement, household cement, cyanoacrylate.	Contact cement, rubber cement, household cement, epoxy, cyanoacrylate.	Rubber cement, contact cement, household cement.	Plastic resin, contact cement, rubber cement, household cement.	Cyanoacrylate, silicone, contact cement, epoxy, household cement, rubber cement, mastic.	Contact cement, epoxy, cyanoacrylate, silicone, household cement, mastic.	PLASTIC LAMINATE (Formica)

*Some plastics are difficult to glue to surfaces with any type of adhesive.

APPROXIMATE AMOUNTS OF FOODS NEEDED TO SERVE TWENTY-FIVE

BAKERY PRODUCTS

Pan rolls — 4 to 6 dozen
Bread, pullman loaf — 2 to 4 loaves
Bread, French — 4 loaves

BEVERAGES

Coffee — ½ lb.
    Cream for coffee — ½ pint
    Sugar for coffee — ½ lb.
Cocoa — 4 oz.
Tea (amount will vary with quality and blend)
    Hot — 1½ oz.
    Iced — 2 oz.
Fruit juice — 3 quarts

CEREALS

Rice — 2 lbs.
Spaghetti — 3 lbs.

DAIRY PRODUCTS

Butter for table — 1 lb.
Ice cream — 1 gal.
Milk — 1½ gals.

FRUITS

No. 2½ cans — 3
8 lbs. or 3 qts. — fresh
Six to eight 10 oz. pkgs. — frozen

MEAT, POULTRY AND FISH

Chuck roast — 9 to 10 lbs.
Meat loaf — 5 lbs.
Ground meat patties — 6 lbs.
Stew with vegetables — 5 lbs.
Ham, baked — 9 lbs.
Shrimp, boiled — 15 to 20 lbs.
Chicken, dressed weight
    Baked — three 5 to 6 lb. hens
    Fried — eight 2½ to 3 lb. fryers
    a la King — two 5 to 6 lb. hens
    Stewed — two 6 lb. hens
Turkey — 15 to 20 lbs.

VEGETABLES

Canned
    No. 303 cans — 5
    No. 2½ cans — 4
Fresh
    Green beans — 5 to 6 lbs.
    Carrots — 6 lbs.
    Lettuce, head — 6 heads
    Potatoes, baked — 25 medium
    Potatoes, to mash — 7 lbs.
Potatoes to scallop — 7 lbs.
Squash — 5 to 6 lbs.
Cabbage, raw — 4 lbs.
Onions, whole — 6 lbs.
Lettuce, garnish — 2 to 3 heads
Potatoes, sweet — 9 to 10 lbs.
Tomatoes, sliced — 5 to 6 lbs.
Frozen
    Six 10 oz. pkgs.

MISCELLANEOUS

Nuts (nut cups) — 1 lb.
Carrot strips — 1½ lbs.
Celery curls — 2 medium stalks
Olives, green — 1 quart
Pickles — 1 lb.
Candies, small — 1 lb.
Jelly — 1½ lbs.

ITALIAN SPAGHETTI

¾ cup olive or salad oil
6 cloves garlic, minced
5 medium onions, chopped
3 pounds ground beef
6 cans tomato paste
4 quarts hot water
1 bay leaf
1 tablespoon sugar
1 tablespoon oregano
2 tablespoons salt
1½ teaspoons pepper
3 pounds spaghetti, cooked and drained
Grated Parmesan cheese

Sauté garlic and onions in hot oil until tender. Add meat. Cook and stir until crumbly. Mix tomato paste, water and seasonings. Stir into meat. Simmer on low heat about 1 hour or until sauce thickens. Serve over hot spaghetti, macaroni or noodles. Sprinkle with cheese.
Serves 25.

The electric roaster is ideal for this recipe. Brown garlic, onions and meat in preheated roaster at 500 degrees. Cover roaster while meat is being browned. Add remaining ingredients and mix well. Cover. Reset temperature control to 375 degrees and cook about 1 hour or until thickened.

POTATO SALAD (Serves 25)

8 cups boiled potatoes, diced
  (8 to 9-pounds as purchased)
1 cup French dressing
8 hard cooked eggs, chopped
3 cups celery, chopped fine
2 medium onions, chopped fine or grated (optional)
1½-2 cups mayonnaise
1 cup sour pickles, chopped or
  1 cup sweet pickles, chopped
2 cups dill pickles, chopped
Juice of 1 or 2 lemons

Mix diced potatoes and French dressing and let stand in refrigerator about 1 hour. Add remaining ingredients and mix well.

Note: Add ½ cup chopped pimiento and/or ½ cup chopped green pepper if desired.

BOSTON BAKED BEANS (Serves 25)

1 pound sliced bacon
6 medium onions, chopped
6 large green peppers, chopped
6 (No. 2) cans pork and beans
1 tablespoon chili powder
¾ cup brown sugar
6 tablespoons molasses
1½ cups catsup
¾ cup water

Cut bacon in small pieces and brown in skillet. Remove bacon from skillet and add chopped onion and peppers. Cook until vegetables are tender. Pour off excess fat. Combine all ingredients and bake at 325 degrees, 1 hour. Remove cover and continue baking for an additional hour or until thick. May bake entire period in electric roaster.

CHICKEN SPAGHETTI (Serves 25)

2 (6-pound) chickens
2 quarts water
2 bay leaves
Salt and pepper to taste
1 cup chicken fat
1 clove garlic, finely chopped
2 large onions, chopped
2 cups chopped celery
2 green pepper, chopped
6 tablespoons browned flour

3 tablespoons Worcestershire sauce
1 (8-ounce) can tomato paste
2 (No. 2) cans tomatoes or tomato juice
1 cup mushrooms, sliced
1 cup olives, chopped
2½ pounds spaghetti
1 cup cheese, grated

Put chicken, water, bay leaves, salt and pepper in covered utensil. Bring to steaming point on high, then simmer on low heat until tender. Remove meat from bone and dice into bite-size pieces. Save broth. Skim off fat. Melt fat in skillet—add chopped vegetables. Cook until tender using medium heat of the range. Add flour, which has been browned on low heat, Worcestershire sauce, tomato paste, canned tomatoes, mushrooms and olives. Transfer to larger utensil (electric roaster) add chicken and simmer 30 minutes. Cook spaghetti according to directions on package—**do not overcook**. Rinse spaghetti. Add spaghetti to chicken mixture. Add enough broth to make mixture moist. Bake in casserole dishes in oven or in the electric roaster at 350 degrees for 30 minutes. When ready to serve, sprinkle over with grated American cheese or Parmesan cheese. This may be prepared ahead of time and baked just before serving.

CHICKEN SALAD De LUXE

2 (5 to 6-pound) chickens
1 cup sliced green onions
6 cups sliced celery with tops
1 dozen hard cooked eggs, chopped
1½ cups coarsely chopped walnuts
2 tablespoons butter or margarine
3 cups salad dressing or mayonnaise

½ cup wine vinegar
1½ cups chicken broth
2 teaspoons salt
¼ teaspoon pepper
2 heads lettuce
½ bunch water cress (optional) or parsley

Simmer chickens in 2-quarts water with salt and pepper until tender. Pull meat off bone and dice. Save broth. Refrigerate. At least 2½ hours before serving: sauté nuts in butter until crisp and golden (about 5 minutes). Drain on paper towels; cool. Combine salad dressing, vinegar, chicken broth, salt and pepper; toss with chicken, eggs, nuts, green onions and celery. Refrigerate until serving time. To serve: arrange salad on bed of lettuce; garnish with water cress.

Makes 25 servings.

Need to cut fats in recipes! Try ingredient substitutions

Jacquelyn Hooter, registered dietitian with Lane Memorial Hospital, prepared a list of ingredient substitutions to help home cooks in lowering fats in recipes.

The list includes several low-fat substitutions for recipe ingredients that are commonly used in preparing autumn party appetizers and treats. *(Reprinted by permission)*

IF RECIPE CALLS FOR:	RECIPE SUBSTITUTIONS:
avocado	asparagus or green peas, pureed
bacon	Canadian bacon
bacon bits	soy bits
baking powder	low sodium baking powder
beef	chicken or turkey without skin or tofu
bouillon cubes	low sodium broth or bouillon cubes
bread crumbs	fat-free bread crumbs
butter	equal amount of apple sauce
cheese	low-fat or fat-free cheese
chicken stock	vegetable stock
chocolate	3-4 tablespoons cocoa and 1 tablespoon canola oil
chocolate sauce	cocoa and apple juice
chips	baked chips
cream	non-fat dry milk
cream cheese	non-fat cream cheese
cream sauce	tomato sauce
cream soups	prepare with non-fat dry milk
evaporated milk	skim evaporated milk
flour and fat	pureed vegetables or corn starch
fudge sauce	marshmallow sauce
granola	low-fat granola or puffed cereal and raisins
gravy	butter-flavored seasoning
half-and-half	non-fat dry milk
honey	frozen concentrated fruit juice
ice cream or ice milk	non-fat frozen yogurt
icing	powdered sugar or non-fat cream cheese blended with pineapple juice
margarine	diet margarine (as a spread) and butter-flavored seasoning (in cooking)
mayonnaise	non-fat mayonnaise
meat	beans
nuts	dry cereal
oils in baking	applesauce
oils in cooking	canola or olive oil
oils in frying	non-stick cookware or spray
oils in sauteing	water or non-fat broth
peanut butter	apple butter
salad dressing	non-fat salad dressing
salt	¼ amount called for
seasoning salts	salt free herb blends
shortening	for each cup required, use ¾ cup canola oil
sour cream	low-fat sour cream or plain yogurt
soy sauce	sodium-reduced soy sauce
sugar substitute	fructose
wine	non-alcoholic wine
whipped cream	fat-reduced whipped cream
white flour	whole wheat flour
white pasta	whole wheat pasta
white rice	brown rice
white sugar	brown sugar
whole egg	2 egg whites or ¼ cup egg substitute
whole milk	skim milk or low-fat milk

INDEX

Addie McCoy's Corn and Shrimp
  Soup 31
Angel Biscuits 60
Angel Cornsticks 50

APPETIZERS
Artichoke Dip 16
Bacon-Wrapped Crackers 9
Baked Crabmeat Dip 17
Barbeque Sauce For Lil' Smokies 9
Broccoli Cheese Dip 18
Broccoli Dip 16
Caponata With Pita Crisps 7
Cheddar Cheese Ball 2
Cheese Crispies 4
Cheese Straws 3
Chex Party Mix 10
Coconut Bananas 13
Crab Dip 17
Crab Muffins 10
Curried Snack Mix 14
Dried Beef Dip 16
Fiesta Dip 233
Football Party Dip 236
Fruit Yogurt Dip 20
Garlic Cheese Rolls 4
Guacamole Spread 233
Hawaiian Brie 2
Herb-Cheese Spread 3
Hot Bean — Venison Dip 21
Hot Crab/Crawfish Artichoke Dip 5
Kozan's Ham and Cheese Rolls 8
Lake Charles Dip 18
Mexican Hot Sauce Dip 15
Mini-Muffaletta 11
Mount St. Helena 19
Oysters Wrapped In Bacon 11
"Philly" Cheese Ball 4
Party Pizzas 6
Party Stroganoff 11
Pita Triangles 5
Queso Dip 19
Quick Shrimp Dip 17
Rolled Tortillas 8
Salad Bar Basket & Cheddar Party
  Onions 20
Sausage Pizza Rounds 10
Shrimp and Mushroom Dip 18
Shrimp Dip I 15
Shrimp Dip II 15
Spiced Pineapple Pickups 13
Spicy Italian Dip 19

Spinach, Feta, and Phyllo Purses ... 12
Stuffed Eggs 9
Stuffed Mushrooms With Crabmeat ... 6
Tiropetes 14
Touchdown Tortillas 13
Vegetable Dip 14
Vegetable Dip 17
Zingy Strawberry Brie 2
Apple Dumplings 185
Apple Streusel Muffins 56
Applesauce Cake 160
Ardeth's Bars 197
Artichoke Casserole 148
Artichoke Dip 16
Artichoke Soup 33
Asphodel Bread 62
Avocado Soup 34
Bacon-Wrapped Crackers 9
Bagna Cotti Dip 156
Baked Crabmeat Dip 17
Baked Duck With Orange Currant
  Sauce 118
Baked Manicotti With Cheese Filling ... 92
Baked Seafood Casserole 130
Baked Shrimp & Artichokes 122
Banana Nut Bread 59
Banana Pudding 181
Banana Punch 23
Banana Split Cake 176
Bar-B-Qued Shrimp 121
Barbeque Sauce 93
Barbequed Brisket 79
Barbequed Shrimp 120
Barbeque Sauce For Lil' Smokies 9
Basic Roux 136
Basic Vegetable Mixture 151
Bayou Bengal Backstrap 117
Becky's Pasta and Crawfish Casserole .. 76

BEEF
Barbequed Brisket 79
Beef Burgundy Stroganoff 88
Beef Chart 78
Grillades 91
Grilled Steak 81
Marinated Brisket 79
Marinated Eye of the Round 80
Natchitoches Meat Pies 90
Party Stroganoff 11
Reuben Sandwich 94
Roasted Tenderloin in Cane Syrup .. 82
Rump Roast 80

Surprise Roast 80
Veal Parmigiana 81
Beef Burgundy Stroganoff 88
Beef Chart 78
Beefy Jalapeno Cornbread 53
Best Dessert Ever 180
Best Yet Slaw 44
Best-Ever Lemon Pie 191
Better Than Sex Cake 163

BEVERAGES
Banana Punch 23
Bloody Mary A La Vivian 26
Cappuccino 23
Cranberry Punch 22
Frozen Margaritas 23
Gelatin Punch 22
Instant Hot Cocoa Mix 25
Instant Spiced Tea 25
Minted Tea 26
Mock Champagne 24
Orange Julius 224
Party Punch 21
Spiced Tea 22
Strawberry Orange Frost 224
Vodka Slush 24
Wassail 25
Wine Cooler Concentrate 24
Wine Punch 21
Big Big Cinnamon Rolls 230
Biscuits 55
Bits N Berries 182
Blind Dates 196
Bloody Mary A La Vivian 26
Blueberry Gelatin Salad 46
Blueberry Muffins 55
Boiled Crawfish 138
Boiled Shrimp 124
Braised Stuffed Pork Chops 101

BREADS
Angel Biscuits 60
Angel Cornsticks 50
Apple Streusel Muffins 56
Asphodel Bread 62
Banana Nut Bread 59
Beefy Jalapeno Cornbread 53
Big Big Cinnamon Rolls 230
Biscuits 55
Blueberry Muffins 55
Cajun Crawfish Cornbread 53
Cheese Braids 58
Christine Denise's Potato Rolls 62
Coffee Can Bread 51
Country Cinnamon Rolls 57

Danny's Hush Puppies 50
Date Nut Coffee Cake 64
Educated Hush Puppies 50
French Bread 67
Granola Muffins 57
Herb Bread 63
Irresistible Biscuits 56
Jalapeno Cornbread 52
Jalapeno Cornbread II 52
Joe Kelly Bread 66
Morning Gloria Muffins 61
Nut Rolls (KALACS) 54
Orange Muffins 61
Pancakes Marney 54
Pogacsa Biscuits 68
Poppy Seed Loaf 60
Rotel Cornbread 59
Sour Cream Dinner Rolls 63
Strawberry Nut Bread 51
Sweet Potato Bread 66
The Best Refrigerator Rolls 63
Yeast Rolls 65
Zucchini Bread 68
Bread & Butter Pickles 220
Bread Pudding w/Amaretto Sauce ... 184
Broccoli Casserole 148
Broccoli Cheese Dip 18
Broccoli Dip 16
Broccoli Salad 42
Brown Sauce or Gravy 96
Brownies 193
Brownie II 210
Brunch Casserole 74
Butter Cream Icing 177
Cacoons 210
Cajun Crawfish Cornbread 53
Cajun Fried Turkey 107
Cajun Squash 145
Cajun Tators 153

CAKES
Applesauce Cake 160
Banana Split Cake 176
Better Than Sex Cake 163
Carrot Cake 170
Cheesecake For A Crowd 175
Chocolate Glaze 172
Chocolate Rum Chiffon Cake 172
Coconut Cake 161
Cream Cheese Pound Cake 170
Crump's Fig Cake 171
Death By Chocolate 175
Devil's Food Peanut Layer Cake ... 160
Featherweight Coffee Cake 225

Fresh Apple Cake 165
Harvey Wallbanger Cake 162
Heavenly Hash Cake 168
Hershey Prize Chocolate Cake 166
Italian Cream Cake 161
King's Cake 158
$25,000 Mardi Gras Cake 164
Marble Cheesecake 174
Milky Way Cake 167
Mississippi Mud Cake 166
Orange Slice Cake 168
Oreo Cookie Cake 185
Pineapple Crush Cake 169
Rum Cake 163
Sock-it-to-Me Cake 173
Sour Cream Pound Cake 173
Strawberry Pecan Cake 171
Tunnel of Fudge Cake 167
Vanilla Pound Cake 162
Vanilla Wafer Cake 169

CAKE FILLINGS AND ICINGS
Butter Cream Icing 177
Custard Cream Filling 177
Filling For King's Cake 159
Frosting For King's Cake 159
Lemon Filling 178
Pineapple Filling 178
Seven-Minute Icing 177
Snow White Icing 177
Strawberry Filling 178
California Spinach Salad 41
Candied Sweet Potatoes 143

CANDY
Ardeth's Bars 197
Blind Dates 196
Caramel Morsel Bars 227
Caramel Apples 226
Chinese Chews 199
Chocolate Covered Banana Pops .. 230
Chocolate Delight 198
Chocolate Dip Strawberries 236
Chocolate Fudge 197
Creamy Pralines ...'............. 195
Creamy Pralines 200
Divinity 195
Fantasy Fudge 203
Fudge Squares 203
Graham Cracker Pralines 195
Hard Candy 196
Heavenly Hash 202
Holiday Rocky Road 205
Jack-O'-Lantern Treats 228
Light Pralines 200
Martha Washington Balls 202

Nut Goodie Bars 201
Nutty Caramel Corn 204
Orange Coconut Balls 205
Peanut Brittle 199
Peanut Butter Balls 196
Praline Popcorn Crunch 204
Rocky Road Halloween Squares ... 198
"Trash Candy" 205
Tunnel of Fudge 198
White Chocolate Fudge 199
Caponata With Pita Crisps 7
Cappuccino 23
Caramel Morsel Bars 227
Caramel Apples 226
Carrot Cake 170
Cheddar Cheese Ball 2
Cheese Braids 58
Cheese Crispies 4
Cheese Straws 3
Cheesecake For A Crowd 175
Chewy Chocolate Cookies 206
Chex Party Mix 10
Chicken & Dumplings 108
Chicken & Rice 110
Chicken and Spaghetti 108
Chicken Casserole 101
Chicken Curry 113
Chicken Divan 111
Chicken Enchiladas 114
Chicken Fajitas 104
Chicken Flambeau 105
Chicken Gumbo 33
Chicken In Mustard Sauce 103
Chicken Jambalaya 109
Chicken Okra Gumbo 34
Chicken Salad 112
Chicken Sausage Jambalaya 102
Chicken Tetrazzini 109
Chicken Tortillas 102
Chicken With Artichokes 110
Chili Pot 91
Chinese Chews 199
Chocolate Almond Coffee Spoons .. 240
Chocolate Chip Cookies 210
Chocolate Covered Banana Pops .. 230
Chocolate Delight 198
Chocolate Dip Strawberries 236
Chocolate Fudge 197
Chocolate Glaze 172
Chocolate Leaves 236
Chocolate Pie 194
Chocolate Rum Chiffon Cake 172

CHOWDER
Fish Chowder 28
Fish Chowder II 28

Shrimp and Corn Chowder 128
Christine Denise's Potato Rolls 62
Christmas Jewels or Thumb Print 211
Christmas Tree Cookies 209
Coca-Cola Salad 47
Coconut Bananas 13
Coconut Cake 161
Coffee Can Bread 51
Cole Slaw 43

COOKIES
   Brownies 193
   Brownies II 210
   Cacoons 210
   Chewy Chocolate Cookies 206
   Chocolate Chip Cookies 210
   Chocolate Valentine Cookies 215
   Christmas Jewels or Thumb Print .. 211
   Christmas Tree Cookies 209
   Creme De Menthe Squares 212
   Famous Oatmeal Cookies 214
   Fantastic Brownies 208
   Fruit Cake Cookies 207
   Heartthrob Cookie Dough 229
   Heath Bars 216
   Magic Cookie Bars 211
   Neiman's $250 Cookie Recipe 206
   Nut Roll 213
   Peanut Blossoms 216
   Pecan Pie Bars 209
   Rolled Sugar Cookies 208
   Scotch Shortbread 207
   Super Chocolate Chip Cookies 214
   The Cake 212
Corn Casserole 149
Cornish Hens 112
Country Cinnamon Rolls 57
Crab and Corn Soup 29
Crab and Eggplant Dressing 127
Crab Dip 17
Crab Meat Quiche 129
Crab Muffins 10
Crabmeat Au Gratin 122
Crabmeat Mornay 125
Cranberry Punch 22
Cranberry Relish 222
Cranberry Sauce 46
Crawfish "Tout Etouffee" 132
Crawfish (or Shrimp) Squash Dressing ... 133
Crawfish and Pasta 135
Crawfish Elegante 137
Crawfish Etouffee 132
Crawfish Fettucini 131
Crawfish Fettucini II 131

Crawfish Rice Casserole 135
Cream Cheese Pound Cake 170
Cream of Peanut Soup 32
Creamy Fruit Salad 44
Creamy Italian Dressing 39
Creamy Pralines 195
Creamy Pralines 200
Creamy Tart French Dressing 39
Creme De Menthe Squares 212
Creole Seafood Seasoning 136
Crockpot Venison Chili 117
Crump's Fig Cake 171
Cucumber Palm Trees 234
Curried Snack Mix 14
Custard Cream Filling 177
Danny's Hush Puppies 50
Date Nut Coffee Cake 64
Death By Chocolate 175
Deep Fried Frog Legs 130
Delicate Grits 72
Delicious Fruit Salad 47

DESSERTS
   Apple Dumplings 185
   Banana Pudding 181
   Best Dessert Ever 180
   Bits N Berries 182
   Bread Pudding w/Amaretto Sauce ... 184
   Desserts From The Ice Cream Freezer .. 186
   Drunken Grapes 184
   Fruit Delight 183
   Fruit Pizza 183
   Hasty Cobbler 178
   Maw Helen's Banana Pudding 180
   Old-Fashioned Cooked Custard Ice
      Cream 186
   Peach Cobbler 179
   Too Easy Peach Cobbler 182
   Uncooked Homemade Ice Cream .. 186
Desserts From The Ice Cream Freezer 186
Devil's Food Peanut Layer Cake 160
Deviled Oysters 134
Dill Pickles 220
Dillybeans 219

DIPS
   Artichoke Dip 6
   Bagna Cotti Dip 156
   Baked Crabmeat Dip 17
   Broccoli Cheese Dip 18
   Broccoli Dip 16
   Caponata with Pita Crisps 7
   Crab Dip 17
   Dried Beef Dip 16
   Fiesta Dip 233

Football Party Dip	236
Fruit Yogurt Dip	20
Hot Bean — Venison Dip	21
Lake Charles Dip	18
Mexican Hot Sauce Dip	15
Queso Dip	19
Quick Shrimp Dip	17
Shrimp and Mushroom Dip	18
Shrimp Dip I	15
Shrimp Dip II	15
Spicy Italian Dip	19
Vegetable Dip	14
Vegetable Dip	17
Dirty Rice	106
Divinity	195
Doris' Chicken	108
Dried Beef Dip	16
Drunken Grapes	184
Duck in Orange Mustard Sauce	117
Dumplings	105
Easy Chocolate Pie	187
Educated Hush Puppies	50

EGGS, CHEESE, AND PASTA

Becky's Pasta and Crawfish Casserole	76
Brunch Casserole	74
Delicate Grits	72
Eggs Benedict	71
Eggs Fillet	224
Fettuccine Alfredo	75
French Omelet	70
Garlic Cheese Grits	72
Ham & Cheese Rolls	73
Pesto	70
Quiche Lorraine With Ham	73
Rice Patties	71
Spinach Quiche	74
Stuffed Eggs	9
Toad in Hole	224
Tortellini Salad	75
Tri Color Cheese Surprise	76
Eggs Benedict	71
Eggs Fillet	224
Escalloped Corn With Sausage	98

FACTS FROM CHEF

Amounts To Serve Twenty-Five	255
Boston Baked Beans	256
Chicken Salad	257
Chicken Spaghetti	257
Italian Spaghetti	256
Potato Salad	256
Herbs and Spices	251
Need To Cut Fats In Recipes	258

Rice Cookery	252
When You Don't Have...Use This Instead	248
Which Glue Should I Use?	254
White Sauces	250
Wine and Alcohol Substitutes	253
Fajitas	104
Famous Oatmeal Cookies	214
Fantastic Brownies	208
Fantasy Fudge	203
Faye's Crawfish Etouffee	134
Featherweight Coffee Cake	225
Fettuccine Alfredo	75
Fiesta Dip	233
Fig Strawberry Jam	221
Filling For King's Cake	159
Finger Paints	226
Fish Casserole	126
Fish Chowder	28
Fish Chowder II	28
Floral Ice Cubes	240
Fluffy Dumplings	105
Fluffy Fruit Dressing	38
Foolproof Pie Dough	194
Football Party Dip	236
French Apple Pie	190
French Bread	67
French Omelet	70
French Onion Soup	36
Fresh Apple Cake	165
Fresh Pear Pie	192
Fresh Strawberry Pie	188
Fresh Strawberry Pie #2	188
Fried Shrimp	121
Frog Legs	126
Frosted Cauliflower	140
Frosted Grapes	239
Frosting For King's Cake	159
Frozen Fruit Salad	45
Frozen Margaritas	23

FRUIT

Coconut Bananas	13
Spiced Pineapple Pickups	13
Fruit Cake Cookies	207
Fruit Delight	183
Fruit Pizza	183
Fruit Salad	45
Fruit Yogurt Dip	20
Fruited Yam Cups	147
Fudge Squares	203
Galashata (Cabbage Rolls)	148

GAME

Baked Duck With Orange Currant Sauce	118

Bayou Bengal Backstrap 117
Crockpot Venison Chili 117
Duck in Orange Mustard Sauce 117
Smoked Duck 116
Venison Marinade 116
Venison Roast With Sausage 118
Garlic Cheese Grits 72
Garlic Cheese Rolls 4
Garnishes 234
Gelatin Punch 22
German Fried Potatoes 150
Giblet Gravy 96
Gloria's Easy Lasagna 86
Golden Broccoli 145
Graham Cracker Pralines 195
Granny's Season-All 136
Granola Muffins 57
Grasshopper Pie 189

GRAVY
Brown Sauce or Gravy 96
Giblet Gravy 96
Green Chili Rice 141
Grillades 91
Grilled Steak 81

GROUND BEEF
Baked Manicotti With Cheese
  Filling 92
Chili Pot 91
Gloria's Easy Lasagna 86
Ground Meat Casserole 83
Hot Pepper Sandwiches 95
Hot Tamale Pie 87
Jerry's Mexican Pie 84
Lasagna 84
Lasagna II 85
Manicotti With Florentine Filling 93
Nell's Husband's Delight 88
Skillet Pizza 94
Tamales 89
Ground Meat Casserole 83
Guacamole Spread 233
Hallelujah Crabs 129
Ham & Cheese Rolls 73
Hard Candy 196
Harvey Wallbanger Cake 162
Hasty Cobbler 178
Hawaiian Brie 2
Heartthrob Cookie Dough 229
Heath Bars 216
Heavenly Hash 202
Heavenly Hash Cake 168
Herb Bread 63
Herb-Cheese Spread 3

Hershey Prize Chocolate Cake 166
Holiday Rocky Road 205
Honey-Cream Dressing For Fruit Salad 39
Hot Bean — Venison Dip 21
Hot Chicken Salad 116
Hot Crab/Crawfish Artichoke Dip 5
Hot Pepper Sandwiches 95
Hot Stuffed Tomatoes 153
Hot Tamale Pie 87
Ice Ring 239
Instant Hot Cocoa Mix 25
Instant Spiced Tea 25
Irresistible Biscuits 56
Italian Cream Cake 161
Italian Marinated Vegetables 144
Italian Soup 30
Jack-O'-Lantern Treats 228
Jackie's Etouffee 138
Jalapeno Cornbread 52
Jalapeno Cornbread II 52
Jerry's Mexican Pie 84
Jezebel Sauce 218
Jo's Potato Casserole 156
Joe Kelly Bread 66
Johnny's Marzetti 98
Kathy's Chicken Sauce Piquant 103
Kentucky Derby Pie 194
Kim's Bar-B-Que Shrimp 120
King's Cake 158
Kozan's Ham and Cheese Rolls 8
Lake Charles Dip 18
Lasagna 84
Lasagna II 85
Layered Chicken Salad 40
Layered Spinach Salad 43
Lemon Chicken 111
Lemon Filling 178
Light Pralines 200
Luau Center Piece 232
Magic Cookie Bars 211
Make Your Favorite Dressing 106
Manicotti With Florentine Filling 93
Marble Cheesecake 174
$25,000 Mardi Gras Cake 164
Margarita Pie 190
Marinated Brisket 79
Marinated Eye Of The Round 80
Marinated Fruit 47
Marinated Tomatoes 140
Marinated Vegetable Salad 145
Martha Washington Balls 202
Maw Helen's Banana Pudding 180
Mexican Hot Sauce Dip 15
Milky Way Cake 167

Mini-Muffaletta	11
Minted Tea	26
Mississippi Mud Cake	166
Mississippi Mud Pie	181
Mock Champagne	24
Morning Gloria Muffins	61
Mount St. Helena	19
Mountain Caviar	144
Mrs. Crump's Cornbread Dressing	115
Mushroom Croustades	150
Natchitoches Meat Pies	90
Neiman's $250 Cookie Recipe	206
Nell's Husband's Delight	88
No Work Chicken	114
Nut Goodie Bars	201
Nut Roll (Kalacs)	54
Nut Roll	213
Nutty Caramel Corn	204
Nutty Putty	227
Nutty Wild Rice Casserole	152
Old-Fashioned Cooked Custard Ice Cream	186
Orange Coconut Balls	205
Orange Currant Sauce	118
Orange Julius	224
Orange Muffins	61
Orange Pineapple Salad	48
Orange Slice Cake	168
Oreo Cookie Cake	185
Oysters Wrapped In Bacon	11
Palm Trees	235
Pancakes Marney	54

PARTY IDEAS

Chocolate Almond Coffee Spoons	240
Chocolate Dipped Strawberries	236
Chocolate Leaves	236
Cucumber Palm Trees	234
Fiesta Dip	233
Floral Ice Cubes	240
Football Party Dip	236
Frosted Grapes	239
Garnishes	234
Guacamole Spread	233
Ice Ring	239
Luau Center Piece	232
Sombrero Salad	232
Watermelon Whale	237

PARTY MENUS

A Summer Evening Repast	vi
Cajun Delight — It's Crawfish Season	v
Candlelight and Elegance	viii
Child's Birthday Party	x
Mardi Gras Magic — Breakfast After The Ball	ix

Tailgating Under The Oaks	vii
Party Pizzas	6
Party Punch	21
Party Stroganoff	11
Peach Cobbler	179
Peach Daiquiri Jam	218
Peach Jam	222
Peach Pecan Pie	189
Peanut Blossoms	216
Peanut Brittle	199
Peanut Butter Balls	196
Pecan Pie	193
Pecan Pie Bars	209
Pecan Rice Dressing	133
Pepper Jelly	218
Pesto	70
"Philly" Cheese Ball	4
$3000 Picante Onion Soup	35
Pickled Okra	221
Pickled Squash	219

PIES

Banana Pie	187
Best-Ever Lemon Pie	191
Chocolate Pie	194
Coconut Pie	187
Easy Chocolate Pie	187
Foolproof Pie Dough	194
French Apple Pie	190
Fresh Pear Pie	192
Fresh Strawberry Pie	188
Fresh Strawberry Pie #2	188
Grasshopper Pie	189
Kentucky Derby Pie	194
Margarita Pie	190
Mississippi Mud Pie	181
Peach Pecan Pie	189
Pecan Pie	193
Pink Lemonade Pie	187
Strawberry Pie	187
Strawberry Pie #2	188
Pineapple Crush Cake	169
Pineapple Fig Conserve	222
Pineapple Filling	178
Pink Lemonade Pie	187
Pita Triangles	5
Playdough	226
Pogacsa Biscuits	68
Poppy Seed Dressing	38
Poppy Seed Loaf	60

PORK

Braised Stuffed Pork Chops	101
Escaliped Corn With Sausage	98
Johnny's Marzetti	98
Pork Chart	97

Red Beans and Rice With Tasso 95
Sausage & Rice Pilaf 98
Stuffed Pork Chops 99
Stuffed Pork Chops 100
Stuffed Pork Loin 99
Texas Barbequed Pork Chops 100
Pork Chart 97
Potato Casserole 154
Potato Salad 41
Potatoes Stuffed With Crabmeat 154

POULTRY
Cajun Fried Turkey 107
Chicken & Dumplings 108
Chicken & Rice 110
Chicken and Spaghetti 108
Chicken Casserole 101
Chicken Curry 113
Chicken Divan 111
Chicken Enchiladas 114
Chicken Fajitas 104
Chicken Flambeau 105
Chicken In Mustard Sauce 103
Chicken Jambalaya 109
Chicken Salad 112
Chicken Sausage Jambalaya 102
Chicken Tetrazzini 109
Chicken Tortillas 102
Chicken With Artichokes 110
Cornish Hens 112
Dirty Rice 106
Doris' Chicken 108
Dumplings 105
Fajitas 104
Fluffy Dumplings 105
Hot Chicken Salad 116
Kathy's Chicken Sauce Piquant 103
Lemon Chicken 111
Make Your Favorite Dressing 106
Mrs. Crump's Cornbread Dressing .. 115
No Work Chicken 114
Savory Cornish Hens 113
Spaghetti Sauce 86
Stuff Chicken With Crab 125
Turkey Shoot Up A La Johnny 107
Turkey Shoot Up A La Ronnie 107
Praline Popcorn Crunch 204

PRESERVES, RELISHES
Bread & Butter Pickles 220
Cranberry Relish 222
Dill Pickles 220
Dillybeans 219
Fig Strawberry Jam 221
Jezebel Sauce 218
Peach Daiquiri Jam 218

Peach Jam 222
Pepper Jelly 218
Pickled Okra 221
Pickled Squash 219
Pineapple Fig Conserve 222
Squash Pickles 220
Tomato Sauce 221
Primevera Salad 156
Queso Dip 19
Quiche Lorraine With Ham 73
Quick Shrimp Dip 17
Ratatouille Nicoise 142
Red Beans and Rice With Tasso 95
Reuben Sandwich 94
Rice 114
Rice and Oyster Dressing 127
Rice Patties 71
Roasted Tenderloin In Cane Syrup 82
Rocky Road Halloween Squares 198
Rolled Sugar Cookies 208
Rolled Tortillas 8
Rotel Cornbread 59
Rum Cake 163
Rump Roast 80
Russian or Thousand Island Dressing .. 38

SALADS
Best Yet Slaw 44
Blueberry Gelatin Salad 46
Broccoli Salad 42
California Spinach Salad 41
Chicken Salad 112
Coca-Cola Salad 47
Cole Slaw 43
Creamy Fruit Salad 44
Delicious Fruit Salad 47
Frozen Fruit Salad 45
Fruit Salad 45
Hot Chicken Salad 116
Layered Chicken Salad 40
Layered Spinach Salad 43
Marinated Fruit 47
Marinated Vegetable Salad 145
Orange Pineapple Salad 48
Potato Salad 41
Primevera Salad 156
Salad Bar Basket & Cheddar Party
  Onions 20
Strawberry Spinach Salad 48
Tex-Mex Cornbread Salad 42
24 Hour Salad 40
Waldorf Salad 48
Watergate Salad 44

SALAD DRESSING
Creamy Italian Dressing 39

Creamy Tart French Dressing 39
Fluffy Fruit Dressing 38
Honey-Cream Dressing For Fruit
  Salad 39
Poppy Seed Dressing 38
Russian or Thousand Island Dressing 38
Sandra's Salad Dressing 46
Thelma's Fresh Fruit Dip 38
Salad Bar Basket & Cheddar Party Onions .. 20
Sandra's Hot Pepper Sandwiches 95
Sandra's Salad Dressing 46
Sausage & Rice Pilaf 98
Sausage Pizza Rounds 10

SAUCES
Barbeque Sauce 93
Cranberry Sauce 46
Orange Currant Sauce 118
Vivian's Barbeque Sauce 96
Savory Cornish Hens 113
Scotch Shortbread 207

SEAFOOD
Addie McCoy's Corn and Shrimp
  Soup 31
Baked Seafood Casserole 130
Baked Shrimp & Artichokes 122
Bar-B-Qued Shrimp 121
Barbequed Shrimp 120
Basic Roux 136
Becky's Pasta and Crawfish
  Casserole 76
Boiled Crawfish 138
Boiled Shrimp 124
Crab and Eggplant Dressing 127
Crab Meat Quiche 129
Crabmeat Au Gratin 122
Crabmeat Mornay 125
Crawfish "Tout Etouffee" 132
Crawfish (or Shrimp) Squash
  Dressing 133
Crawfish and Pasta 135
Crawfish Elegante 137
Crawfish Etouffee 132
Crawfish Fettucini 131
Crawfish Fettucini II 131
Crawfish Rice Casserole 135
Creole Seafood Seasoning 136
Deep Fried Frog Legs 130
Deviled Oysters 134
Faye's Crawfish Etouffee 134
Fish Casserole 126
Fried Shrimp 121
Frog Legs 126
Hallelujah Crabs 129
Jackie's Etouffee 138

Kim's Bar-B-Que Shrimp 120
Oysters Wrapped in Bacon 11
Pecan Rice Dressing 133
Potatoes Stuffed With Crabmeat ... 154
Rice and Oyster Dressing 127
Seafood Pasta 137
Seafood Squash 122
Shrimp and Corn Chowder 128
Shrimp and Pork Egg Rolls 123
Shrimp Creole 121
Shrimp or Crawfish Thermidor 124
Shrimp St. John 124
Shrimp, Tomato and Feta 128
Stuff Chicken With Crab 125
Stuffed Shrimp 123
Tuna Burgers 225
Seafood Gumbo 30
Seafood Gumbo III 32
Seafood Pasta 137
Seafood Squash 122
Seasoned Potatoes 143

SEASONINGS
Basic Roux 136
Creole Seafood Seasoning 136
Granny's Season-All 136
Seven-Minute Icing 177
Shrimp and Corn Chowder 128
Shrimp and Corn Soup 29
Shrimp and Mushroom Dip 18
Shrimp and Pork Egg Rolls 123
Shrimp Creole 121
Shrimp Dip I 15
Shrimp Dip II 15
Shrimp Gumbo 31
Shrimp or Crawfish Thermidor 124
Shrimp St. John 124
Shrimp, Tomato and Feta 128
Skillet Pizza 94
Smoked Duck 116
Snow White Icing 177
Snowy Mashed Potatoes 149
Sock-It-To-Me Cake 173
Sombrero Salad 232

SOUPS AND GUMBOS
Addie McCoy's Corn and Shrimp
  Soup 31
Artichoke Soup 33
Avocado Soup 34
Chicken Gumbo 33
Chicken Okra Gumbo 34
Crab and Corn Soup 29
Cream of Peanut Soup 32
Fish Chowder 28
Fish Chowder II 28

French Onion Soup 36
Italian Soup 30
$3000 Picante Onion Soup 35
Seafood Gumbo 30
Seafood Gumbo III 32
Shrimp and Corn Soup 29
Shrimp Gumbo 31
Tortilla Soup 35
Yellow Squash Soup 36
Sour Cream Dinner Rolls 63
Sour Cream Pound Cake 173
South La. Red Beans 149
Spaghetti Sauce 86
Special Twice Baked Potatoes 151
Spiced Pineapple Pickups 13
Spiced Tea 22
Spicy Italian Dip 19
Spinach Casserole 151
Spinach Madeleine 146
Spinach Quiche 74
Spinach, Feta, and Phyllo Purses 12
Squash Casserole 141
Squash Delight 140
Squash Pickles 220
Steamed Rice 152
Strawberry Filling 178
Strawberry Nut Bread 51
Strawberry Orange Frost 224
Strawberry Pecan Cake 171
Strawberry Pie #2 188
Strawberry Pie 187
Strawberry Spinach Salad 48
Stuffed Chicken With Crab 125
Stuffed Artichokes 155
Stuffed Baked Potatoes 147
Stuffed Eggs 9
Stuffed Mushrooms With Crabmeat 6
Stuffed Pork Chops 99
Stuffed Pork Chops 100
Stuffed Pork Loin 99
Stuffed Shrimp 123
Super Chocolate Chip Cookies 214
Surprise Roast 80
Sweet Potato Bread 66
Sweet Potato Casserole 155
Sweet Potato Loaf 143

TABLE SETTING
Buffet 244
Buffet Server 245
Informal and Formal 243
Napkins, Folding 246
Tips For Table Setting 242
Tamales 89
Tangy Marinated Vegetable Kabobs ... 142

Tex-Mex Cornbread Salad 42
Texas Barbequed Pork Chops 100
The Best Refrigerator Rolls 63
The Cake 212
Thelma's Fresh Fruit Dip 38
Tips For Table Settings 240
Tiropetes 14
Toad In Hole 224
Tomato Sauce 221
Too Easy Peach Cobbler 182
Tortellini Salad 75
Tortilla Soup 35
Touchdown Tortillas 13
"Trash Candy" 205
Tri Color Cheese Surprise 76
Tuna Burgers 225
Tunnel of Fudge 198
Tunnel of Fudge Cake 167
Turkey Shoot Up A La Johnny 107
Turkey Shoot Up A La Ronnie 107
24 Hour Salad 40
Uncooked Homemade Ice Cream 186
Vanilla Pound Cake 162
Vanilla Wafer Cake 169
Veal Parmigiana 81

VEGETABLES
Artichoke Casserole 148
Bagna Cotti Dip 156
Basic Vegetable Mixture 151
Broccoli Casserole 148
Cajun Squash 145
Cajun Tators 153
Candied Sweet Potatoes 143
Corn Casserole 149
Frosted Cauliflower 140
Fruited Yam Cups 147
Galashta (Cabbage Rolls) 148
German Fried Potatoes 150
Golden Broccoli 145
Green Chili Rice 141
Hot Stuffed Tomatoes 153
Italian Marinated Vegetables 144
Jo's Potato Casserole 156
Marinated Tomatoes 140
Marinated Vegetable Salad 145
Mountain Caviar 144
Mushroom Croustades 150
Nutty Wild Rice Casserole 152
Potato Casserole 154
Potatoes Stuffed With Crabmeat ... 154
Primevera Salad 156
Ratatouille Nicoise 142
Rice 114
Seasoned Potatoes 143
Snowy Mashed Potatoes 149

South La. Red Beans	149
Special Twice Baked Potatoes	151
Spinach Casserole	151
Spinach Madeleine	146
Squash Casserole	141
Squash Delight	140
Steamed Rice	152
Stuffed Artichokes	155
Stuffed Baked Potatoes	147
Sweet Potato Casserole	155
Sweet Potato Loaf	143
Tangy Marinated Vegetable Kabobs	142
Vegetable Casserole	146
Vegetable Casserole	146
Vegetable Dip	14
Vegetable Dip	17
Venison Marinade	116
Venison Roast With Sausage	118
Vivian's Barbeque Sauce	96
Vodka Slush	24
Waldorf Salad	48
Wassail	25
Watergate Salad	44
Watermelon Whale	237
Watermelon Whale Pattern	238
White Chocolate Fudge	199
Wine Cooler Concentrate	24
Wine Punch	21
Yeast Rolls	65
Yellow Squash Soup	36
Zingy Strawberry Brie	2
Zucchini Bread	68

Froggy Bottom

549 Kenilworth Parkway
Baton Rouge, Louisiana 70808

Please send me _____ copies of **Froggy Bottom** at $11.95 per copy, plus $2.00 for postage and handling per book. Louisiana residents add 8% sales tax.

Enclosed you will find my check or money order for $_____

NAME _____

ADDRESS _____

CITY _____ STATE _____ ZIP _____

Froggy Bottom

549 Kenilworth Parkway
Baton Rouge, Louisiana 70808

Please send me _____ copies of **Froggy Bottom** at $11.95 per copy, plus $2.00 for postage and handling per book. Louisiana residents add 8% sales tax.

Enclosed you will find my check or money order for $_____

NAME _____

ADDRESS _____

CITY _____ STATE _____ ZIP _____

Reorder Additional Copies

Froggy Bottom

549 Kenilworth Parkway
Baton Rouge, Louisiana 70808

Please send me _____ copies of **Froggy Bottom** at $11.95 per copy, plus $2.00 for postage and handling per book. Louisiana residents add 8% sales tax.

Enclosed you will find my check or money order for $_____

NAME _____

ADDRESS _____

CITY _____ STATE _____ ZIP _____

- -

Froggy Bottom

549 Kenilworth Parkway
Baton Rouge, Louisiana 70808

Please send me _____ copies of **Froggy Bottom** at $11.95 per copy, plus $2.00 for postage and handling per book. Louisiana residents add 8% sales tax.

Enclosed you will find my check or money order for $_____

NAME _____

ADDRESS _____

CITY _____ STATE _____ ZIP _____

Reorder Additional Copies